Website Design using AI

By Neal Hettinger

Flint Group Publishers

Cover design: D. Hettinger.

ISBN 979-8-9929481-1-0 | Paperback

Genre: Website Design

COM100000 COMPUTERS / Artificial Intelligence / Generative AI

DES007010 DESIGN / Graphic Arts / Advertising

BUS043000 BUSINESS & ECONOMICS / Marketing / General

Printed in the United States of America.

FlintGroup

PUBLISHERS

This book is intended to help creatives with website design in partnership with AI.

AI cannot replace HI.
Artificial Intelligence can generate content but it needs Human Ingenuity to make an effective website.

The goal is not to replace marketers and website designers. These professionals have the education and experience you need.

If the budget or time require self creation, then it is better to produce a workable website than an ugly waste of time.

Enjoy designing—it is fun!

Preface

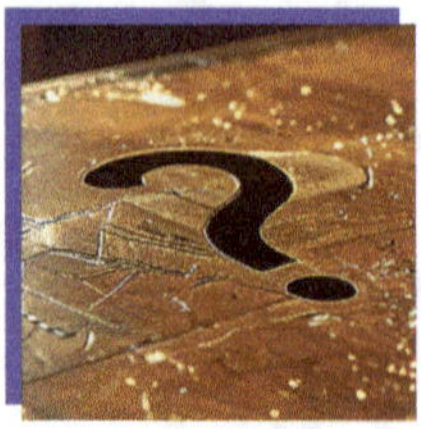

This foundation-level book introduces website design principles alongside modern artificial intelligence (AI) tools. The book is specifically written for creatives who want to understand the basics of website program design. It explains how to build websites that clearly communicate trustworthiness and are discoverable in search environments. It will benefit experienced designers in expanding AI-assisted workflows.

Visitors need to have trust established by the website design to become a user.

Business owners and marketers will learn how to use AI to save time and reduce costs. They will discover that building websites requires establishing long-term business goals first. Design students develop website concepts and assets that demonstrate professional judgment, clarity, and strategic use of AI. Readers will understand what attracts the right audience, earns trust, and motivates meaningful action.

The artificial intelligence created images include the prompt and identifies the AI generator. These examples are references to demonstrate the prompting techniques and show the strengths and weaknesses of different AI generators. Human ingenuity is identified with the software and a short description of the action.

INTELLIGENCE IS NOT THE POINT

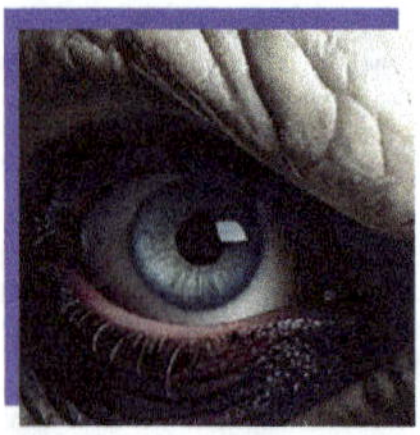

AI has changed how we create. This distinction matters deeply in design, communication, and how work is discovered and inspired. It can generate images in seconds, write paragraphs on demand, analyze data at a scale no human could match, and organize information with remarkable efficiency.

For many people, this has sparked excitement. For others, anxiety. Much of that tension comes from how AI is framed—as something that competes with human intelligence rather than something that complements human ability.

Throughout these pages, AI is treated as what it truly is: a powerful tool for assisting with complex tasks that once required significant time and labor. It assists with complex tasks that once required significant time and labor.

INGENUITY IS THE POINT

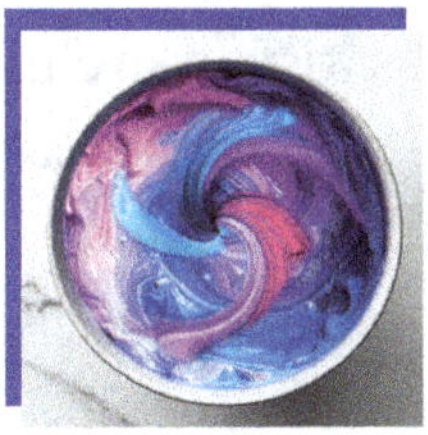

Tools do not decide what matters. That role belongs to humans. To make that distinction clear, I use a second term alongside AI—HI, which in this book stands for Human Ingenuity. I intentionally avoid the phrase human intelligence.

Intelligence—whether artificial or biological—has increasingly come to mean the same things as AI with pattern recognition, logic, optimization, and structure. These areas are precisely where AI now performs well.

Framing the conversation as "AI versus human intelligence" places both on the same axis and turns progress into a competition. When AI and HI are treated as competitors, both are diminished. When they are treated as collaborators, each becomes more powerful.

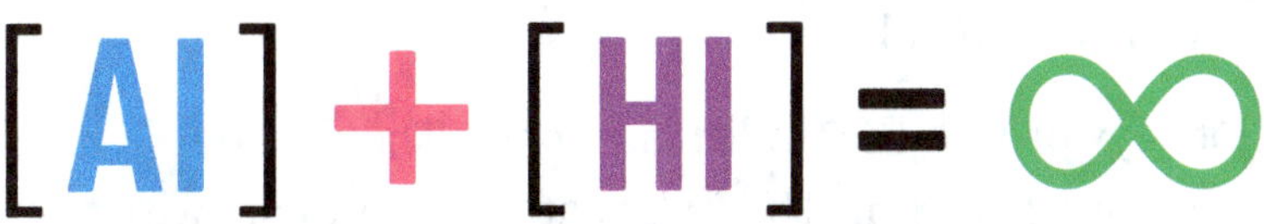

Figure P.4 AI and HI working together in a collaborative framework

Human ingenuity operates on a different axis entirely. It is not about processing power. HI is about creativity and adjustment. Ingenuity is the ability to ask the right questions, recognize nuance, apply judgment, exercise taste, and make ethical decisions. Humans assign meaning, determine relevance, and decide why something should exist—not just how it can be produced.

AI can generate while HI chooses. AI can assist but HI directs. The synergy between artificial intelligence and human ingenuity accelerates design without sacrificing judgment. Artificial intelligence excels at structure, speed, and scale. Human ingenuity provides intent, judgment, and meaning.

Search results are not based on keywords. Now they are based on trustworthy content.

For many years, success on the web was framed as a technical problem: choose the right keywords, structure pages correctly, and satisfy search engine rules to rank higher in search results. While those mechanics still exist, they no longer tell the full story. Modern search systems evaluate relevance first, then observe human behavior—attention, engagement, clarity, and trust.

SEARCH RESULTS NOW

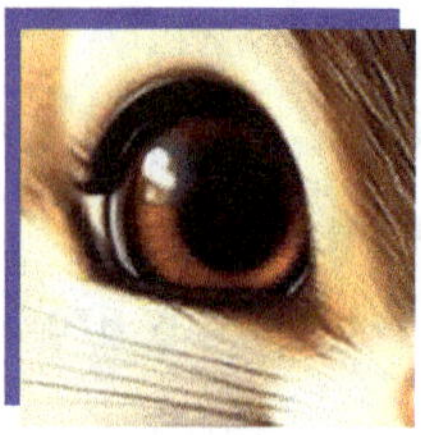

With the advent of AI-generated search results, there has been a major paradigm shift in search engine results. Previously, keywords and phrases that a user typed into a search field defined SER. The queries brought back results with those keywords. Now for high-ranking search results, keywords are out, and AI indirectly relies on Hookwords.

Hookwords are not keywords in the traditional sense. They are not structured to "match" an algorithm. They are written to resonate with people. Hookwords are the words and phrases that signal clarity, credibility, and intent to a human reader—and, as a result, to the systems observing that reader's behavior.

Human ingenuity, not automation, creates Hookwords. AI can help structure language, variations, and ideas. Only HI can determine which words feel honest, which messages build trust, and which signals align with real human needs.

Optimizing for people is being understood—and rewarded—by machines. This is the philosophy behind the chapters in this book that explain SEO and SER in the AI sphere.

Readers will not find arguments about whether AI is good or bad or predictions about replacement and obsolescence. Instead, they will learn how to work with AI deliberately, responsibly, and creatively.

The goal is not to use machines' strengths and adjust with creativity, the human strength. This philosophy is the foundation this book is built on. If designers approach artificial intelligence as a tool guided by human ingenuity to design a website design that fosters trust, everything will follow. Design decisions will become clearer, more effective, increasingly ethical, and discoverable in search results.

DEFINITIONS

Human Ingenuity (HI) Used in this book to describe the distinctly human capacities for intent, judgment, creativity, ethical reasoning, and contextual understanding that guide and give meaning to AI-assisted output.

Hookword Framework (Hettinger, 2025) A visitor-first alternative to keyword-centric SEO that emphasizes trust, engagement, and behavioral validation as primary signals in AI-mediated search systems.

INSETS

FIGURE P.1

Inset of old ways of learning

AI Practicum} Firefly Prompt: Question mark scratched into a vintage school desktop.

FIGURE P.2

Inset of AI tension

AI Practicum} Firefly Prompt: Scary photoreal closeup of monster staring out.

FIGURE P.3

Inset combination of AI and HI

AI Practicum} Express Prompt: View from above a mixing bowl with swirling colorful liquid and raw color dyes of blue, purple, pink.

FIGURE P.4

AI and HI working together in a collaborative framework

HI Practicum} InDesign formula representation.

FIGURE P.5

Inset of AI and HI happy results

AI Practicum} DeepAI Prompt: 3D anime of squirrel smiling at viewer.

Table of

contents

C

List of Figures

INDEX OF FIGURES

LIST OF FIGURES

LIST OF FIGURES

LIST OF FIGURES

LIST OF FIGURES

Acknowledgments

Thank you to every one of my friends, family, and business partners for bearing with me while writing this manuscript. My focus was just on creating a manuscript and everything else had to float by itself.

To write this book I consulted with many experts. Paul Webb has taught me about bringing a project online and all the problems that will occur. Sheryl Ralston worked as a software workflow liaison showed me how to speak to a user in English instead as a developer in Techlish. Jack Werner, PhD patiently explained the real differences between marketing and advertising. Keith Steincamp, CPA, CMA, CSCA, attended my AI seminars and asked me great questions which I addressed in this book.

I truly appreciate my wife who patiently listened to me speaking about the different subjects in this book. The time spent in a closed office typing and sketching was probably a vacation. She enjoys reading about topics that are interesting to her, but I know AI in graphic design is not at the top of her list.

In the classes I teach on AI, there is confusion between AI, Cybernetics and Robotics. Many of the students, who range in age from 18 to 80, are concerned about the negative ramifications of AI. There are no assurances but the use of AI is helpful in so many areas of life I welcome it.

No matter your thoughts on AI, if you do not keep learning, you will be left behind.

When Machines Learn

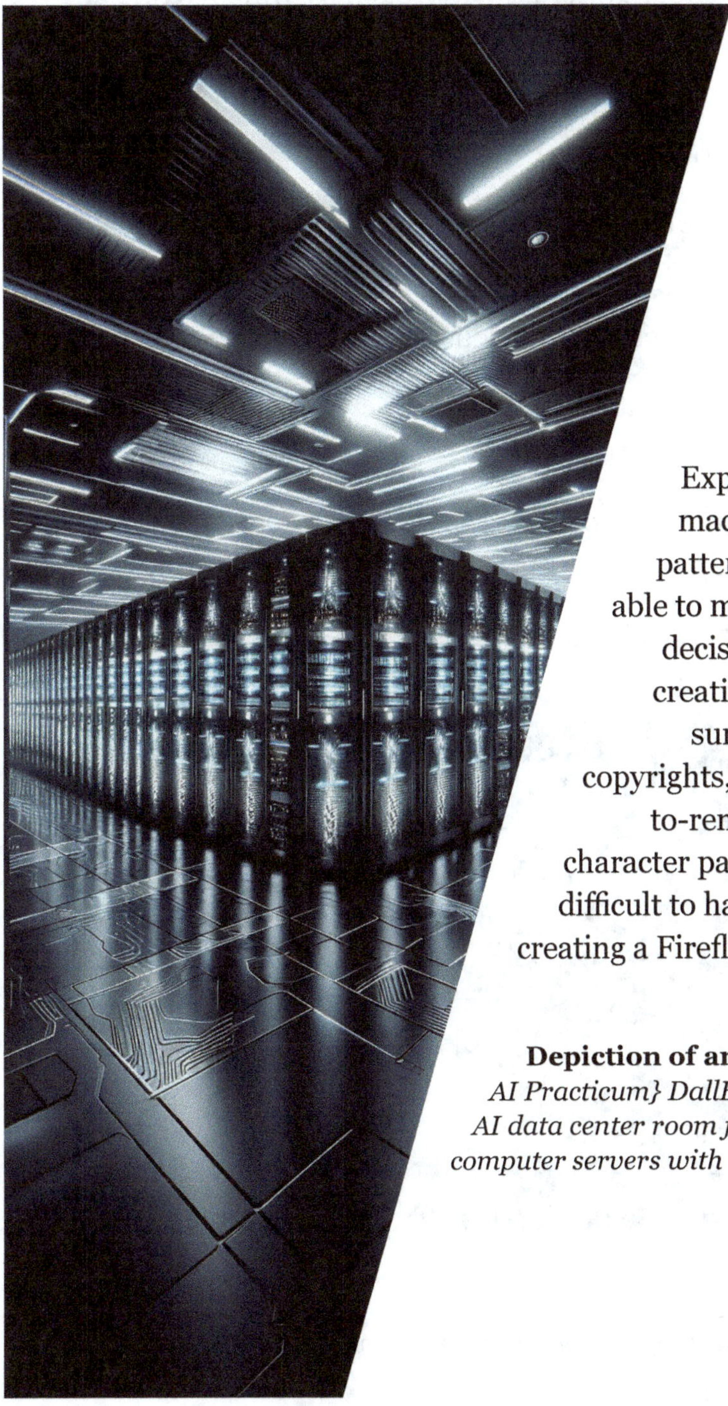

C1

OVERVIEW

Explanation on how machines learn with patterns, data and are able to make predictions, decisions, and output creative images. Short summary of AI and copyrights, setting up easy-to-remember multiple character passwords that are difficult to hack, and demo of creating a Firefly website image.

FIGURE 1.1

Depiction of an AI Data Center

AI Practicum} DallE-3 Prompt: Large AI data center room filled with glowing computer servers with dramatic lighting.

PROFESSIONAL TERMINOLOGY

AI Learning: The manner and approach by which artificial intelligence acquires knowledge.

Browser: The application internet searchers use to access websites and information.

Chatbot: An interface visitors use to get answers via text without leaving the website.

E-commerce: A website that sells products on the internet.

HI: Human Ingenuity—The ability to create an original, clever, or inventive concept or idea.

Natural Language: The format that AI uses to understand the human language.

TLD: The Top-Level Domain in a website address, the domain extension.

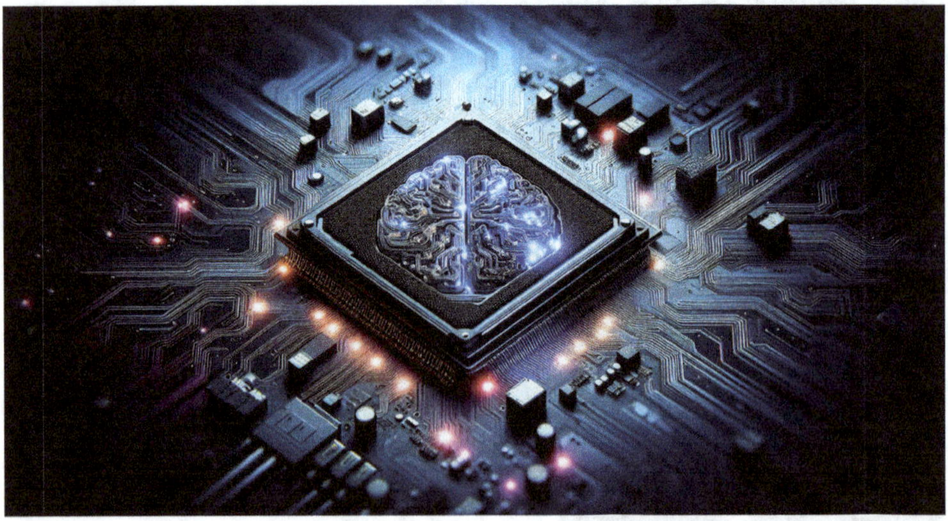

FIGURE 1.2

Board Brain AI GPU

AI Practicum} Adobe Firefly Prompt: Computer board with GPU that looks similar to the human brain.

UNDERSTANDING ARTIFICIAL INTELLIGENCE

Artificial intelligence is defined as a computer processing system that performs tasks that are generally thought of as requiring human intelligence. It was developed by the combined efforts of mathematicians, scientists, data analysts, and visionaries who could put together a team to generate new ideas to develop technologies.

Tremendous energy sources and resourceful funding were needed to configure AI. Decisions had to be made based on these resources on what to include and what to leave out in the data loading. This naturally created limits and bias.

When artificial intelligence became accessible and inexpensive for everyone to use, the models used machine learning to automate jobs, look at data, plan social media postings, and verify grammar and spelling. AI has gotten better at making content. People call it "creating new content headlines and writing," but it's really simply new to the user and comes from the model's sources.

The AI model retrieves information from a data source based on the natural language prompt. This kind of prompt makes it possible for almost anyone to use the AI without using a coding format.

As a result, individuals and businesses alike can generate engaging material without needing extensive writing skills. The accessibility of such technology is transforming how to communicate and share information in the digital age.

The basic term "artificial intelligence," which initially referred to studying ways machines can simulate human intelligence, originated in 1956. It should not be confused with terms such as "cybernetics," which refers to robotic machines. At that time, artificial intelligence was researching how to program a machine to learn, solve problems, and use language to communicate instead of coding. AI started as an academic discipline studying intelligence by machines but has evolved into 3 main types of AI that are used today.

AI Tools

Software that uses artificial intelligence to help complete tasks more quickly or efficiently is referred to as AI tools. They support users rather than independently creating new work. Features can be assistive, task-focused, user-driven, and considered productivity boosters. They are used for editing content, analyzing data, organizing information, content creation, query searching, and automating processes.

Examples:

Grammarly: The text is changed to make it simpler to read by using clearer words.

Word: Full proofreading for punctuation and spelling mistakes.

QuillBot: A lot of ways to make your writing better, including grammar and punctuation.

ChatGPT: Good for checking spelling and making sentences better.

Zapier AI: Programs apps and tasks integrate automatically.

AI Generators

Artificial intelligence generators are systems that create or combine content based on prompts. This type of AI can generate text, images, audio, code, video, and designs. They find and curate information to produce new solutions. To accomplish this, the artificial intelligence model uses large datasets to learn patterns, and the user must be able to properly prompt for AI generation. Today they are used for writing blogs, generating graphics, designing logos, creating sound effects, making videos, producing ads, etc.

Examples:

ChatGPT: Writes in a way that sounds like a person, yet it often adds distracting emojis.

DALL·E: OpenAI that turns prompts into detailed pictures,

Runway: An innovative AI promotional tool that makes videos, animations, and special effects.

Canva: Makes graphics using templates and a blank canvas.

Adobe Firefly: Creates photos and maximalism styled images and with effects that are similar to those in online Photoshop.

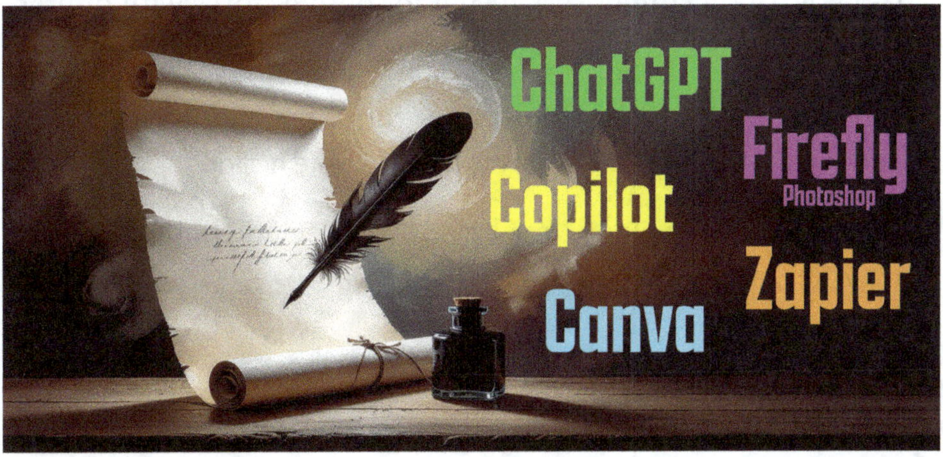

FIGURE 1.3

Content generators

AI Practicum} Firefly Prompt: A painting of an old-fashioned artwork featuring a rolled parchment and a quill pen on a swirling dark background. Leave space on the sides for additional elements or text. Retouched and effects with Web Photoshop through Firefly.

AI Agents

AI agents are independent programs that can act on their own to complete tasks. They can plan, take steps, complete tasks, interact with software, and work toward a goal based on their programming. The AI agents can be used to schedule appointments, write and send emails, analyze data with summaries and key takeaways, run automations, update spreadsheets, manage workflows for production and marketing, and even write and test software.

Examples:

AutoGPT: Handles many tasks, plans, with reasons to carry them out with a little HI guidance.

Devin: A task in language-based software engineering that makes code

Tidio: A free customer service bot for online stores with limited functionalities and easy setup.

Zoho SalesIQ: Figures out what visitors want and uses clever, rule-based sales funnels to get them to take action.

Tripnotes AI: Develops travel plans that include hotels, food, activities, and route planning.

AI tools enable non-designers and train graphic designers to achieve credible design results without deep UI/UX training. Marketers and business owners on limited budgets can now have professional-looking websites based on the principles and theories of visual design. However, AI does not actually understand how the visuals can persuaded an individual. It is up to the AI user to prompt and guide the AI to generate impactful solutions.

Artificial intelligence is trained to understand and respond to using learning methods like deep learning. This allows the general user to instruct the AI model to generate a solution. With the human language, the prompts are much easier than learning how to set up code to direct AI to a solution.

FIGURE 1.4
US Report

COPYRIGHTING AI CONTENT

A large section of the professional creative community were pretty sure that AI-generated content and prompts were not copyrightable. In January 2025, the US Copyright Office agreed. From a graphic design perspective, the report *Copyright and Artificial Intelligence, Part 2: Copyrightability*[1] clarified that if artificial intelligence is used as a tool to create effects or stylize the human-generated work, that content is copyrightable. The report also concluded that "Copyright protects the original expression in a work created by a human author, even if the work also includes AI-generated material." The following summary is what has been determined by creatives after reading the report.

The 42-page report was an overview and analysis of how

copyright law today applies to artificial intelligence and human creativity as two separate concepts. Human writing is copyrightable, and AI-generated writing is not. However, AI tools such as grammar and spelling correction used on human compositions may be eligible for US legal protection. When generating content and images, it is important to keep all multilayered prompts to show human input and direction.

The Copyright Office acknowledged that AI-generated content was new and further evaluation would be needed since the use of this technology would continue to evolve. At this time, the deciding factor would balance on human input and the origin of the content. This explanation is not a legal analysis or a legal memorandum. Consult a copyright attorney if there are questions.

The report sees AI and human creativity as two separate elements. When AI creates an image or composes a draft, it analyzes its data and draws from thousands of concepts to generate a solution based on the prompt. The final curated prompt solution is not creative but a mixture of data in a pleasing manner, either visually or as readable content.

When a graphic designer stares at a blank screen and then starts laying out a design, the ideas come from what they have seen, experienced, learned, and been taught. That process leads not to a completely new concept. The solution is an inspired composition that may have been used many times before or seen as a new approach.

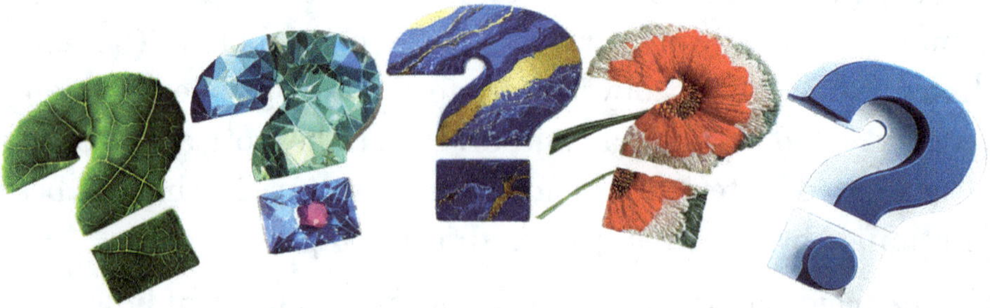

FIGURE 1.5

Question Marks

AI Practicum} Adobe Express Prompt: Using artwork, illustrate 5 different question marks that are slightly rotated n a shallow curve.

The question is whether this is different than how AI generates images and writes an essay or if these processes are similar. Scientists develop new ideas, engineers devise new components, and medical professionals experiment to find new medicines. Their solutions are based on previous solutions.

These human inventions are patented by either the developer or their employer. The employer provided funds to allow the engineers to invent, but the employer did not create the end result. How is this unlike a human prompting artificial intelligence? If the human pays for the AI-generated solution, then, similar to a patent, why should they be excluded from owning a copyright on the solution?

ACCURACY OF ARTIFICIAL INTELLIGENCE

A user needs to be aware that AI is not all-knowing and many users do not check the source of a response. Artificial intelligence generators can save time, which equals money. At lectures and seminars, a common question asked is if AI and the internet search engines are rewriting history and to give an example. *Rewriting* is not the correct term, but a number of individuals believe what they read and do not take into account bias or fact checking. Here is one example:

When simple short domains were becoming limited, other TLDs were proposed. A query on what was the first city TLD, Google will respond it was ".berlin." However, website designers at that time found the first city available as a TLD to use was ".vegas. Therefore, it was before any other city, including ".berlin" and ".tokyo." Further Google search results querying the date that ".berlin" was available do not agree with answers that vary from sometime in 2013 to March 2014. According to Google, ".vegas" was available later in March, followed by other US cities.

SCAMS, SLIPS, AND CONUNDRUMS

AI can be leveraged to research targets, discover encrypt data, and identify system vulnerabilities. Artificial intelligence can accurately guess passwords by listening to keystrokes.

Scammers use artificial intelligence to mimic voices and create fake videos. A number of different cons such as the elderly scam where their grandchild will call their grandparent needing cash right away. Someone will show up at the door and pick up the cash for the grandchild.

Banks have to worry about scams since they grow their money by investing their depositors' saving. Sometimes they are led to believe an investment is real and it turns out to be fake

Emails and texts are huge sources of scams. One way to spot them is that it's perfectly spelled and professional sounding, but sometimes the words just don't quite make sense, as if it's from the translation. They will send fake invoices or legal proceedings or try to get money for a past due invoice. Websites have SSL security sockets, but even so, there are a number of legitimately professional websites that you will enter go to put in your credit card information, and it won't be real. They will even have chat. Bots to represent customer service. Artificial intelligence can generate fake IDs, passports, and badges. One of the strongest forms of identity theft is taking your password and using that along with the user ID.

Individuals, to protect themselves, should never click on an email to go to a site. They should always go to it on their own. They need to verify that is a legitimate website check the spelling of the domain; that is one way they will fake out prospects create a 16 character password do not trust images, videos, or voices at face value.

Many times, scammers will take over a website to put their own information on it and if the website master is not watching the website, it could go days weeks or even months before is found out that has been taken over.

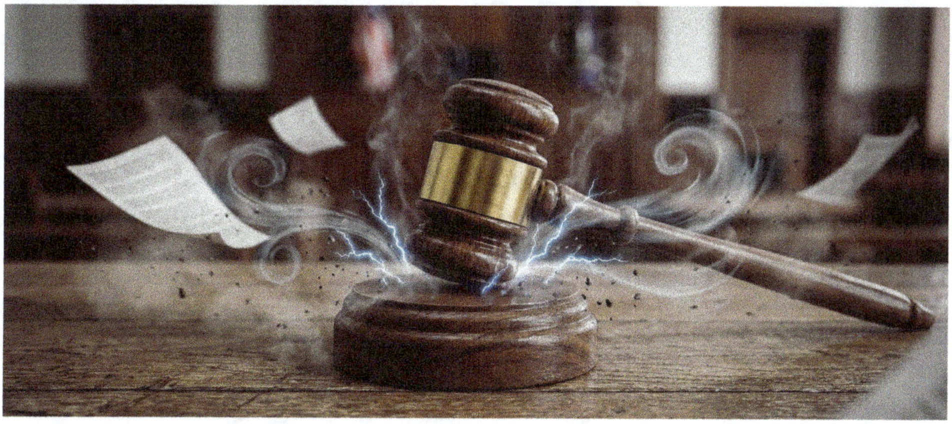

FIGURE 1.6

AI guilt trips

AI Practicum} Google Gemini Create Image Prompt: Photo of judges gavel smacking the desk and small bolts of lightning and wind coming out.

Lapse in judgment

New York City launched a chatbot without adequate beta testing. Intended to help business owners with information, the chatbot advised illegal solutions.[2]

Example of bias

For over four years Amazon worked on developing a recruiting AI tool to filter resumes down to the best applicants. Since it was men who trained the artificial intelligence, the system taught itself that the best results were male candidates.[3]

Fake videos

The list of AI-generated luminaries includes influencers such as Kim Kardashian, Gordon Ramsay, Taylor Swift, and Oprah. Recently, a scam sold a weight loss supplement with an AI fake Oprah.[4]

Legal briefs

A number of attorneys have allegedly cited false legal cases in their briefs due to AI. They supposedly used artificial intelligence to help write their documents and judges are not happy.[5]

SPAM EMAIL BOX AND PASSWORD CREATION

The most effective solution is a truly randomized password with uppercase, lowercase, numbers, and punctuation. Most organizations and institutions have started using a multi-function password where, after the username is entered along with a password, a code is texted or emailed to the individual. There is no logic to this process. Security insurance companies do not seem to understand that if someone has accessed your device, they have access to your text messaging and emails.

Websites that need a security password usually list three requirements:

√ Uppercase and lowercase letters

√ Between 6 and 32 characters with no spaces

√ Contain a number and a symbol or punctuation

Secure and reasonable

The dilemma in password security is that to be truly random and 16 characters, it will be difficult to be remembered. If it is written down and saved somewhere where it can be easily retrieved, it is not secure.

People choose passwords and formulate them using many of the same options. They may use phrases such as their favorite sports team's cheers or reverse their favorite sports team's names, use their children's names, or use their children's initials or birth dates. They may have the letter 'E' in their password and change it to a three, an 'H' becomes a 4, and a five takes the place of the letter 'S.'

AI can discover an incredible amount of private information about an individual across the Internet in milliseconds. Where a person lived in first grade, the name of their dog, their childhood sweetheart, and the list goes on.

Increasing the number and type of characters increases the possible combinations an attacker has to try. A 16-character password is more secure and resistant to attackers, even with the assistance of artificial intelligence.

Brute force attacks use automated software to try every possible combination until it finds the correct target. These attackers are looking for a non-secure or low-security account, WiFi networks, or encrypted files to access. Hackers will run programs that will try thousands to billions of guesses per second on just one target.

There are two ways to set up passwords that are secure. Using a password manager system that requires an individual to submit a password to the manager through a secure access point.

A second option, since an individual still needs a password, is to use the formula explained in the next section. It is a way to enter a password through a secure site that is created and can be remembered without recording it. If is too complicated or too simple, then AI can figure it out. It also needs to be typed easily, but it has to be made up of unrelated words and characters. The password needs to be more than eight or 10 characters that make sense only to the individual.

Any password can be broken if the hacker has unlimited time and assets. Here is a simple format for a 16-word password that can be remembered. Do not copy it exactly. This formula is presented as an idea of what to do. Options are to add another word or number to make it even longer. The words can be six letters or another punctuation mark such as #, $, %, or _ can be used.

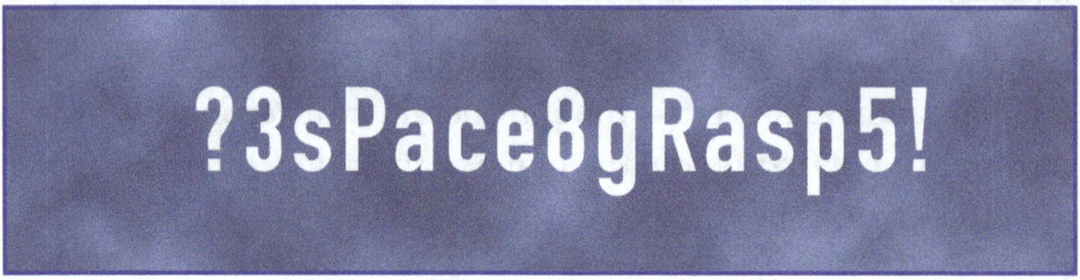

FIGURE 1.7

Password formula

HI Practicum} Designed in Adobe Photoshop

1. Start with punctuation such as a question mark because the password is being asked again, and the first response is to ask why every time?

2. Choose a number between 1 and 9. Do not use a zero because it may be confused later with a letter "O"

3. Decide on a random lowercase five-letter word that is easy remember. It can be in a different language than what is spoken in your location and not an obvious choice.

4. Capitalize the second or third letter of that word.

5. Choose another number between 1 and 9.

6. Use another five-letter word and capitalize one of its letters. Five-letter words are easier to remember than longer words.

7. Capitalize the second or third letter as you did in step 4.

8. Now add or subtract the two numbers that were used and put the solutions the fourteenth character .

9. Add another punctuation mark.

10. For the sixteenth letter, choose from the URL of website that is being visited. Do not include the top-level domain, the domain extension such as a ".com." As an example, use the "L" in learn-ai.website or choose the last letter before the dot, so it would be an "I" as the 16th character of the password.

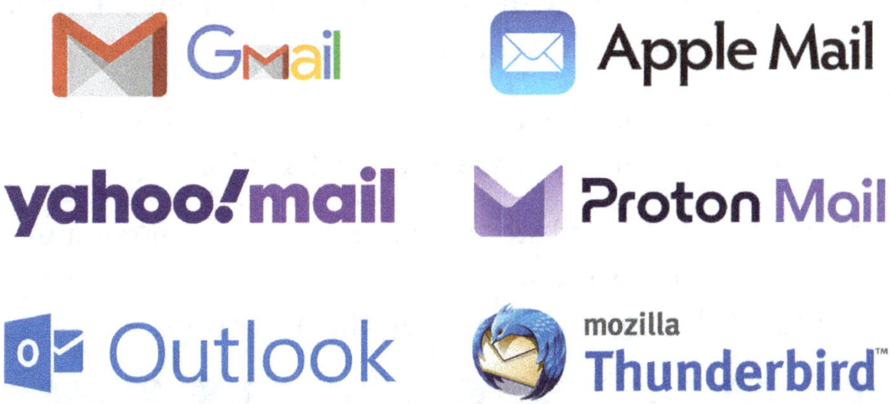

FIGURE 1.8
Free email services
HI Practicum} Layout in Adobe Photoshop

Free email accounts.

For a spam/junk email box, use a different email service than the one(s) you are presently using. If you have a Gmail account, then choose another provider so you do not get mixed up as to which to use or supply it to businesses that are asking for it to send you information. Check the email box monthly to delete the junk and spam. If you do not visit the email regularly, they may close the account.

Proton is a strong Swiss service that is heavily encrypted, but what you gain in privacy and security, you lose in storage—it has a limited storage space.

Gmail offers a highly efficient spam filter and access from the app and online and works well with other Google products and services.

Apple Mail is perhaps the most user-friendly and works seamlessly with its apps, products, and devices with strong security.

Outlook works well with the other Microsoft apps, but the storage is limited, and you may have ads.

Yahoo Mail is not the most secure option, but it has large storage, so you do not have to clear it as often.

Mozilla Thunderbird stores your emails on your computer so you can access them when you are offline. The interface appears to be older looking than the other services.

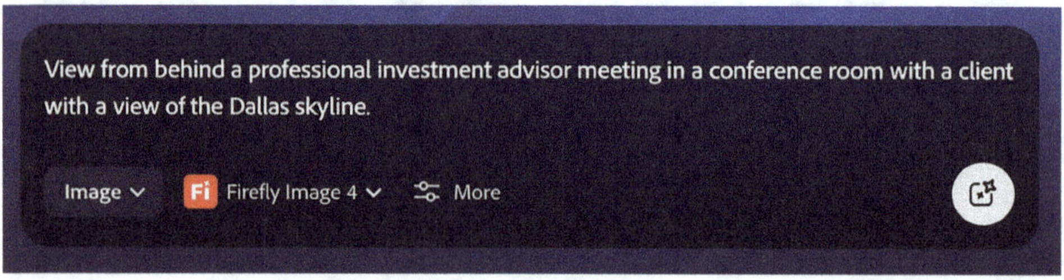

FIGURE 1.9

Firefly prompt window with options

Select image to choose video or image. The next selection gives the options of different Firefly Image builders and Google.

Demo Firefly—Creating a website image

Sign into Adobe Firefly. See Chapter Seven for this process and for image settings. Write out the goals and a brief description of the image or images to generate.

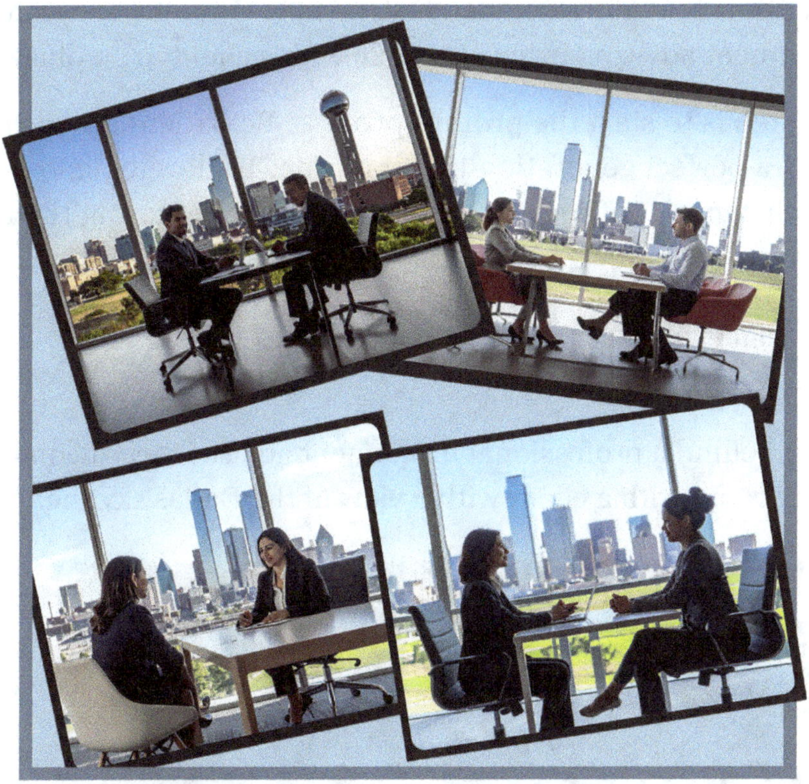

FIGURE 1.10

Firefly first prompt image options for a webpage

The first step is to decide what elements need to be in the visual solution. To get an effective AI generative solution, take the time to write down the following list and descriptions:

Subject: Financial Investment Company

Role: professional investment advisor

Audience: Investor

Setting: Office in a high-rise building

Goal: Show a face-to-face meeting reviewing a report.

Format: Website horizontal landscape image 4 wide by 3 tall.

First draft: Start with a simple sentence "Investment advisor meeting with client at a table."

Second draft: Add more detailed instructions "View from behind an investment advisor sitting at a table with a client in an office."

The next step is to start the prompt process. Be patient and do not expect a perfect generation the first time. To develop and curate the prompt, put together the words before entering them into the prompt field.

Choose the photo as the content.

Prompt 1: Figure 1.10

View from behind a professional investment advisor meeting in a conference room with a client with a view of the Dallas skyline.

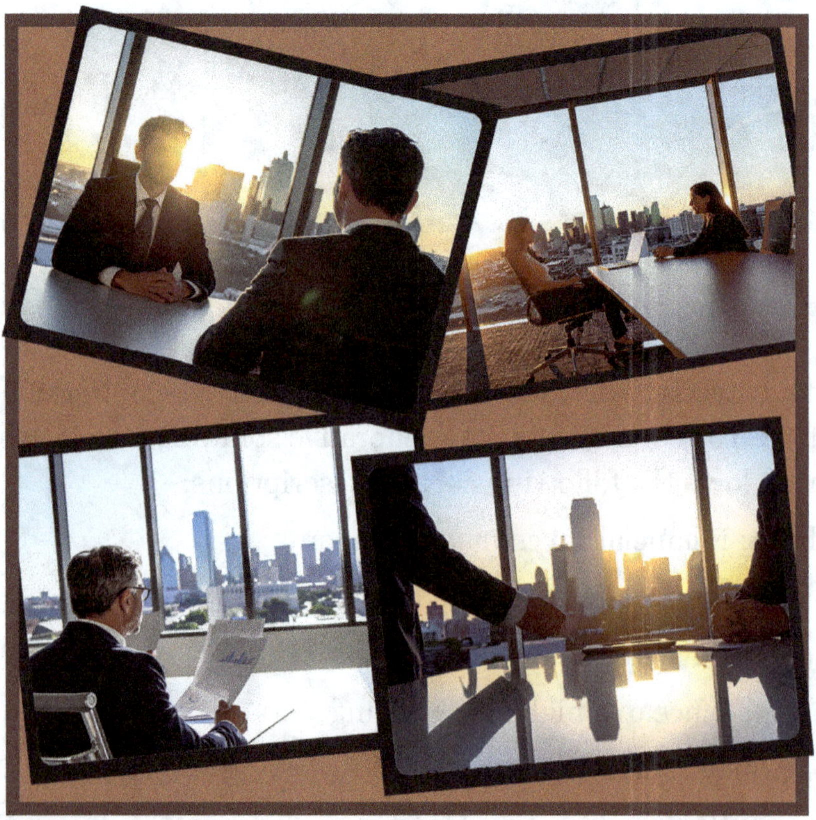

FIGURE 1.11
Firefly prompt 2 image options for a webpage

Prompt 2 includes more details

Tight crop looking over the shoulder of an older adult male professional investment advisor meeting with a client in a conference room, with a large window offering a view of the vibrant Dallas cityscape.

Compare the images and narrow your options down to the one that is close to what you are trying to achieve. Finesse the prompt more, or if it is quicker, you may just need to use Photoshop.

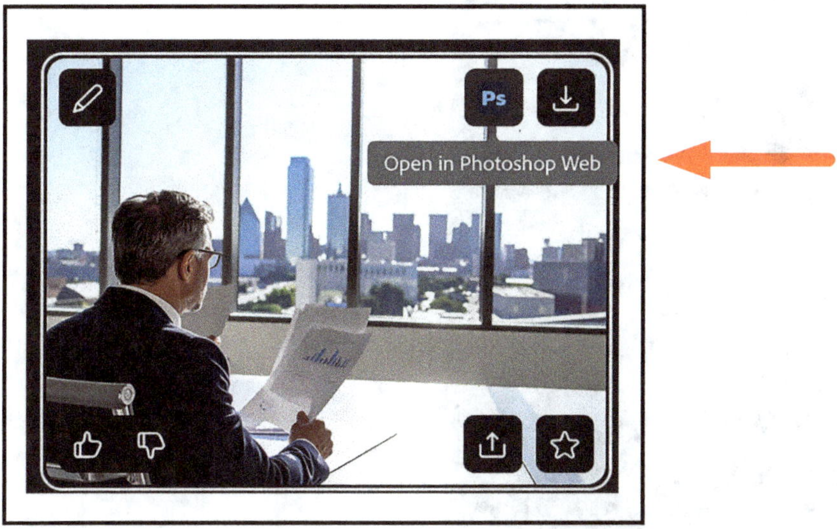

FIGURE 1.12
Firefly to the internet Photoshop options
Hover over image with cursor to see options.

Using Web Photoshop

Trying to generate the final image through Firefly was difficult. It could not configure a daytime background with two businessmen in the foreground without more time spent on curating the prompting. However, there were two images with the elements needed if they were put together. Manually combining the images, seemed the fastest option.

Firefly can seamlessly open the images in the web version of Photoshop by selecting the option in the upper right corner (See Figure 1.12). The tools in this version of Adobe Photoshop while similar somewhat limited are perfect for combining the images.

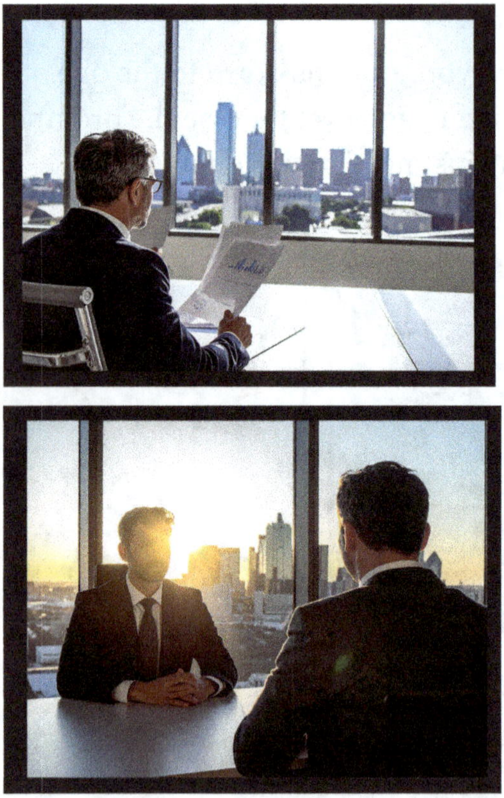

FIGURE 1.13
Firefly selected image

1. Choose one of the options to be the main image to work on.

2. Select the download icon, and then select the option to open it in Photoshop.

3. Add the second image.

4. Instruct Photoshop AI to combine the images.

5. Download the image as a jpg.

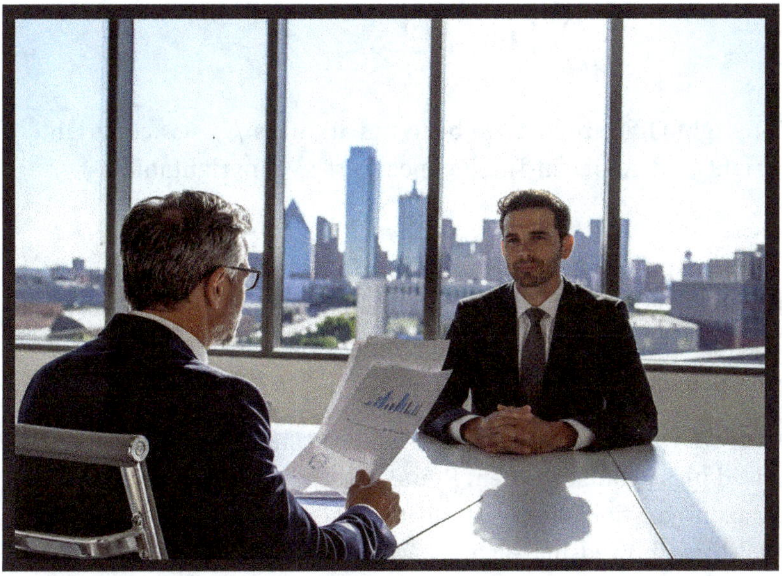

FIGURE 1.14

Combined images, note Photoshop took the glare off one of the businessman.

AI Practicum} Used AI generative tool in Photoshop

AI generators have limitations and strengths. Knowing the goal will help decide which AI to use to efficiently generate the image needed.

When using a new AI generator for the first time, it is recommended to make a list of its techniques and styles. Since the final goal is a visual solution, taking a screen grab to place in the list may help.

As part of the workflow, reference the list. Noting which AI is free, which ones need a subscription, size limitations and style options.

Realizing the limitations of AI in Firefly saved time. Knowing the internet version of Photoshop also had AI capabilities solved the problem without frustration.

The image will need to be optimized for the web. If it is not adapted for the internet, viewers may not wait for the large image to load—especially if there are more than one. See Chapter 7.

REFERENCES

1. The US Copyright Office report can be found at: https://www.copyright.gov/ai/Copyright-and-Artificial-Intelligence-Part-2-Copyrightability-Report.pdf

2. Allen, J. (2024, April 4). NYC mayor defends its chatbot pilot, as the Al tool continues to dish out illegal advice. Reuters. https://www.reuters.com/technology/new-york-city-defends-ai-chatbot-that-advised-entrepreneurs-break-laws-2024-04-04

3. Dastin, J. (2018, October 10). Insight - Amazon scraps secret AI recruiting tool that showed bias against women. Reuters. https://www.reuters.com/article/us-amazon-com-jobs-automation-insight/amazon-scraps-secret-ai-recruiting-tool-that-showed-bias-against-women-idUSKCN1MK08G/

4. Blake, S. (2024, January 16). Taylor Swift, Oprah Social Media Scams Cost Americans Billions. Newsweek. https://www.newsweek.com/celebrity-deepfake-scams-lost-money-taylor-swift-oprah-1861255

5. BUSSEWITZ, C. (2025, October 30). Mistake-filled legal briefs show the limits of relying on AI tools at work. The Associated Press. https://apnews.com/article/artificial-intelligence-tools-work-errors-skills-fddcd0a5c86c20a4748dc65ba38f77fa

Configuring Websites

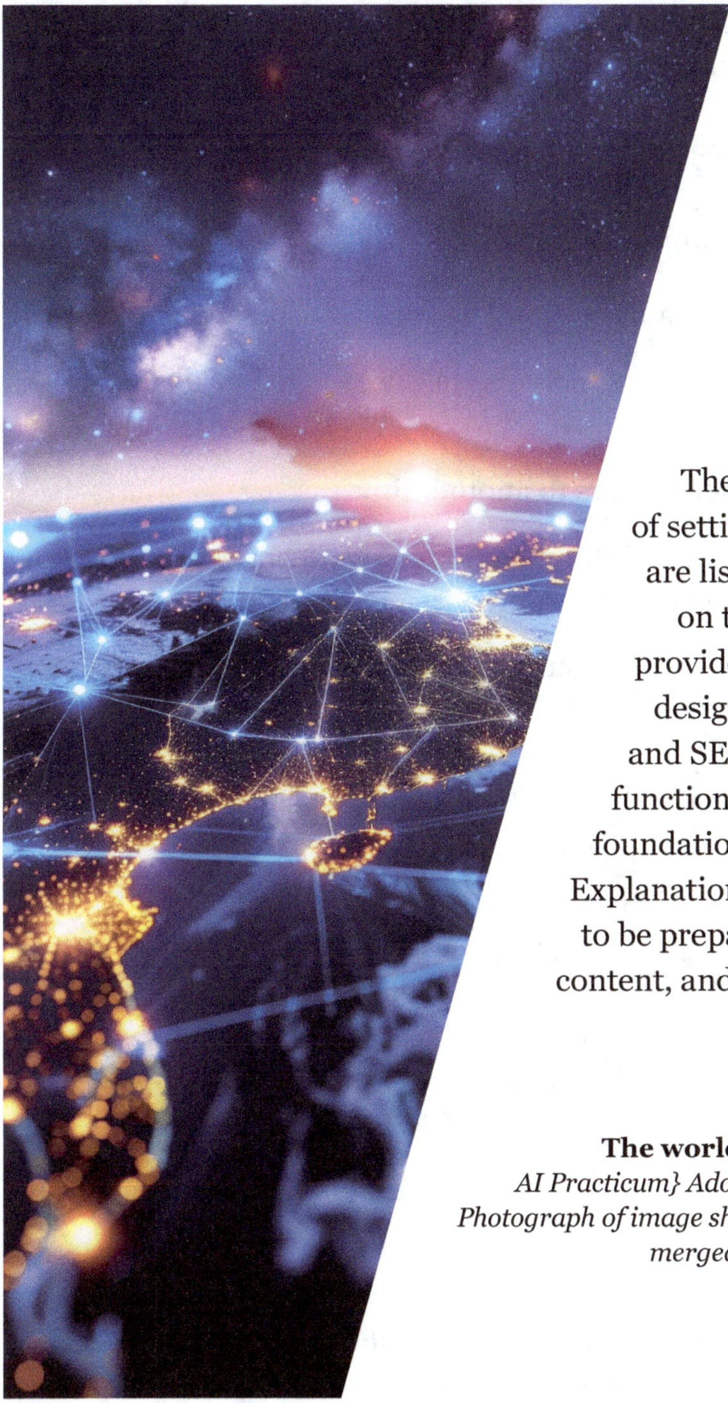

C2

OVERVIEW

The essential steps of setting up a website are listed. Discussion on the best hosting providers for security, design, e-commerce, and SEO to establish a functional, professional foundation for a website. Explanation of what needs to be prepared for design, content, and future growth.

FIGURE 2.1

The world of the internet

AI Practicum} Adobe Firefly Prompt: Photograph of image showing the internet merged around the earth.

PROFESSIONAL TERMINOLOGY

CMS: Content Management Systems are platforms that design a website without coding.

CSS: Cascading Style Sheets are the code that controls the visual layout of a website.

Domain: The address typed into a URL for a website

Open-source: Available to public use and usually at no cost.

Plugin: An additional tool used in the design and actions on a website.

Redirect: Sends visitors to another link.

SEO: Search Engine Optimization refers to building a site that search robots can easily index.

SER: Search Engine Results are based on many characteristics that need to be input into the backend of a website.

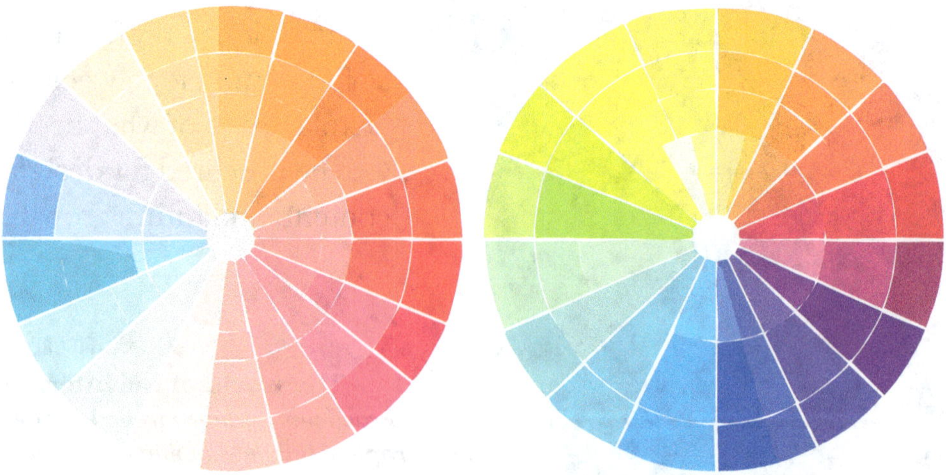

FIGURE 2.2

Rendering of color mode wheels per media

AI Practicum} Adobe Illustrator Prompt: Print and Internet Color Wheels.

WEBSITE DESIGN & PRINT DESIGN

When creating a flyer or business card, the designer has more control over the visual elements than when designing a website. A flyer size is a set, unchanging marketing piece, while a website varies from monitor to monitor and brand of mobile device. The designer will not be able to set the composition with spacing, font choice, or even format—vertical or horizontal.

The color palette is a different system since print is limited to the colors mixed with the inks, and monitors use lights in a palette that mixes red, green, and blue. The printed color is close to what the designer intended, but the monitor color will vary based on the type of monitor and its age.

Fonts are chosen for print marketing but are limited to what the viewer may have on their computer or browser for a website. The flyer is designed with the goal for a viewer to be attracted to the design and pick it up, while a website has to not only entice the viewer to stay on the page but also have images that must be optimized to load the website quickly, or the viewer will leave.

Browsers may portray the website differently. The flyer is static with very little interaction, while a website is built to involve the viewer with hovering components and button links to select.

The list goes on, with the main difference being that the flyer must be distributed as part of the marketing process and a website must be set up in the marketing process to be found by the viewer. Print designers have close to perfect control of the visual, while a website designer does not have that kind of control and must design with flexible visuals.

Visually, a web design is a box within a box. Curves, diagonals, and circles are shapes placed in boxes. Space is set up with padding, fonts have to be embedded to be downloadable for the viewer, and links have to be obvious, or they will not be found.

Both types of design need to be eye-catching and memorable. A successful design uses space, alignment, and most importantly contrast. Contrast can be achieved with scale, color, fonts, images, and textures.

HOSTING WITH A DOMAIN

The TLD, also known as a domain extension, should be easily remembered and apply to the service, product, or business. The standard has become ".com" even though".net" was registered first in 1985. However, there are very few short domain names available with ".com" as the extension. At one time there were four-letter domains with .com but there are none available now in English.

To allow for shorter and specific domains, nearly 1600 different TLDs have been made available. Before setting up hosting for the website, choose an appropriate domain and the TLD.

Here is a short list:

.com is short for commercial

.edu is used by educational websites such as universities, and they must have proof to use the TLD

.org usually reserved for non-profit companies

.us is the country code for the United States and .ca for Canada

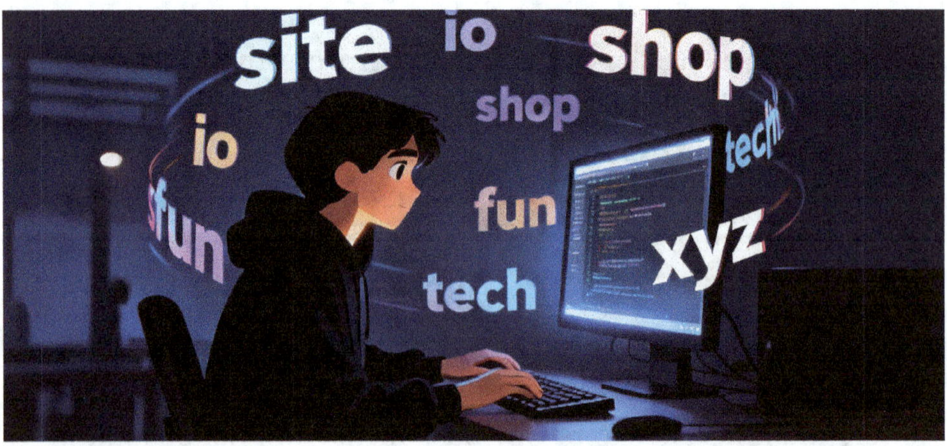

FIGURE 2.3

TLDs floating around a person's head

AI Practicum} Picsart Prompt: Illustration of the words site, io, shop, tech, fun, xyz floating around a designer seated at a computer in a dark room.

A few of the more popular new TLDs are .online, .site, .io. .shop, .tech, .fun, and .xyz. Occupations such as plumber, contractor, dentist, attorney, florist, designer, and art are available.

Choosing a domain can be stressful. Many business owners will use the name of the company, while others will choose something easy to remember that has to do with the company. As an example, a roofing company could use the name toughestroofs. com. Hosting providers may register the first year of a domain at a reduced price but make sure to research the cost for the following years.

The domain should be easy to remember, short, pronounce, and spell. It is recommended the domain be made up of three words or less and under 15 characters. With more than one word, it can be marketed with a cap to start each word since browsers will read it as lowercase.

It should reflect the company brand now and for the future. Check options in social media, and if applicable, search other countries. There are AI domain name generators such as NameBoy.

Avoid numbers, hyphens, symbols, and punctuation. Name generators will not have difficulty spelling the domain and using double letters. For potential customers, double letters are prone to typing errors, such as learnnewwords.com so make sure not to set the domain up with them.

Common mistakes are to choose trendy words or create a domain that only makes sense when it is seen spelled out. It should be relevant to what individuals think about when using a search engine.

Domain Checker Tools

WhoIsLookup and ICANN can be used to check the availability of a domain, to discover who it is registered to, when it was set up, and when it will expire. Sometimes the history can be checked for free in case an available domain with a bad reputation.

DomainTools and Wayback Machine are paid options to see if the domain was used for scams, spamming, and phishing. They can even check the backlinks.

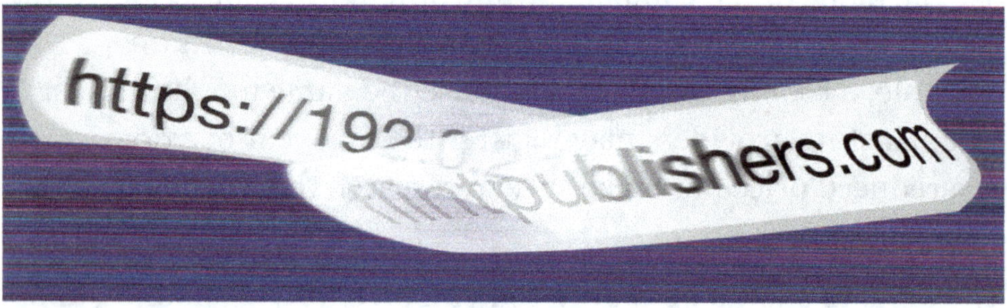

FIGURE 2.4

URL field with IP numbers changing into words

HI Practicum} Photoshop: Set type, used warp edit, blurred and masked.

Uniform Resource Locator explained

At the top of the Internet browser is a field where a query or a web address can be entered. This unique address will take an individual to either a resource such as an amateur file or a webpage. The Uniform Resource Locator (URL) today is secure if at the beginning of a website address or resource are the letters HTTPS. This address will be unique for a website or as a link to a resource such as a PDF or image.

HTTPS, Hypertext Transfer Protocol Secure, is a verified website's server encryption through an SSL, Secure Sockets Layer, certificate This security is an additional paid service that must accompany the hosting package to be a positive factor used by Google in search results. Many browsers, such as Firefox, Chrome,

Safari, and Edge, will show a "not secure" icon in the URL, which will stop most internet searchers. Atlas, the OpenAI ChatGPT internet browser, does not specifically use SSL certification in deciding the results of a search; since it uses the combination of multiple search engines such as Google and Bing, it does affect the results.

The web domain, is a human-friendly address that a browser uses to visit a website by translating the domain into numbers known as an IP address. Type the numbers 142.250.190.78 into the URL field and watch it convert to the name of the domain as it goes to the address. Try 172.217.194.113.

Apple owns the entire 16 million IP 17.0.0.0/8 address range. Amazon is 72.21.211.176, and Facebook's IP is 66.220.149.25.

Domain Registration

Registering domain names originally began with a US government agency. In 1998 a nonprofit company, ICANN, the Internet Corporation for Assigned Names and Numbers, began to oversee the registration and Domain Name System.[1] A DNS reads the domain name and the matching IP address to point the browser to the website.[1]

Sometimes it is easier to purchase and register a domain with the hosting provider. If an individual knows how to edit a DNS record, then they should shop around. Consider what TLD to use and make sure it is included when a domain search is conducted. Check for pricing not just for the first year but for years following. The AI Honey discount app can apply discounts for domain and hosting to some of the registrars.

> **NameCheap:** As the name implies, it is one of the most affordable options. Started in 2000 in Los Angeles, it has grown into one of the top three independent domain registrars globally. Free WHOIS privacy on most domains

GoDaddy: Started in 1977 in Tempe and has grown to be the largest registrar. Will email the latest big domain discounts—a lot.

Cloudflare Registrar: Does not mark up the cost of domains but does not offer hosting. Started in 2018 in San Francisco.

Hostinger: An accredited worldwide registrar that began in 2004 in Lithuania. Offers many low-cost domains and is free the first year with hosting.

Google Domains: Acquired by Squarespace in 2023 with no upsells and considered one of the most reliable on DNS speed.

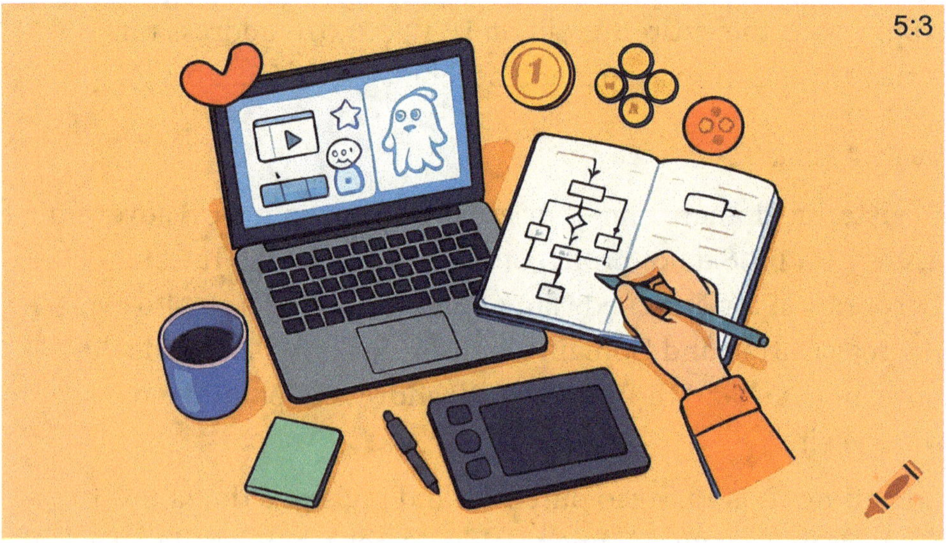

FIGURE 2.5

Websites start with a planned idea

AI Practicum} Craiyon Prompt: flat art of a website being planned in a 5x3 format.

WEBSITE BUILDERS

Business owners planning to build their own websites or marketers developing a landing page for a product or service look for three main functions in a site builder. It has to have a fast learning curve, be easy to use, and not take up valuable time designing and optimizing. After all, if they are not concerned with these points, the businessperson can hire someone who is trained and skilled in design and setting up a website.

Graphic artists, marketing designers, and website creators need a building platform that allows them to see how the page will appear as it is designed, and the layouts must be very customizable. Time is always a factor, and this group is used to learning new technologies. Their struggle may be learning the optimization of the website for search engines such as Google.

Not counting the setup and the go-live steps, webmasters fall into two groups. Many want to start with a blank canvas where they can add visual elements and written content they and AI have generated. The other group prefers to start with an existing modern template that they can change out most of the elements and even revise the page structure.

These groups have common qualities: they do not want to write code, they do not know how to optimize the site, they have creative talents, and they have deadlines.

There are four platforms to build a website: code, template, or visual editor. The fourth platform will be discussed later. Website builders can have drop-and-place elements in most of these options.

Content Management System

A CMS is a platform that builds a website without using code. It allows the designer to organize, edit, and publish the elements of a website visually. All of the website builders listed are CMS.

Template Platforms

Wix, Squarespace, Weebly, GoDaddy SiteBuilder, and Webflow are great for beginners and businesses that want simple designs and some SEO and SER capabilities. Wix has a larger customer base than Squarespace, which is still large and has grown from being started in a University of Maryland dorm room in 2004.

Wix is the easiest CMS platform for small businesses. A website can be built and then maintain itself. Squarespace is almost as easy to use and good for simple store businesses. Weebly is good for landing pages and very small websites. GoDaddy Site Builder is very simple and quick. Webflow is a good starting builder for designers.

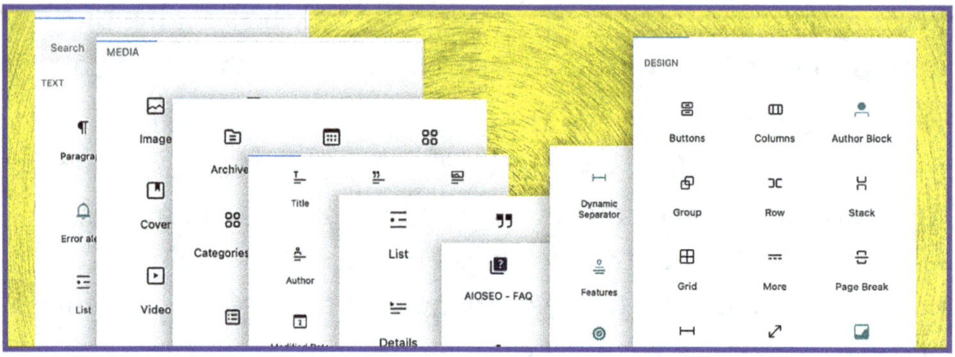

FIGURE 2.6
WordPress Backend page
Screengrabs of WordPress page editing.

Visual Builders and E-Commerce site builders

While WordPress is considered a visual builder, one look at the page and a designer will struggle with the code-like tools. It is estimated that over 40% of the websites in the world use WordPress but no one seems to know how accurate that statement might be and if that is only because it is a good personal use platform and not reliable or secure enough for large companies.

Divi from Elegant Themes, Elementor, Beaver Builder, WP Bakery, and Brick Builder are themes that are added to WordPress and allow the designer to visually lay out the pages. These visual builders are perfect for webmasters that want the most control over the look and feel of a website.

Visual builders allow the designer to see on the screen what the elements will look like in relation to one another. Unlike coding, where the developer has to save the written code and then look at the design in another browser. Visual builders have a plethora of templates to start with and revise and use, such as 404 error pages. SEO can be easily added for search engines, and basic items such as the navigation, buttons, and animation can be selected and placed with a few clicks instead of hours of coding.

The following is a short reference list:

.com stand for commercial

.edu is for educational website such as universities, and they must have proof

.org usually reserved for non-profit companies

.us is the country code for the United States and .ca for Canada.

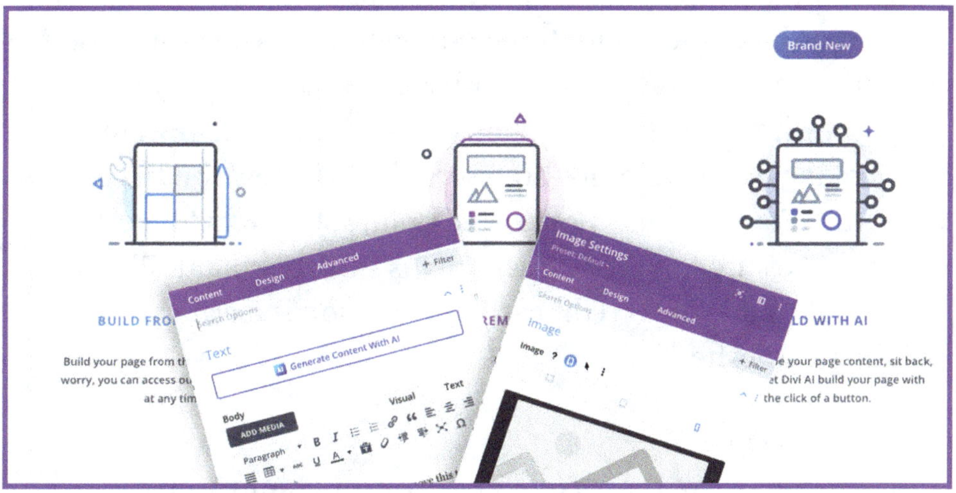

FIGURE 2.7

Divi Visual Designer Page

Screen shot of a Divi page for editing.

Wix, Squarespace, and WooCommerce are good, easy-to-use online shopping platforms. They have templates to follow with some customization. Since the management of e-commerce has to have built-in security and credit card compliance, customization is limited. Shopify has the best security and allows customization.

WooCommerce is an open-source platform, has the most do-it-yourself setup, and has free themes to use. The business owner handles most security via hosting & plugins.

Squarespace has a better look and feel, but the design options are not as flexible as Wix. Their templates are professional and developed for non-techies.

Cost is relatively the same for Squarespace and Wix, and both completely handle the SEO. WooCommerce is the least expensive since the basic site is free, but the plugins can add a cost quickly. Shopify is more expensive, but it comes with all the e-commerce features most businesses need.

One business strategy for keeping a low budget is to start with a more affordable shopping store and then migrate over to Shopify when the inventory and customer list grow. Use a drag-and-drop platform where the design is shown in real time rather than saving and looking at it in another browser. Check reviews on the ease of the setup. For small businesses and online stores that take credit cards, make sure the hosting security is PCI compliant. Planning how to take and store credit card information is a critical step in building a website.

AI website builders

Adobe Express and Canva use AI to assist in building a multi-page website. They do not create an entire multi-page, robust website. It will take a number of prompts to build sections of a website that will need to be uploaded or dragged into a visual builder such as Divi.

AI-generated Websites

The fourth website builder platform is AI-built, such as Wix ADI and Hostinger AI. They can build a fully functional website from a prompt that is uploaded onto their hosting platform. Even though AI website builders can set up the images for bots, add good content, and choose images and colors, humans must finish the website to make it unique, easy to read, and copyrightable.

AI does not understand the concept of space or realize the emotional response of colors and font styles. Therefore, a designer will need to revise, update, and change the layouts to make them human-friendly and impactful.

Google looks at a number of items related to a website as to where to rank it in searches. The main factors in a search result are the amount of traffic, the age of the information on a website, when it was last updated, the quality of the content, the speed of the download of the website pages, how the metadata and keywords are set up, and backlinks that show the bots how highly rated a business or person is considered.

To be found by search engines and reflect the company goals, the AI website will still need at minimum 35% of the content and metadata edited or completely revised. When time is an issue, usiing AI is a good way to start and then learn the nuances of SEO.

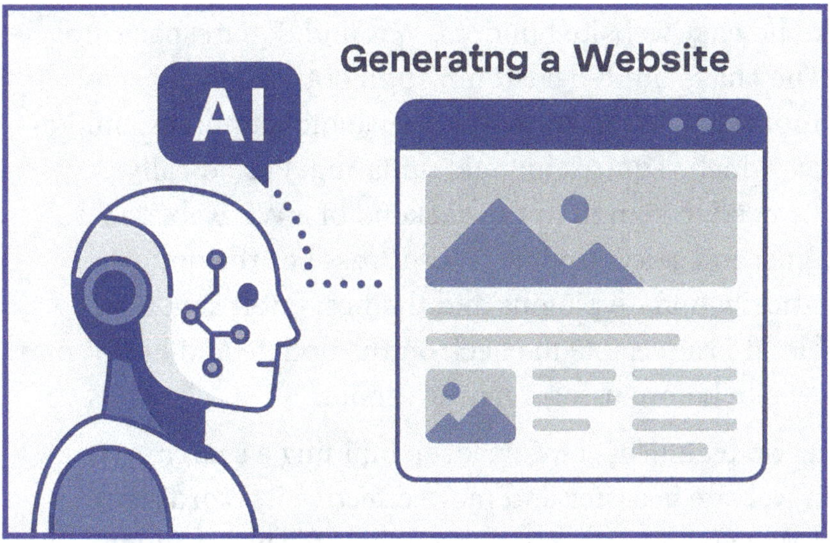

FIGURE 2.8

Spelling and GPT

AI Practicum} ChatGPT Prompt: create an image of AI generating a website.

HOSTING PROVIDERS

The following list is a breakdown of a few of the less expensive web hosting providers. They have a user-friendly setup process, can include WordPress, and have a free setup of the SSL certificate:

IONOS: Least expensive with limited customization options. Best for learning how to build a website.

NameCheap: Value option with an easily accessible control panel. Best for small sites and blogs.

DreamHost: A little more expensive but has extra tools. Good for businesses and designers.

Hostinger: Affordable and includes AI tools. Good for beginners to professionals.

Bluehost: Slightly pricier. Good for agencies and larger businesses.

For quick and easy website builders, Wix and Squarespace are options. They have limited customization options and cost as much or more than WordPress, but they handle updates, unlike WordPress, which requires manual updating. Periodically, individuals need to sign in to the backend of a WP website, go to Plugins, and select update. WordPress has the option to automatically update plugins and themes, but it is not dependable. It is advisable to check on the update and how it may affect a website before using a newer version.

Depending on technical comfort level, building a search-optimized website is easier and more effective in WordPress than with Wix and Squarespace. WP allows for better plugin integration and keyword snippets. It gives the webmaster more control and is flexible. The downside is it was originally built for blogging and not for building a website, so some of the features are antiquated and slow down the design process.

Wix is the solution if a business owner needs a platform that is easy to use, has the drag-and-drop feature, prefers the automatic plugin updating, and plans on using a mostly visual website. Keep in mind that Google bots do not exactly see pictures but read alternate content, file names, and meta descriptions.

Squarespace has modern templates and automatic updating. The search results are weaker but can be manipulated. Since it is a visual solution, the templates are more attractive to visitors, and it can be more effective. A good choice if building a website for credibility and not concerned with bringing in customers through search results.

Getting started

Usually, hosting plans will break the plan down to monthly cost, but they will charge for the entire subscription. If a 12-month plan is chosen, multiply the monthly cost by 12, and that is what the hosting company will charge to get the site files and folders ready on a server. For example, if the cloud startup is chosen at $9.95 per month for 12 months, the cost is $119.40. Make sure to note the renewal rate, which is usually two to three times the initial rate. For this reason, many website developers will choose the longest option to get that rate. For Hostinger, that total cost is $357.60, or broken down to equal $7.45 a month.

If the goal is to just learn how to build a website, keep all elements and content backed up, and plan on redesigning the site on another plan. Choose the 1 month and then pay an increased monthly fee until the project is finished. Once a site is closed, it will not be accessible; take screenshots of all pages for later when the website is rebuilt to go live. Another option is to migrate the practice website to another hosting service.

Hosting platforms have a similar setup process. If Hostinger is chosen, the middle plan includes daily backups, compared to the lower plan which only has weekly backups. Most likely, the website will be worked on more than once a week, and in case something happens or the site is inadvertently deleted, it is nice to be able to go back one day and reinstall a backup. The dedicated IP is a benefit, as is the 24/7 support, but most of the support questions can be solved by searching the internet.

Almost all of the plans include a free domain for one year, but it will need to be renewed after the 12-month period. It is recommended to check to see if the domain is available before signing up.

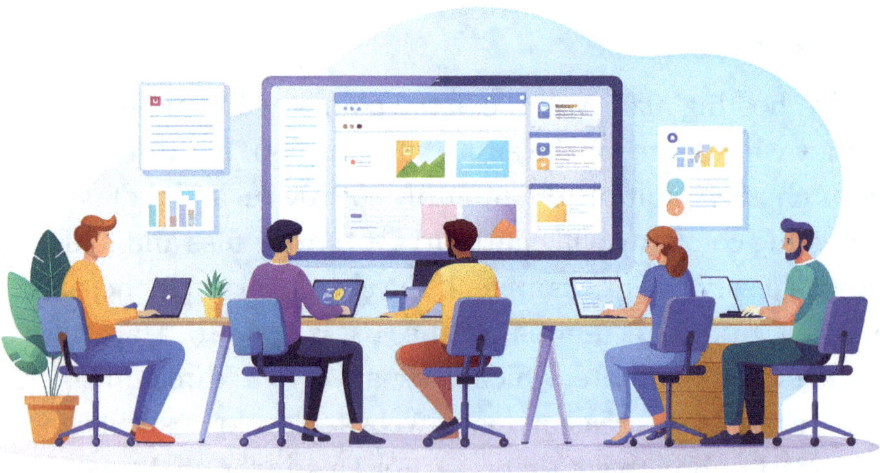

FIGURE 2.9

AI can do a lot but still need HI

AI Practicum} Firefly Prompt: Create an image of AI generating a website.

In the "Find a domain" section, type in the domain and select search. The next window will show its availability and the renewal cost. For example, BestPainterOKC.com is available for free and then $19.99 in 12 months. It is recommended to purchase the domain for 3 years, which helps in search results and to make sure the price is locked in. Usually, a list of other domain extensions will be shown.

Before starting to design, a website builder platform needs to be added to the website. Many hosting companies have their own web builders, which do not need code. To use a visual builder that relies on WordPress, the site needs to be prepared first with the WP files. Then, when the site is ready, add the visual builder into the themes section.

AI and Regular Pricing Plans

Signing up with a hosting company is basically the same process. As an example, here are the Hostinger steps to use WordPress:

1. Visit the Hostinger website and go to pricing.

2. Under Type of hosting, select Managed hosting for WordPress

3. Under the Length of subscription dropdown, select at least 12 months. To show up in search results, it is better to have at least a 36-month term.

4. Choose the "Business + AI" plan, which includes 5 free mailboxes per website per year.

5. In the next window, make sure the length of the plan is correct, or it can be changed in the dropdown.

6. Fill in the domain that has been selected.

7. Register and add in the billing and payment details.

8. Verify the domain email address by retrieving the email from the address listed.

9. Choose the closest country for the server location.

10. The host will automatically install WP and send a notification to the administrator's email on file.

11. When the site is ready, it gives the option to also install plugins that may be used.

12. Log in to the control panel of the host account, select "Create a website," and follow the prompts.

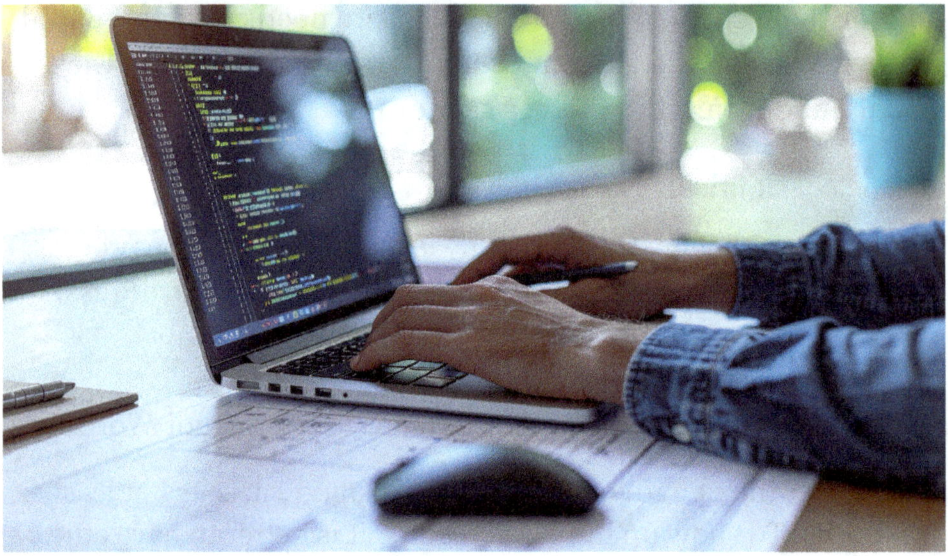

FIGURE 2.10

The Age of AI

AI Practicum} Firefly Prompt: Illustrate how AI generates a complete website.

Demo with ChatGPT—creating a headline

ChatGPT Plus does not have a steep learning curve and can easily create a Headline 1 for a website. This is the main title on a web page that attracts visitors and tells search engines the main goal of the page. It needs to communicate with visitors to keep them on the page and not select the back button. It will give the reader an impression of the page content, such as friendly, creative, or informative, or selling a product or service.

Each page should have one H1 headline. A page can have smaller, less important headlines H2 and H3, but the H1 explains a benefit to the visitor without being to "sales oriented" or full of information.

To create a strong H1 headline with ChatGPT:

1. In a short phrase, explain the business and the target market.

2. Make sure to give details such as which page it is being used for and the goal.

3. Add a keyword for customers and search engines.

4. Ask for at least 5 ideas with a defined tone.

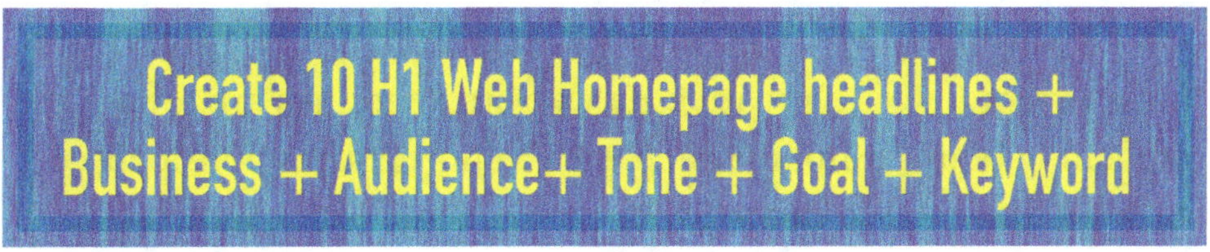

FIGURE 2.11

The magic headline prompt formula

HI Practicum} Designed in Photoshop by creating a textured background using noise and motion filters with a border set as a color burn layer blend.

Headline formula explained:

The business description needs to be short, such as just the industry.

A. Define the customer in as few words as possible.

B. The goal can be a call to action to create conversions.

C. Tone can be friendly, creative, bold, energetic, simple, or sales-oriented.

D. The main search word or phrase is the keyword.

These prompt examples demonstrate clear-toned verbiage:

Create 10 creative H1 website headlines for a book publisher that helps new authors self-publish.

Create 10 creative H1 website headlines for a book publisher that helps new authors self-publish.

Audience: new authors.

Tone: creative and inspiring.

Goal: increase clicks on the 'Send More Information' button.

Include the keyword 'self-publishing.'

Also include a short subhead under each option.

The results

These examples of 10 creative H1 website headlines are for a self-publishing book company, each with a short conversion-focused subhead designed to drive clicks on the "Send More Information" button.

10 H1 Headline Options (with Subheads)

1. Bring Your Book to Life Through Self-Publishing
Start your author journey today with expert guidance every step of the way.

2. Your Story Deserves to Be Published—Let's Begin.
Get professional help turning your manuscript into a beautifully self-published book.

3. Self-Publishing Made Simple for New Authors.
We guide you from idea to finished book with clear direction.

4. Publish Your First Book the Right Way.
Easy, supported self-publishing designed specifically for first-time authors.

5. Turn Your Manuscript Into a Published Book.
Get everything you need to self-publish with professional quality.

6. Ready to Become an Author? Start with Self-Publishing.
Take the next step with expert support built for new writers.

7. Your Voice. Your Book. Your Self-Publishing Journey.
We help you create a book you're proud to share with the world.

8. A Better Path to Self-Publishing for New Writers.
Skip the confusion—get clear, simple guidance from start to finish.

9. Publish Your Book with Confidence.
Professional self-publishing support to help you launch your story.

10. Make Your Dream of Becoming an Author Real.
Get step-by-step self-publishing help designed for beginners.

ChatGPT offered these follow-up options:

If you want, I can also create:

- A/B testing variants
- Homepage hero text
- Button/CTA options
- SEO-friendly meta descriptions
- A full homepage section layout
- Just tell me what you need!

The homepage hero text, CTA button, and SEO meta are content to get now. Consider that instead of a human guessing what an AI bot is looking for in SEO, it would make more sense to have an AI platform such as GPT decide what the AI bot should read.

Once a headline is decided upon, this is a good time to ask for even more subhead options.

REFERENCES

1. Internet Corporation for Assigned Names and Numbers, https://sk.sagepub.com/ency/edvol/newmedia/chpt/internet-corporation-assigned-names-numbers.

The Power of UX/UI

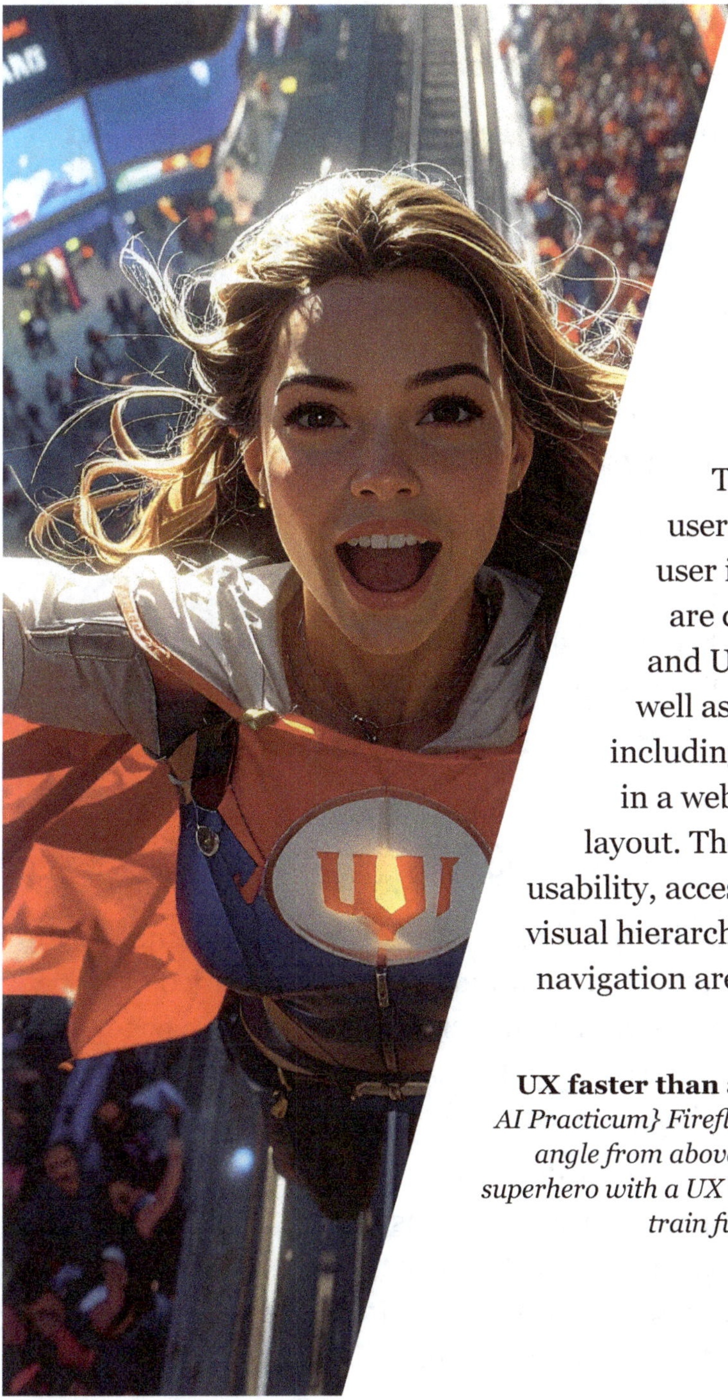

C3

OVERVIEW

The principles of user experience and user interface design are determined. UX and UI are defined as well as the reasons for including that approach in a website design and layout. The importance of usability, accessibility, layout, visual hierarchy, and intuitive navigation are differentiated.

FIGURE 3.1

UX faster than a speeding train
AI Practicum} Firefly Prompt: Camera angle from above showing a female superhero with a UX icon flying above a train full of cheering fans.

PROFESSIONAL TERMINOLOGY

Accessible: A website that is designed for everyone, including the disabled, to interact with the contents.

Brand: The look and feel of a company across all media and marketing.

Site Map: A breakdown of a website's structure.

Tagline: A short, strong message to let visitors know about your company.

Template: A pre-designed layout of a website with fonts and colors that can be customized.

UI Design: User Interface is the look and feel of a website to the visitor.

UX Design: User experience is how easily a visitor can understand the message.

USERS

UI design utilizes the visual structure, the space elements take up, the space around these objects and shapes, and their colors. The user interface design focuses on building an attractive page that is easy to process and scan by the reader. The brand is portrayed consistently on all pages in color and placement.

UX design focuses on how the visitor moves around the website. They want to quickly navigate the website, find what they need, and leave. The designer wants to make this a short trip and not a journey. The minute the visitor feels scanning the site will take too much time and effort, they will leave.

User-friendly design is intuitive. It should be effortless in focusing the user on the product in a natural and easy way. Intuitive design will use the visitors existing knowledge and expectations to engage them.

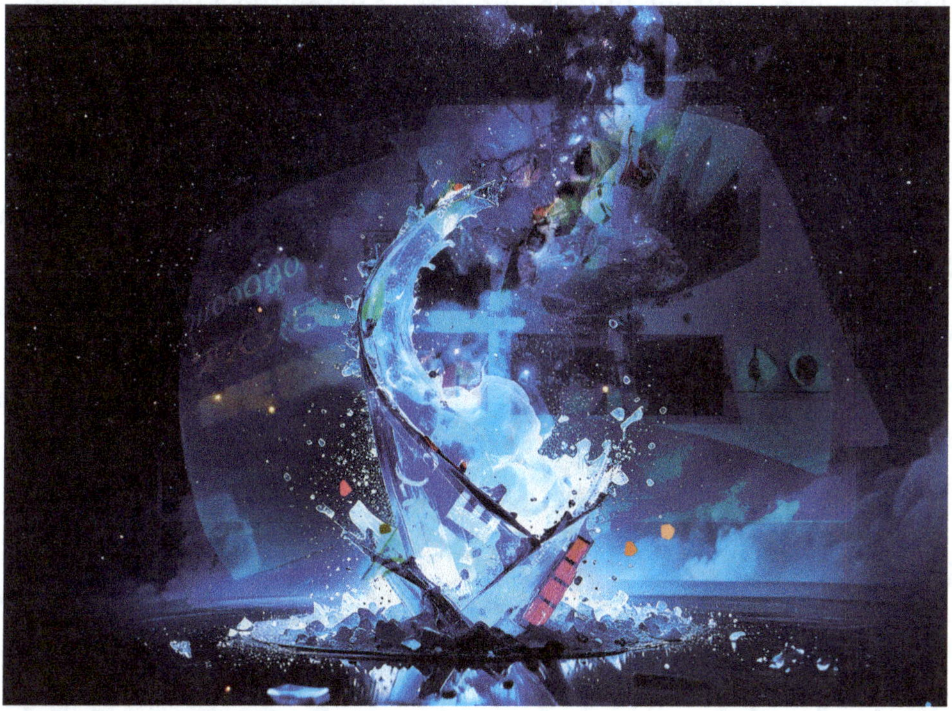

FIGURE 3.2

Without SEO the site implodes

AI Practicum} Firefly Prompt 1: Create a visual image of an image of a futuristic website on glass. Firefly Prompt 2: Visual image on blue of SEO destroyed. HI Practicum} Combine in Photoshop.

Common patterns and easy to follow actions that require minimal explanation is centered on user. It balances created problem-solving without conscious effort. The users to understand the information immediately due to consistent layout features the user prioritize during their scan to come back and focus on.

The design needs to place information and feature such as buttons and links where a visitor will instinctively look. This is where negative space is extremely important. The visual will reduce any friction that could cause the visitor to leave. White space around the text and images, should prevent overwhelming the user as a scan the page for critical information and the CTA.

Links such as buttons that change colors when the cursor hovers them, known as a rollovers, are effective for a CTA.

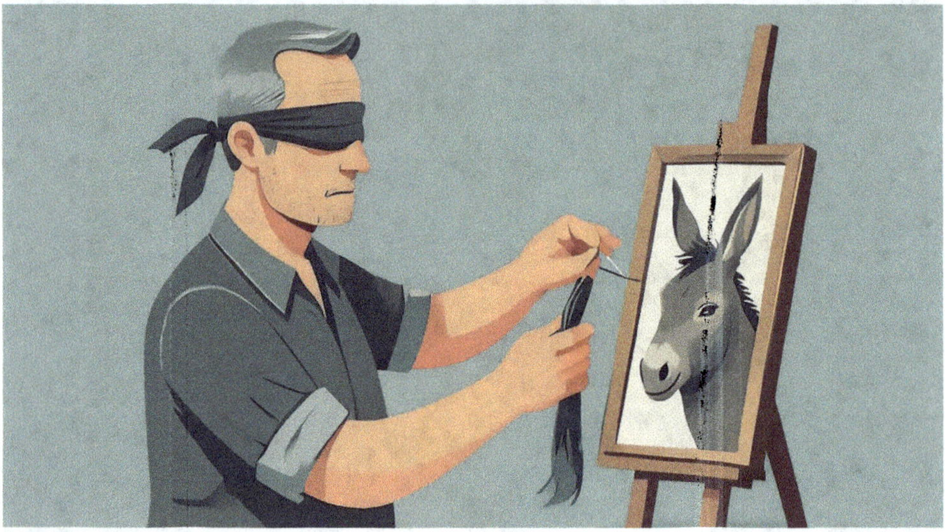

FIGURE 3.3

Pinning down an audience

AI Practicum} Creator Prompt: flat art of a blindfolded middle-aged man pinning a tail onto a picture of a donkey.

DEFINING THE TARGET MARKET

When developing a website, before creating content and artwork, the simplest and most critical step is to define the target market. This step will allow the creative to successfully curate headlines, define the message, and research the keywords for SEO and brand strategy; the design must be aimed at the audience to establish a budget level.

Start with the fundamentals. Identify the existing customers, which includes age range, gender, location, income level, job roles, industry, and education level. These demographics identify who the design is aimed to engage. Understand what makes them care about a product or service. Identify what motivates them and what value they put on the company.

Now turn attention toward new customers. Decide why they are coming to the website. It could be to find a solution for a problem or compare prices. Find out if these visitors trust the company and its products/services, or if the website will need to establish this as part of the sales information.

Drill deeper and figure out if the potential customer can afford what the website offers and if the audience is large enough to support the business. The target market may need to be expanded.

If possible, establish if the visitors are just gathering information so more information through a contact form or phone call can be offered. If they have authority to make the decision, decide what avenues will be needed to close the deal.

By establishing a target market, the website messaging can be decided. The direction of the design can be driven by these answers. The main headlines and content should reflect the problems and solutions that have been defined.

The website should clarify who it's for and what the CTA should be, such as booking a call or finding pricing. The SEO keywords should align with how and why the visitors search.

DESIGNING FOR IMPACT

A single, purpose-driven website created for one action is the most difficult website to design. It is natural to add more images and more information after the visitor has been convinced.

There are five principles in website design that work together to create confident, satisfied users and form the foundation of outstanding UX/UI design. The goal is to have strong engagement and memorable brand perception.

The first principle is to design a website that invites visitors to read and explore more about the information being provided. The information needs to be straightforward. This basic design approach will reduce user frustration and improve retention.

Ensure the website experience is user-friendly to all individuals, including those with disabilities. This second principle is not only responsible but also expands the target audience.

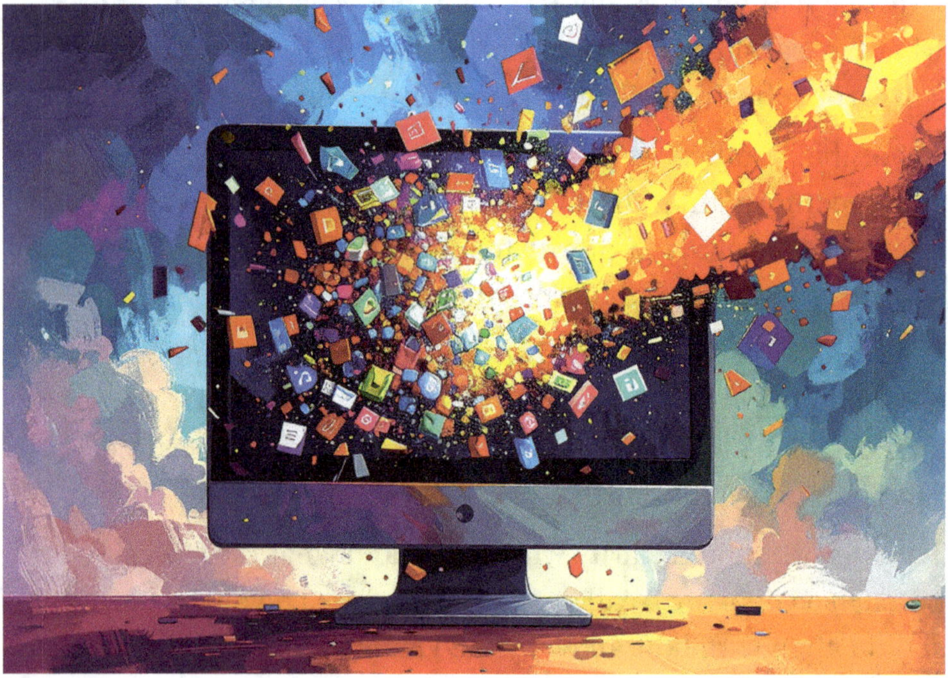

FIGURE 3.4
Grabbing attention
AI Practicum} Firefly Prompt: Cartoon of a website bursting out of a monitor; an abstract concept for the internet.

The third principle is to arrange the elements with a consistent approach, such as a systematic structure, element spacing that is not congested, which could overwhelm the visitor, and grouping elements that are related.

Remember, visitors who found your website in a search are looking for something and will quickly leave if it is not readily available. To accomplish this, utilize design elements such as size, color, and contrast to direct user focus. This fourth principle enhances the ease of scanning and comprehending the message.

The fifth principle is that the navigation needs to be simple to use. Well-defined paths and simple menus enable users to navigate the website pages effortlessly.

These significant principles of UX/UI design will produce a website that sells the product and service while creating a memorable brand. Contented users are the result of the fundamental basis of exceptional UX/UI design, resulting in increased engagement and enhanced brand perception.

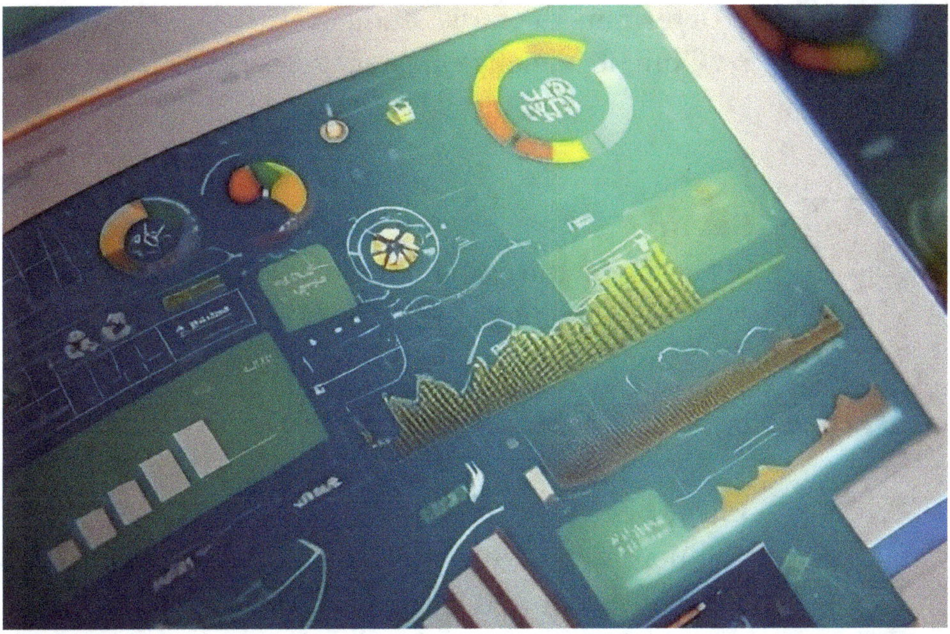

FIGURE 3.5

Website stats and traffic visuals

AI Practicum} Craiyon Prompt: Long color page showing multiple statistics and graphics.

MATCHING MILESTONES WITH GOALS

Before placing the first word on a website, the designer would set up a simple list of the items that need to be covered and create a timeline. Sometimes an individual will get stuck at some point in the website development. Having a timeline focuses them on each step of the process so nothing is missed and creates deadlines to help them recognize when it is time to move on.

A schedule assists in starting and finishing the website project. A step-by-step list of what is involved could include:.

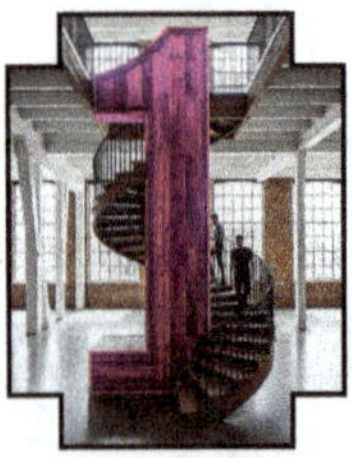

Define

Identify the purpose and goals
Determine the target audience
Obtain feedback from stakeholders

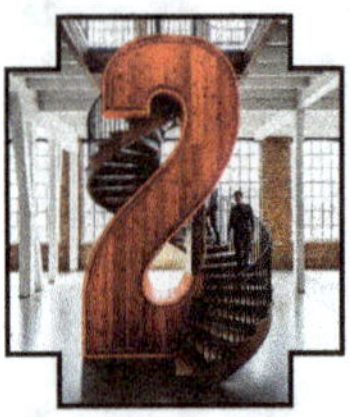

Set up

Decide on the domain name
Create a Web hosting account
Configure the server environment

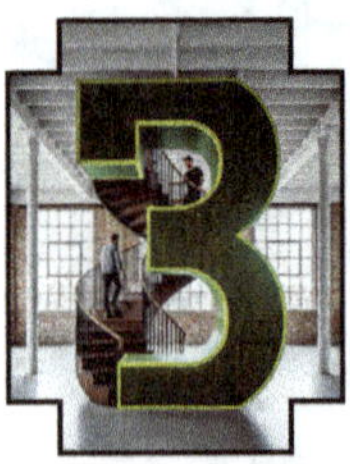

Plan, prepare, execute

Blueprint website's structure, pages, navigation
Create optimized visual design elements
Write content, metadata, and alt text
Layout and Design
Back up the website files and database

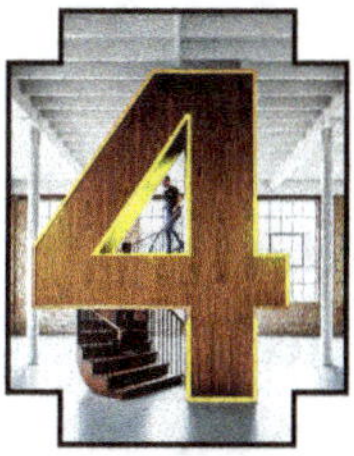

Test and check

Functionality on browsers
Adjust for multiple devices
Review and correct content
Download speed

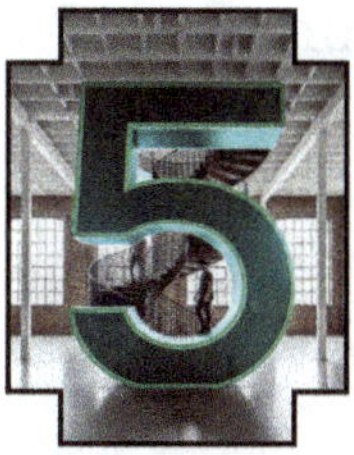

Announce and monitor

Systematically check and correct issues
Discover system update errors post-launch
Regularly update the website with fresh content and maintain security

PAGE FLOW

When laying out a website, the design is based on knowledge. Individuals read from left to right, and they are trained to start at the top of the page. When they first visit a website, the larger and darker elements are more important, and these elements are grouped if connected and have space to set them apart.

For the reader to be comfortable with the design and focus on the message and not leave, the pages must be related visually and readable. People will read paragraphs set in lowercase instead of caps, and headlines are much easier to understand if kept short and do not run across the page.

Overworked designs or pages that appear to not be finished will chase away a potential customer. Professional web developers will study each page and finesse the place, size, and color of each element to make the page inviting. The page must be easily scanned by the visitor trying to find the answer they have searched for that led them to the website.

Another design flaw is extending a page to allow for the spacing of information. Why not let a page go on and on? Hardly anyone but the designer and client wants to scroll more than three times to find what they want. In the days of newspapers, they knew the area above the fold is what would entice a reader to buy the newspaper and put the "grabbers' above the fold. The same principle works with a webpage. On a desktop monitor, place the three items that will hook a reader where they can be seen without scrolling. Size them according to importance and use font weight and color to lead the reader.

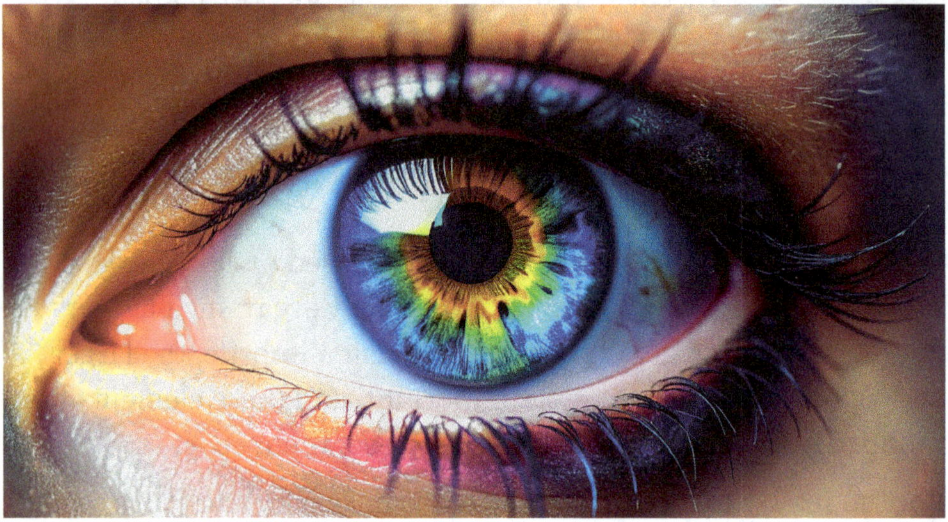

FIGURE 3.6

Eyeful of color

AI Practicum} Firefly Prompt: Photo of color reflecting in a person's eyes.

COLOR

Color is an underappreciated eye-attracting and tone-setting technique used by graphic designers. Many professionals tend to stick with black and white and do not fully understand the appeal of color. The understanding of how color influences emotions, directs attention, enhances readability, and conveys meaning makes it one of the most effective techniques in graphic design. Even Apple has revised their animated logo with color to attract viewers.

A well-crafted color palette will give the layout a visual hierarchy. Designers can direct the reader to the most important information and communicate the meaning of the words before they even read them.

The color palette should sell the message. Just as a website selling spas should use calming light blues and aqua accents, a sports website should use bold reds contrasted with blacks and white space to sell energy and excitement.

Branding utilizes color as an emotional way to build trust and create an appeal to a visitor. Consistent usage of color will make the logo recognizable when the visitor has left the website. In other marketing avenues, the brand color will strengthen its perception.

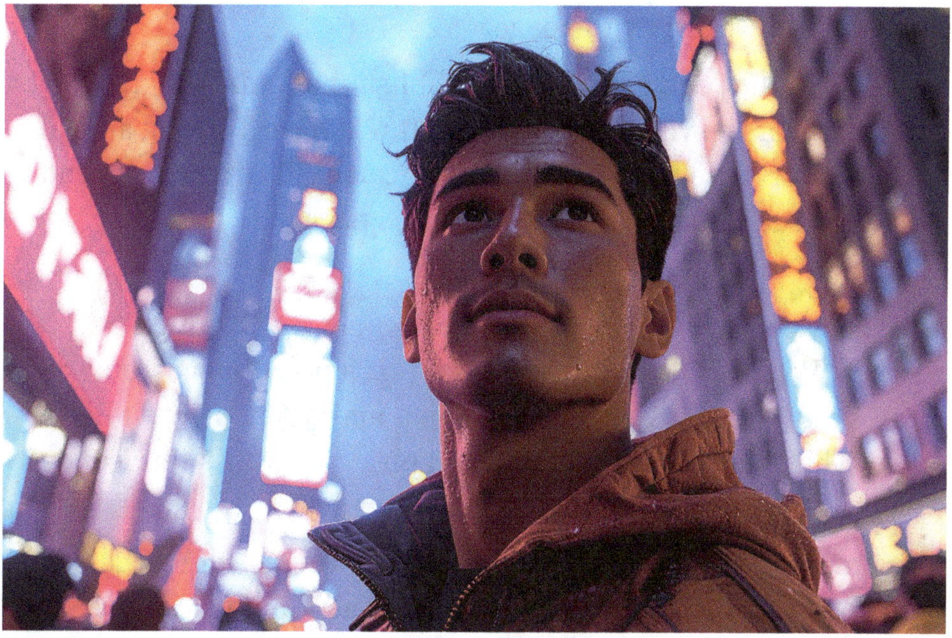

FIGURE 3.7

UI to the rescue

AI Practicum} Firefly Prompt: tight shot of a male superhero with a UI icon standing in a city street with a crowd cheering; the camera view is looking up at the scene.

SPACE

Space will make a page more inviting to a visitor. This principle is without a doubt the least understood but most important aspect of website design.

Clients and designers tend to feel uncomfortable with space and will fill every possible inch with information. They are so enamored with their design, they cannot step back and look at the page with an unbiased opinion. The easy trick is to know there is too much for the reader to look through and leave.

The best benefit of website design to a graphic artist is the information can be alluded to and linked to another area. If the reader is truly interested, they can click on the link that may take them down the page or to another page. If they are not interested, they can keep scanning the page.

Space gives the page a professional polish that makes it attractive and easier for the visitor to navigate. It will have a strong appeal to the visitor since they will think they can easily find or not find what they searched for to end up on this page.

CTA

Dr. Jack Werner stated it very clearly: "If a potential customer cannot find out how to contact you in a marketing piece, it has failed. The effort to educate a person on a company's services or products is wasted if the customer cannot act on it."

This step is the culmination of everything. Do not forget the point of the website and direct the visitor to an action. Make it easy for them to take the next step. Be bold, use color, and have space around the CTA. Have them do it now and not think about it. Keep the call to action short, easy to understand, and easy to find.

TYPES OF SITES

UX and UI are defined as elements that guide that journey, and thoughtful UX/UI design improves satisfaction. However, this type of design revolves around one definable point—the type of website being created should have a single, purpose-driven design for one action.

A brochure website explains what the company does or can provide to the visitor. The site should make it easy to contact them.

An e-commerce site should make it easy to browse the products. Similar to a print catalog, visitors should be able to purchase the products online with a secure interface.

A portfolio showcases samples of creative professionals but also demonstrates a company's products. Unlike an e-commerce website, a portfolio does not directly sell what it is displaying.

Educational, news, or information websites have regularly published written content to share with the target market.

A booking platform is service-oriented, allowing visitors to read about their offerings and schedule them. It should have a calendar with optional times or a contact form that includes the best way

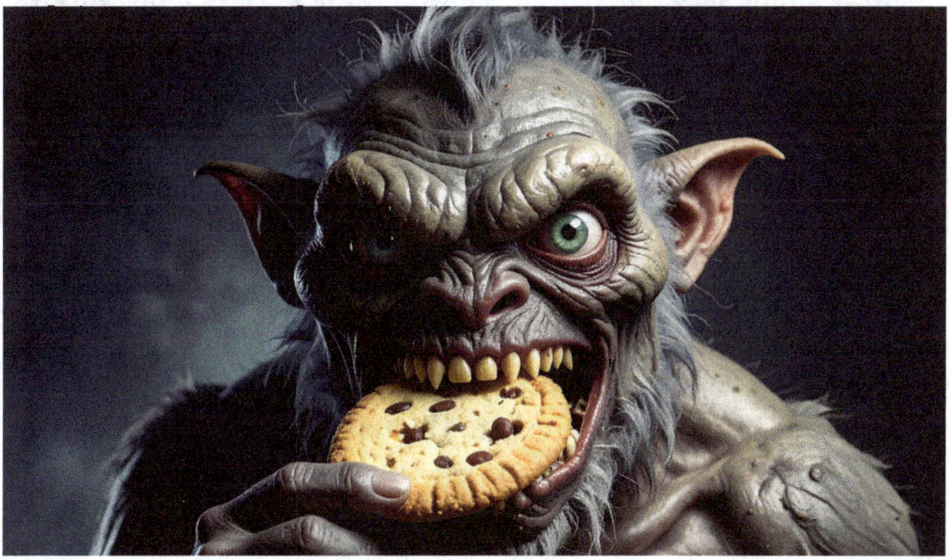

FIGURE 3.8

Cookies have a purpose

AI Practicum} Express Prompt: Photo of monster eating a cookie and looking at the camera.

COOKIES

Website cookies are small text files saved on a visitor's device to store information for future use. They are not software programs and cannot execute code—they are purely data files. Cookies help websites remember user preferences, login details, and other session-related information.

There are two basic types of cookies. Essential cookies are used without the visitor's consent to make the website function. They load automatically. Personal cookies are used to remember preferences, track how a visitor interacts with the website for analytics, or follow a visitor to other websites and show targeted ads.

Visitors do not need to allow cookies, but they may not have a fully functional experience on the site. Shopping carts, logins, and personalized content may not work as well.

In short, cookies range from essential tools for site operation to mechanisms for marketing and analytics. Understanding their purpose helps users make informed decisions about consent and privacy.

SOCIAL MEDIA TRACKERS

Trackers are small pieces of code that are built into webpages. They can be pixels, scripts, or plugins. The social media trackers are used to track and record what visitors do on websites and link that activity to the user's profile or behaviors on the social networking site itself.

They let businesses and platforms customize and improve

content. The code gathers information about visitor interactions, including pages visited, buttons selected, the amount of time spent on a website page, and what purchases were made. The social media site then puts all of this information together and analyzes it. This process lets platforms construct a complete profile of user internet habits and interests.

If the visitor is logged in, the code adds it to their account. If not, it matches the code with the device or browser. This method allows platforms to build a full picture of a visitor's online habits and interests.

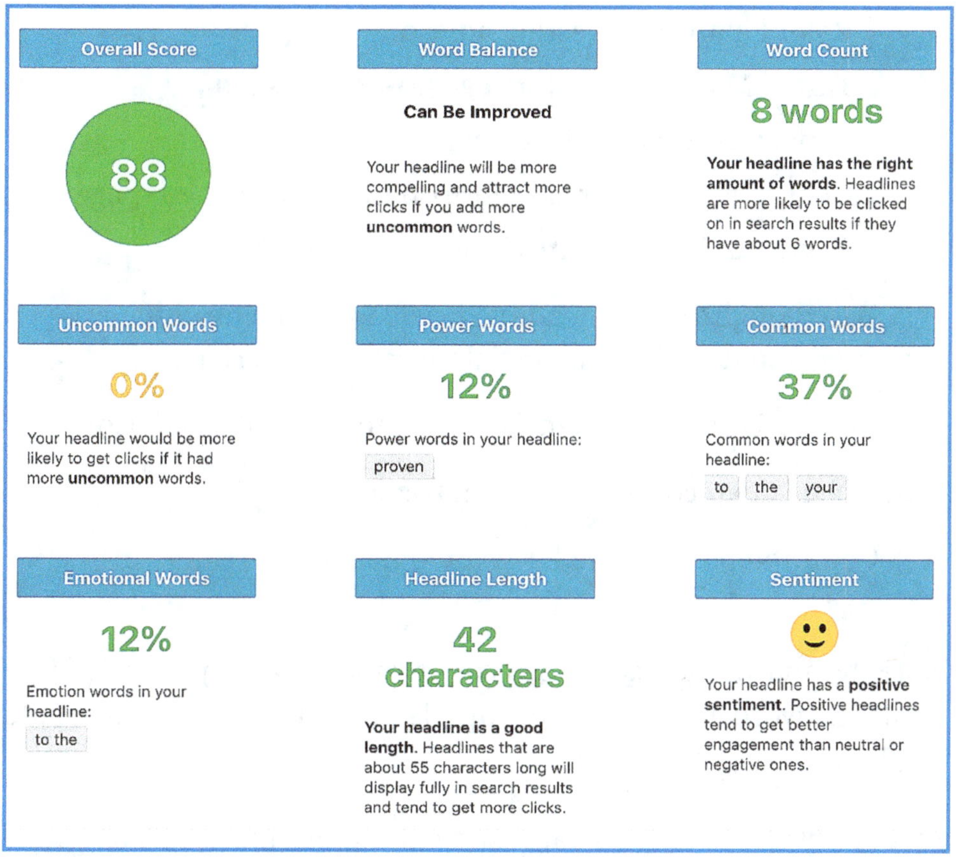

FIGURE 3.9

Screen Grab of IsItWp Headline Analyzer results.

Demo of how to test a headline

To test two headline approaches, one will be human-written, and one will be from Microsoft Word. Each will have the same goal of capturing the visitor's attention to inspire them to read more of the web page.

Approach 1

Test a headline written by human intelligence.

1. Set up the UX/UI framework of the headline for human intelligence to write and for artificial intelligence to generate.

   Role: Financial investing advisor

   Target Market: Investors age 30-45 years old

   Tone: Corporate, safe, calm

   Goal: Visitors will read more on the advisor's web page

   Keyword: Financial Advisor

2. Based on the above headline brief, a website headline was written about selling a financial investor's experience.

3. Result: Trust your financial future to the proven advisor.

4. Open isitwp.com/headline-analyzer

5. Copy and paste in the HI-written headline.

Note the analysis looks at word count, emotional impact, use of numbers, word choices, use of superlatives, and provides alternate headlines.

Easy Peasy also provides a suggestion to improve the headline:

"The headline can be improved by reducing the word count,

adding emotional depth, incorporating numbers, enhancing word choice, and possibly using superlatives. A more concise and emotionally engaging headline with quantifiable benefits could increase its effectiveness."

Easy-Peasy supplies these headline options:

- § "Secure Your Financial Future with a Trusted Expert."
- § "3 Proven Steps to Trust Your Financial Future."
- § "Unlock Confidence in Your Financial Future Today!"
- § "Your Best Financial Future Starts with a Trusted Advisor."
- § "Choose the Top Advisor for Your Financial Peace of Mind."

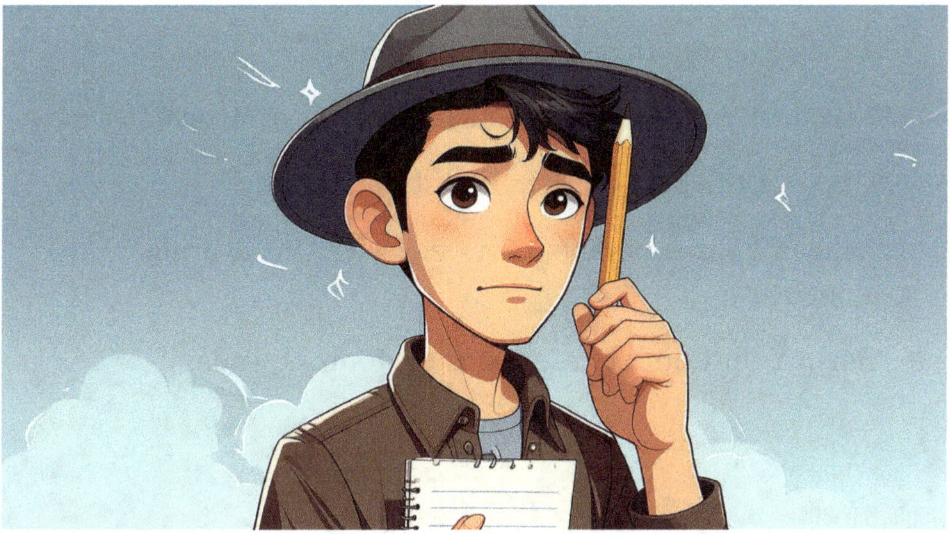

FIGURE 3.10

Trying to be creative

AI Practicum} Express Prompt: Cartoon of man trying to think with hat pushed back and holding a pencil with a notepad.

Approach 2

Test a headline written by artificial intelligence.

1. Prompt Microsoft Copilot in the sidebar:

Create an inspiring short H1 website headline for a financial investing advisor that helps new investors set their investment strategy.

2. Result: Start Investing with Confidence

3. Open easy-peasy.ai/templates/headline-analyzer

   Copy and paste in the HI-written headline.

This time the word count is too short; it approves of the emotional impact of the word "confidence," needs to use numbers, the word choice of "start" is somewhat generic, and provides alternate headlines.

Easy-Peasy also provides alternate headlines:

- "5 Easy Steps to Invest with Confidence"
- "Kickstart Your Investing Journey with Confidence"
- "Discover the Best Ways to Invest Confidently"
- "Launch Your Investment Strategy with Unwavering Confidence"
- "Begin Your Confident Investment Journey Today!"

INSETS

FIGURE 3.11 -3.15

Step of the schedule

AI Practicum} Gemini Prompt: Design the number 1, 2, 3, 4, 5 as columns circled by a staircase. HI Practicum} Use Photoshop to have the number stand out with color overlay, use generative fill to add to the image tip and sides, added cornered border in InDesign.

Beyond Aesthetics

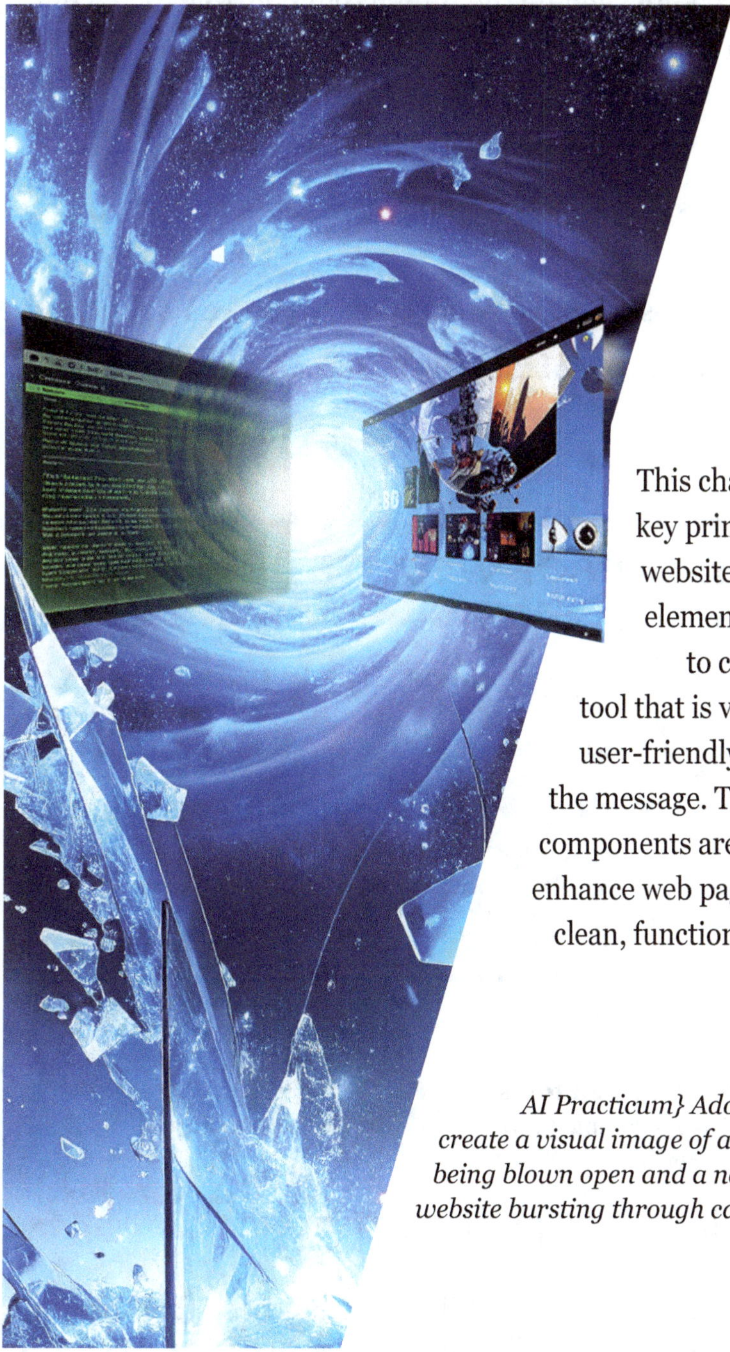

C4

OVERVIEW

This chapter explores the key principles of effective website design. All of the elements work in unison to create a marketing tool that is visually appealing, user-friendly, and focused on the message. The specific design components are covered that can enhance web pages, making them clean, functional, and engaging.

FIGURE 4.1

Look at us now

AI Practicum} Adobe Firefly Prompt: create a visual image of a website from 1990 being blown open and a new fresh 2025 style website bursting through causing debris to fly.

PROFESSIONAL TERMINOLOGY

Backend: The area not seen by the public that controls the layout and content of a website.

Frontend: The visual elements users see and interact with on a website.

Hamburger: 3 lines on a mobile or tablet website that open the navigation menu.

Responsive: The website adapts and changes based on device.

Wireframe: A quick layout of the website for navigation and page design.

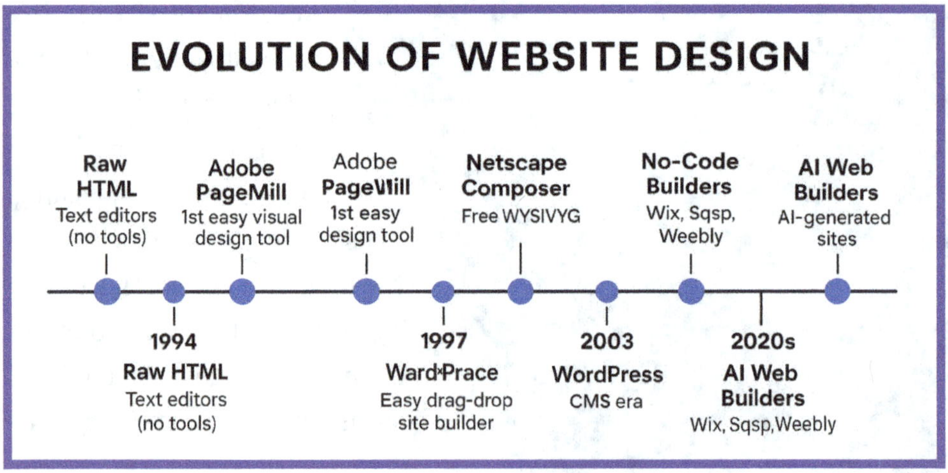

FIGURE 4.2

Evolution of website design tools

AI Practicum} ChatGPT Prompt: Create a timeline graphic about website design tools in a then vs. now visual.

EVOLUTION OF WEBSITE DESIGN

Throughout science, a common philosophy has been that the inventor must know the history and understand the location in the present day to develop something for the future. Website design is similar. A creative should not follow a design because it looks like a style they recognize. It may not be cutting edge, but in reality, it's old, and due to a lack of layout tools and skills, the layout was necessary. If an individual sees a website design in search results, they may think it is a new approach. If they have a timeline, then they will know it is not.

Up until the mid-1990s, websites were developed by software engineers who used code to produce text for the content and links. Type was black on light, usually white, backgrounds, and links were a royal blue and underlined. The end product was intended to provide information that was available to everyone and everywhere. It was nicknamed the information superhighway

In 1992, a website "design" seminar was limited to adding a digital image that was barely recognizable, using the return key to add space, and typing words, all flush left. Paul Hebron, a well-known California designer at the seminar, commented that until designers can actually lay out the elements, websites will not be developed to attract attention or create memorable compositions.

The inherent problem was the design was based on what software engineers comprehended about visual principles, color, and fonts. The same problem exists for designers today since they use the design programs that have fonts and colors loaded into the layouts for them to choose from. If the graphic designers do not create their own libraries of these two key elements of effective design, they are limiting themselves. Anyone who designs a visual layout needs to learn the basics of design to create a professional, communicative website.

Software such as FrontPage and PageMill allowed a visual designer tocreate without writing code. While the sites were simple and limited due to the internet speed at that time, these programs began the evolution to today's drag-and-drop font selection that is automatically coded to allow a browser to download when visiting a website and images with motion.

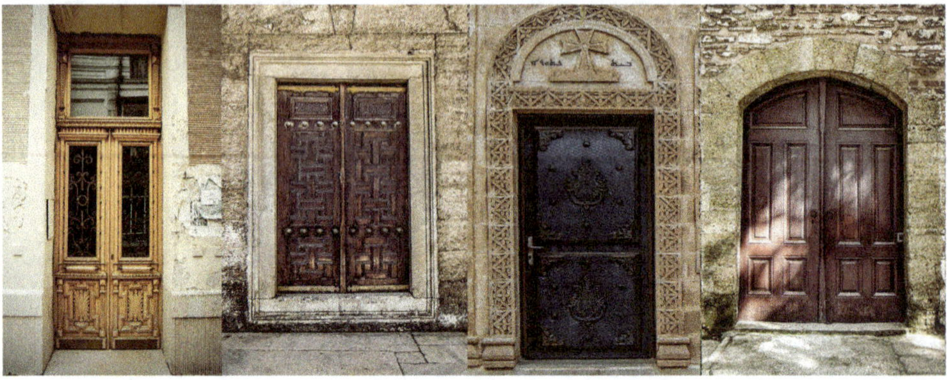

FIGURE 4.3
Door of any design is still a door
Adobe Stock photo.

DIFFERENCES BETWEEN DESIGN AND DEVELOPMENT

The look and feel of a website is the creative side. This is not just about color fonts, image imagery, and layout structure, but also the branding. The user experience has to be overall easy and inviting.

Web development is the part you don't see, which is coding using different types of codes. This is referred to as the backend of the website; visitors don't see the servers that his website is connected to or the security.

When designing and developing a website's layout, think of it like a house. Although invisible, the electrical and plumbing parts need to function. Although they are not visible, the beams and frame are an integral part of the construction. The outside, its coverings, and the color of the paint all contribute to curb appeal. The inside flow from one room to another allows the visitor to move easily. The door styles create a mood and appearance, and they must function as intended. The insulation in the house should make it comfortable. The designer of the house is an architect, and the developer of the home is the general contractor.

Web design decides how the pages look and feel. Web development dictates how the pages work and perform.

ANATOMY OF A WEBSITE LAYOUT

The digital storefront starts with a wireframe, which is usually a black and white sketched layout of the website. Colors can be used to indicate areas and elements—not style and design. The main purpose is to create a blueprint that will show the placement of images and elements to engage the visitor. It will show the size of the header in relationship to the size of the page. It will indicate where the hero image should be placed and its approximate height. Buttons, content blocks, and sections are drawn in to show the general hierarchy.

A wireframe is intended to plan the layout and solve any usability issues. Make sure it has a logical flow. This blueprint can be used by designers and developers. The trick is to keep the sketches loose and rough; at the next stage, create more detailed sketches and drawings. The wireframe does not show style.

On a higher level, there is the site framework, which starts with the navigation to the pages. Search engines like to see an individual homepage, an about page, a services page, and a contact page. A professional website should not be one long page but rather many pages with minimal scrolling. The navigation should be crystal clear and not be hidden.

A website is made up of HTML, or HyperText Markup Language, which is the code used to create websites. JavaScript is coding that makes web pages interactive. A good design program will create these code structures automatically.

The time it takes to load a website when searched is a determining factor in being found in search results. The website's loading should be tested by the search engines before getting too far into the design.

When a menu or header moves down a page during scrolling, that is called sticky navigation. This way the visitor does not need to scroll up to the menu. However, it can be distracting, and another option is to add an arrow on the right or left that points up and is linked to the top of the page for quick access to the navigation. Another option is to have side features bulleted on the right for quick linking to specific information.

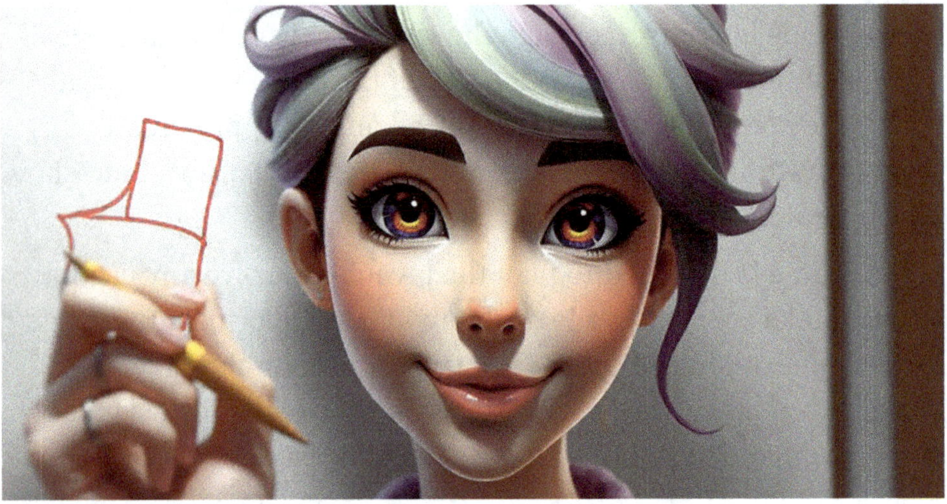

FIGURE 4.4

You must first learn the principles

AI Practicum} DeepAI Prompt: Cartoon of a teacher drawing a shape on a white board

Readability With Personality

The designer has to struggle between choosing typography that has flair and typography that can be easily read. Images cannot be too large, and they have to allow space for content. Type that goes over images has to be readable. Headlines can just be legible, but body content must be readable. The spacing between the lines, also known as the leading, is too tight and difficult to read.

It is very easy to set type center, but it is more difficult to read than flush left. Balancing centered headlines with flush-left content takes a keen eye. More than 5 lines of center type become very difficult to read if choosing center type, trying to make sure it does not have a shape unless it is intended to mirror another element. A shape created by text can be distracting and passed over.

Types Of Images

Real photos build trust, credibility, and an emotional connection. They show images of products, services, and employees that customers can associate with the brand. Actual company members rather than models found in stock photos lead to higher engagement.

Studies have shown that customers purchase more apparel when a website shows real people in a situation than a stock photo of a model.[1]

Custom photographs can help create a connection of the brand with visitors on a more human level. Conversion rates go up if using real people instead of stock photos by as much as 20%.[2]

Photos are supposed to show the company to the potential customer. Stock photos are generic, and visitors can be suspicious of a website that has no real photos. As a designer, helping customers connect to the brand is important. Photographs need to be good quality, well lit, and retouched where needed. Lifestyle shots of employees in action at work show the visitors the people behind a company, which is more interesting than posed photos.

Stock and AI photos are a quick solution, and the more authentic they are, the greater impact they will have on a visitor. When budgets are limited, stock photos are a good resource. Make sure they're sending the correct message and help establish the brand by avoiding cliché type. When posting for social media and articles on the website, stock photos may be the best solution based on budget, time, and goal.

Planning Pages And Menus

Since computers have large monitors, it is only natural to start the design of a website with the desktop format. However, more internet surfers use mobile devices than desktops. Designers should start with the smaller canvas of a phone, but showing a website on a computer is a much stronger presentation. Usually, after the desktop site is finished and approved, the responsive site is then edited for the mobile phone.

The importance of mobile-first layouts and the mobile-first philosophy cannot be overstated. Not only is everything smaller, but also space is less, and navigation patterns are different. A finger or fingers are used and not a cursor.

Images sized for a desktop site can be reduced to fit on a mobile device without any degradation to the image. However, if an image is sized for a phone but then enlarged to fit on a desktop, the image will appear soft and pixelated.

PRINCIPLES OF DESIGN

Website design can present attractive, memorable compositions. However, the control of space and scale is still limited. Colors, logos, and fonts tell your story on a website. Nothing is haphazard. Each element relates to another, and the space dictates that relationship. Visitors are attracted to large, medium, and small images and type. A design that does not have contrast will not be interesting, and it takes time to adjust the different parts of the layout to create the perfect relationship of all the elements.

Each word is carefully wordsmithed to be as short and effective at communicating the goal of the site page. Artificial intelligence can not only be an additional tool but also be used to validate the usefulness of the content.

Polished Design Solutions

Design should be engaging. If a layout has no space to rest the eye and nothing fits, the website failed. Space, visuals, photos, and typefaces must portray the message. An acronym that describes how to achieve engaging design is B.U.L.L.I.T.S.

Balance helps a layout appear finished.

Use three fonts or less even though thousands of fonts are available.

Large, medium, and small elements help visitors know quickly and easily where the answer is to their query.

Light, medium, and dark tones work effectively when a layout has complementary but contrasting colors.

Inspiration from all visual research leads to a mental library of well-designed websites.

Typos ruin designs more than any other error.

Solve the problem of the best design to engage the visitor and the website is a success.

The above limitation on fonts does not include the fonts used in company logos. The brand is a visually distinctive element, but it is no longer unique if a website uses the same font. If struck choosing a font style, look at the family. Type will be easier to use with multiple options, including a bold option that is darker and a thinner light type.

Misspellings will be embarrassing, especially with AI to check for them. Clients and anyone else who notices a misspelled word are merciless. Check for spelling by reading out loud.

In page design, uniform sizing of the elements is the easy way to lay it out but is boring and not eye-catching. The scale establishes a visual hierarchy to lead the visitor. Using a contrast of size, weight, color, and space on a marketing website will grab attention and then engage the potential customer.

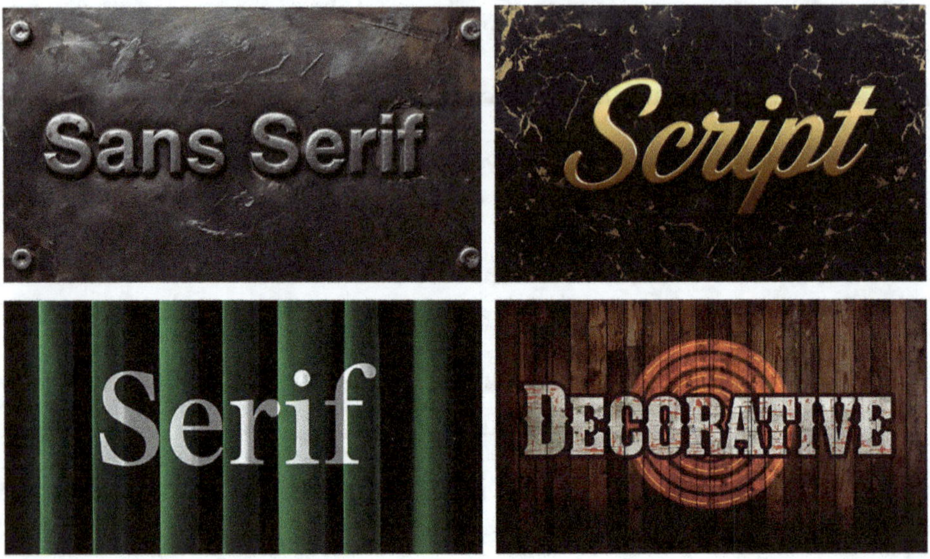

FIGURE 4.5

The four main font categories

AI Practicum} Canva Prompts: The word Decorative in a western font painted on wood; The word Serif in a serif font on a green curtain; The word Sans Serif in the helvetica condensed font embossed into metal; The word Script in the commercial script font floating over marble wall.

Crafting Clear and Compelling Web Visuals

Creators falling in love with their masterpieces is an age-old story. Anyone creating a website must know they should not be impressed with their design and fall in love with the layout. If they do think it is the best solution just because they created it, these builders will not objectively critique the final compositions to see what is not correctly placed, sized, or in the appropriate color. One of the most difficult tasks for anyone who creates a website is to stand back and, with unbiased vision, analyze the page visually and verbally.

AI doesn't know how fonts make people feel a specific way. It doesn't know how color makes people feel; thus, it's up to you as the designer to utilize these techniques. One of the main ways to do this is to not replace the copywriter but have AI generate content that pulls from diverse sources, finding words that get the message narrowed down. Then use the words in the brief to the copywriter, or if you go with a different AI writer, use the words in the prompts.

Color is emotional theory

Colors and tones give a design character and depth. They remove the message from the elements, make things look better, and keep things the same. Color makes things easier to read, see, and understand, and it helps people remember your brand.

Adding gray to a color makes tones lighter or darker. They have an effect on the look, feel, and mood of the design. Tones create harmony, balance, and contrast in a work.

Using light and dark colors can give a design depth and contrast. A light source lets the commercial artist apply light to one side and shadows on the opposite and then blending tones slowly or making them stand out with sharp shadows.

Color draws people in. Tone-based lights and darks can give the reader energy and direction. Colors that are bright, different, and full of passion get people's attention.

Space fundamentally creates a safe page

An undervalued design technique is to make a page visually inviting and not overwhelming. Based on the space, a visitor will decide to read more or go to an easier website to scan. The space will immediately let the visitor know how professional the website will be, and the product or service will be subconsciously evaluated. Too much space will have an adverse effect in breaking up the train of thought and verbal flow.

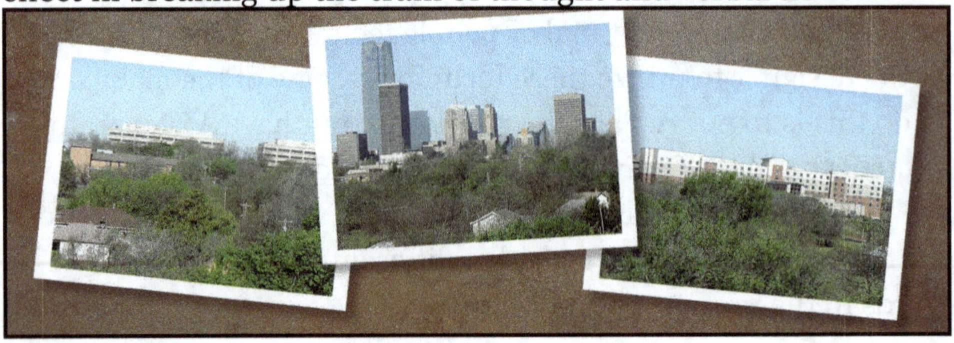

FIGURE 4.6

Screenshots of icons and upload option.

Demo on how to retouch images online

Adobe Firefly offers an online version of Photoshop as part of the subscription. While it is limited, for many graphic artists, it has more tools than should be needed.

In this project, instead of having a header with a gradation or solid color as the background, a cityscape will be used. One of the main issues is creating an image that is wide but not tall.

The second goal is to create an interesting image even though it must either be dark enough for light type to read on or light enough that dark type is legible.

To build the wide image, three photos were taken of a city. Each photo showed a part of the city that when combined will make a panoramic view for the header.

1. Open Firefly in a browser, and from the top icon menu, select PS, which will open Photoshop (See Figure 4.7).

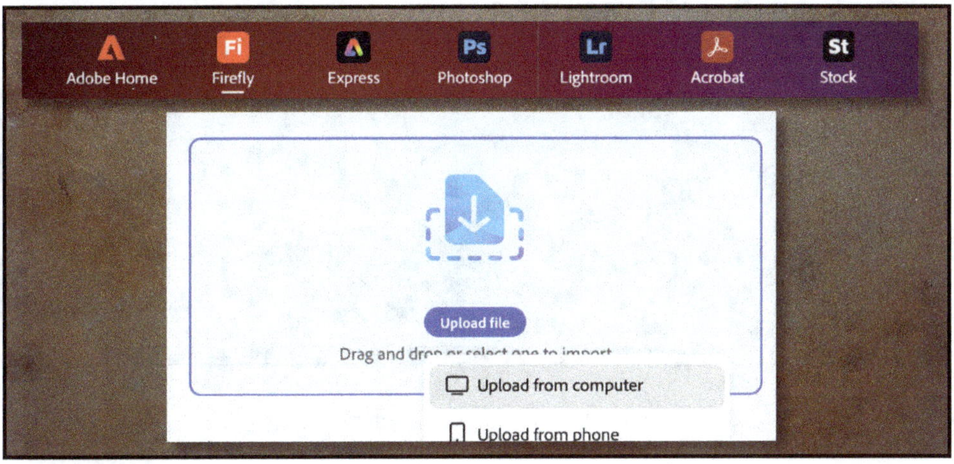

FIGURE 4.7

Steps 1 and 2

2. Select the image upload and either drag or choose an image from the computer.

3. Use the crop tool to extend the canvas.

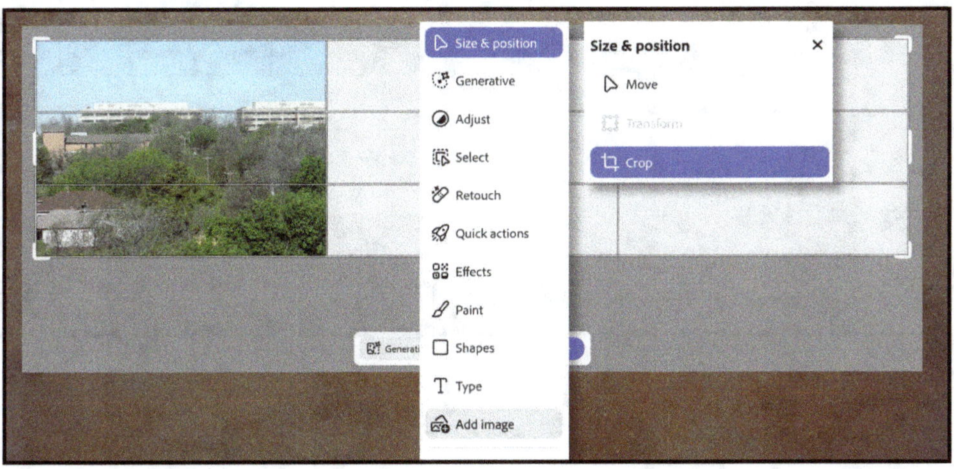

FIGURE 4.8

Step 3

4. Place and position additional photos.

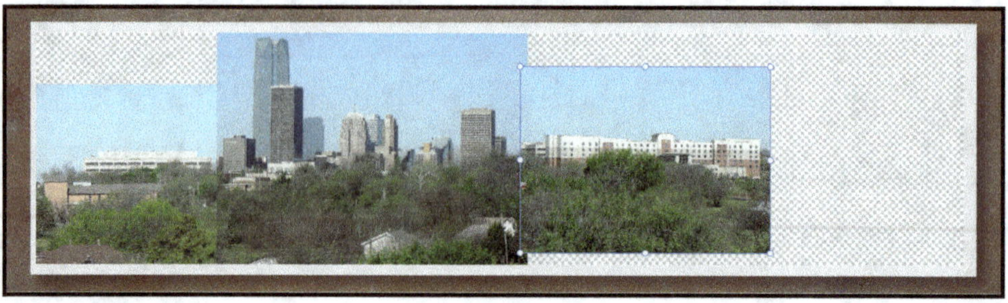

FIGURE 4.9
Step 4

5. From the ***Size & position*** menu, using the ***Crop*** tool, drag the corners to change the canvas size to the width of the images.

> Double-click on the layer name and change it to ***Compiled images***.

> At the bottom of the canvas select ***Merge Layers*** option.

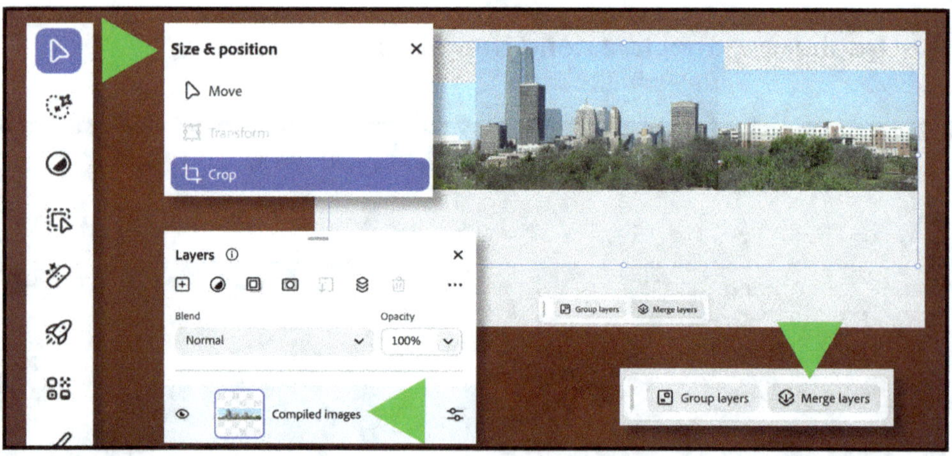

FIGURE 4.10
Step 5

6. Note that moving the cursor over the image will select areas of background, foreground, and middle images with pink masks.

7. Right click with your mouse and duplicate the layer to work on. This will allow the original to be available if needed.

> Click on the ***Eye*** icon on left side of the original layer, Compiled images, to hide the layer.

> On the duplicate layer, edit the layer name to ***Working City.***

8. Choose the ***Brush*** tool.

> Hold down the Option Key (Alt Key for PC) which will select the ***Eyedropper*** tool.

> Click to choose the left sky color.

> Paint the missing areas of the sky and where the skies merge.

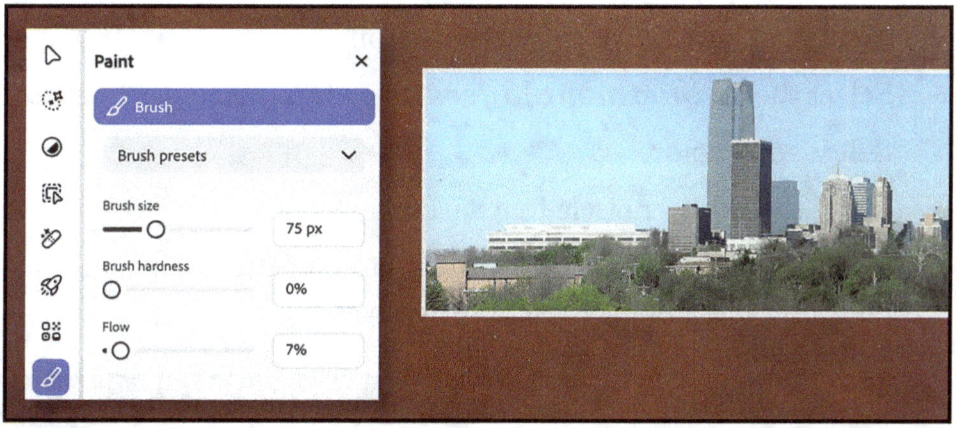

FIGURE 4.11
Step 8

9. With the adjustment tool, select ***Black & white***.

> In the properties menu, adjust all the colors as shown to create a high contrast black and white image.

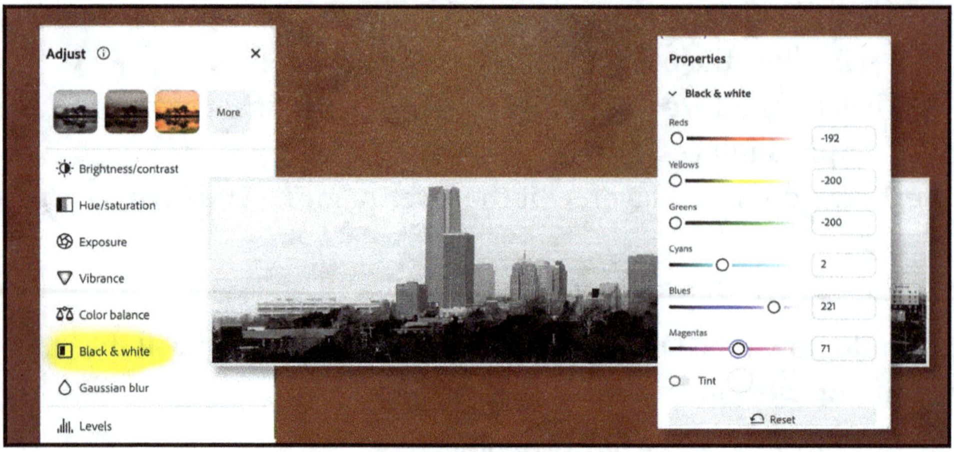

FIGURE 4.12

Step 9

10. Create a new layer selecting the + icon.

> Select the ***Adjustment layers*** icon at the top of the menu.

> Select solid color.

> Move the chooser circle to a dark blue.

> Add the color to Swatches at the bottom of the menu and click off onto a blank area of the canvas.

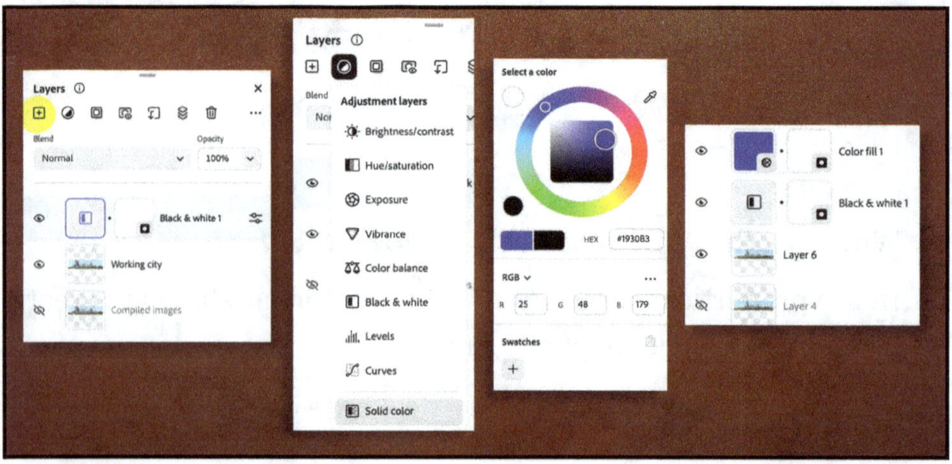

FIGURE 4.13

Step 10

11. While the layer is selected, choose a blend, Multiply, and an opacity, 74%, that allows the cityscape to show through.

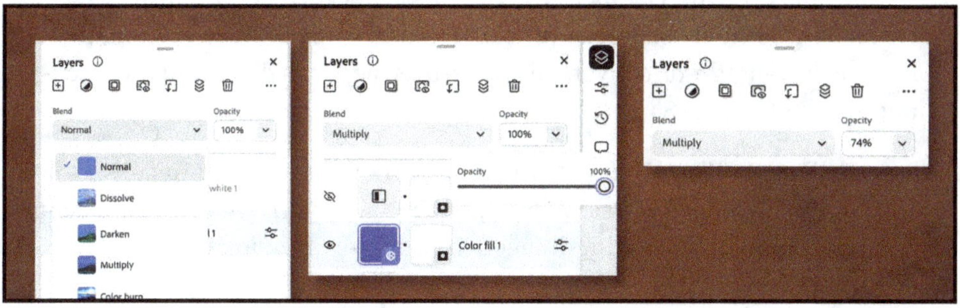

FIGURE 4.14
Step 11

12. Duplicate the layer. Use the blend Color with opacity at 100%.

13. Download either the file in layers to adjust in the desktop version of Photoshop or as a JPG.

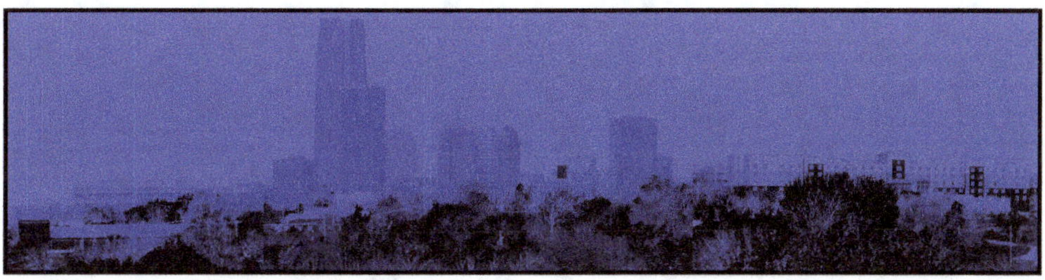

FIGURE 4.15
Step 13 Final Image

REFERENCES

1. Dean, T. (2016, October 24). The Battle of Conversion Rates—User-Generated Content vs. Stock Photos. Medium. https://medium.com/the-mission/the-battle-of-conversion-rates-user-generated-content-vs-stock-photos-7bc8f3c76ea8

2. Tolliver-Walker, H. (2017, April 19). Proof That Adding Images Improves Conversion Rates. What They Think. https://whattheythink.com/articles/84937-proof-adding-images-improves-conversion-rates/

Visitor Engagement

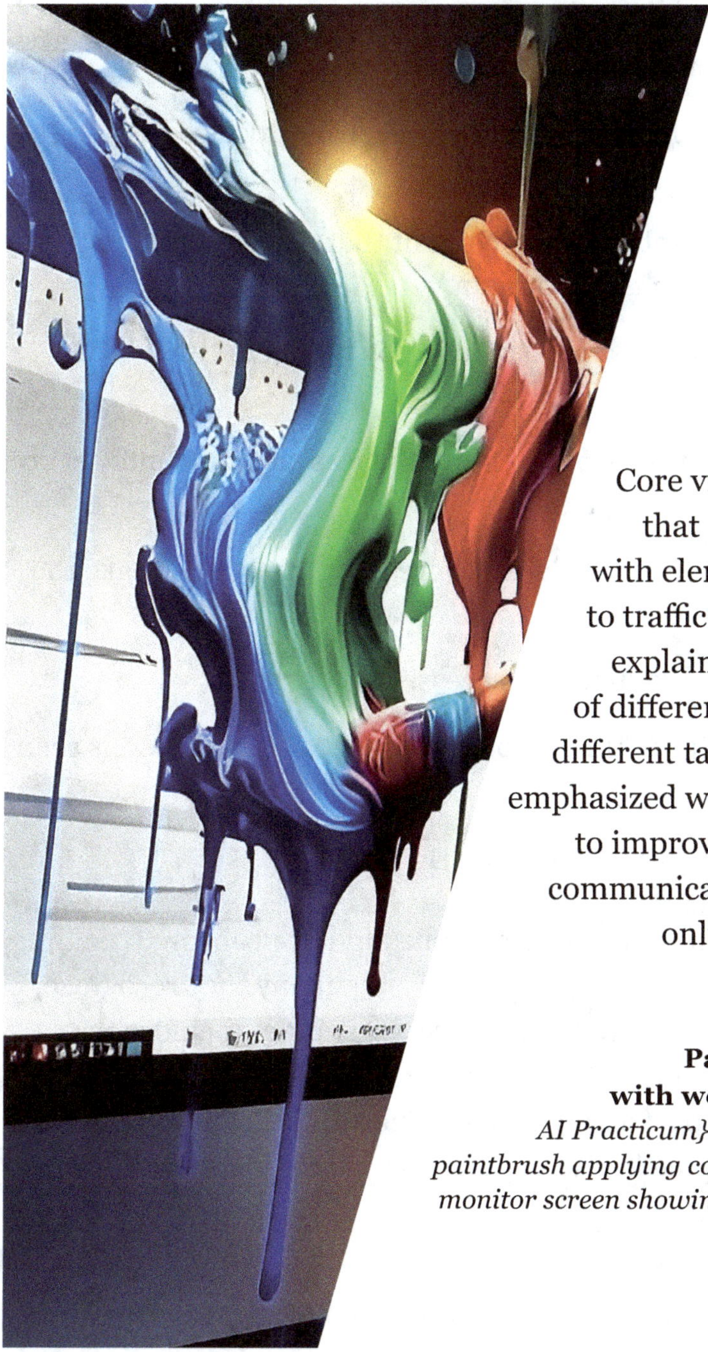

C5

OVERVIEW

Core visual principles that shape a design with elements that lead to traffic conversion are explained. The appeal of different font styles to different target markets is emphasized with suggestions to improve usability and communicate an engaging online experience.

FIGURE 5.1

Painting a brand with words and color.

AI Practicum} Craiyon Prompt: paintbrush applying colorful acrylic to a monitor screen showing a website page.

PROFESSIONAL TERMINOLOGY

CTA: Call to Action: Prompts viewers to interact with a company or product.

Conversion: When a visitor takes a specific, desired action to a business goal.

Dynamic Content: Website content that changes automatically based on user behavior or data.

Homepage: The first page reached by typing in the domain name.

Grid System: A layout system that places elements into sections and on subsequent pages.

Layout: Elements are placed to create contrast and make the website memorable.

Visitor: An individual who accesses a website.

Views: Number of times a page on a website loads and is seen by a searcher.

THE FIRST GOAL IS TO CREATE INTEREST

Surfers on the internet think of a question or problem, type the key phrase into a search engine, see a company they recognize, and go to it, or find a website where the snippet includes the subject of interest and navigates to it. It is like dropping acorns to lead a squirrel to a feeding trough. The snippets are explanations using demographic key search words with the same words on a page of the website.

Visitors will expect a website page to load quickly and be easily scanned. If the site loads slowly or is too difficult to scan, the users quickly move back to the search results.

If the page design creates visual interest and a focal point to attract a viewer, they stay. Some users are tab searchers, which means they know to open the search result section in a new tab and go down the list of search results and then quickly look at each option.

There are a number of design techniques used to tell the story of the company, product, or service, but they all start with understanding a visitor. The structure helps them quickly figure out the message and decide if they want to see more or select the back button.

The design must involve the visitor. Their eyes are drawn to impressive layouts, whether it's with the placement of the elements or the use of space around those items. The structure helps them quickly figure out the message and decide if they want to spend more time on the website.

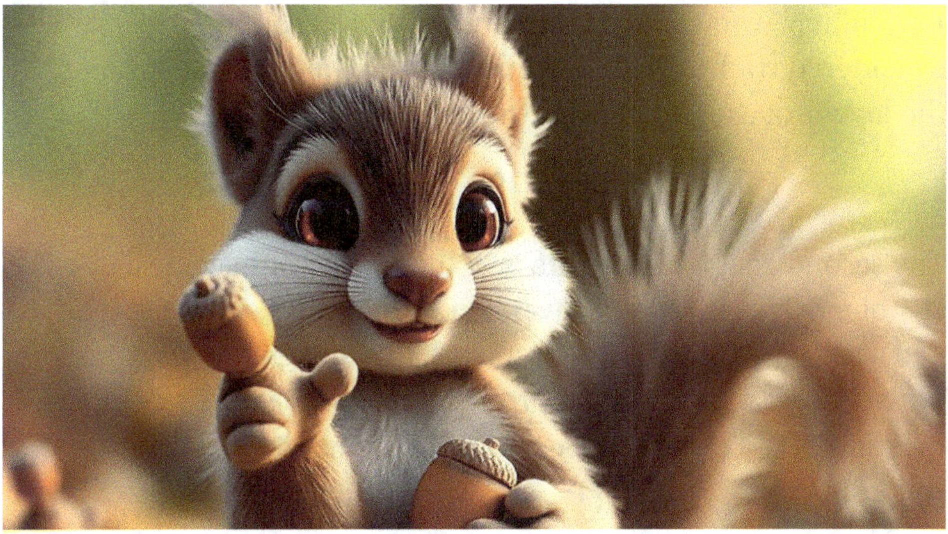

FIGURE 5.2
Not falling for that trick.
AI Prompt} DeepAI Prompt: A squirrel holding acorns and shaking a finger at the viewer.

To attract a viewer to a layout, it must use different colors, shapes, and images on the page to create contrast. Items that are too close in size and color will not make them unattractive. Viewers will look for recurring shapes and images that make a layout interesting. This repetition comes through unity and consistency in alignment, color, texture, and space.

New designers center everything, which creates a symmetrically balanced composition. At first glance, this arrangement looks pleasing to the builder, but when a surfer goes from one website to another, the website needs to stand out and make the visitor stop. Centered is boring and the common solution. The visual designer will use more time to craft an interesting page that is not centered but still balanced. To create an asymmetrically balanced layout takes looking at the design with a visitor's eye and making adjustments. The solution will have more impact, create more interest, and grab the visitor.

Individuals who stay at a website for more than five seconds are considered traffic. The page must have an answer for them in the layout of the visuals and the content.

CONVERT VISITORS INTO CUSTOMERS

The second goal for a website is to have a visitor become a customer. This is called conversion. While a website tracks traffic and actions, the company must track the conversion of customers. Conversion can be buying a product, scheduling a service, or meeting with a company. See Chapter 8 for details.

When it comes to website design, there are generally three main creative strategies: Dominant Visual, Hard Sell, and Information-Driven (Problem-Solving). Most successful websites focus on one strategy and use parts of the others to back it up. Effective websites often blend these approaches with uncomplicated layouts.

Dominant visual website methods work best when perception, emotion, and brand identity are more important than precise explanations. This lets images and design communicate value before words do. The disadvantage of this approach is it easy for a designer and marketers to become enamored with the design and forget the goal is to sell or inform through trust.

Strategy	Industries	Approach	Goal
Dominant Visual	Branding, fashion, art, portfolio	Perception-first motion-led	Visual hierarchy leads to CTA
Hard Sell	E-commerce, contractors, product introduction, retail, real estate, events B2B, Landing pages, promotions, lead generation	Direct CTAs, urgency, offers, price-driven, social proof	Conversion-led, action-first CTA
Information-Driven	Healthcare, technical, political, news, legal services, financial firms, educational	Explains the problem, process, solution	Credibility, trust, clarity leads to and action

Table 5.1 | Design based on the intent

Hard-sell website methods work best in industries where people are more interested in short-term results than creating long-term trust. This is because people are more likely to act quickly than do a lot of study. Hard-sell approaches risk emphasizing urgency over reassurance, which may turn off visitors who need to build trust before making a decision.

Information-oriented website strategies are most effective in sectors where establishing trust, clarity, and comprehension is essential prior to taking action, and where visitors are evaluating expertise rather than focusing on price or urgency.

Information-driven methods can put more emphasis on extensive explanations than creating an action, which can delay decisions longer than intended.

These methods are based on well-known models of advertising and persuasion that separate emotional, transactional, and cognitive decision-making. If a designer is enamored with a website layout, they can ask themselves whether or not the website solves the goal of selling or establishing trust.

RESPONSIVE DESIGN

The normal workflow in website development is to design the desktop site and then, after all the kinks and strange spacing concerns are fixed, shrink the mobile site down. This mistake can result in losing both searchers and Google's bots.

The best workflow is to start with the mobile device and move up, but that is not practical. To work on a desktop site with a large monitor and start designing a small area seems counterproductive.

Developing the largest site first is the historical method. While separate sites for each device can be built with a code to open the one set for the device, search engines prefer one responsive website. Separate mobile and desktop versions will have duplicate content issues and affect search results.

Different solutions for different schemes

During the original website planning, outline the page requirements based on the device type rather than on how a page can be scaled down. Users searching on different devices are looking for varied responses based on the specific device they are using. Consider the purpose of their search.

The desktop user has time to investigate and the ability to open up multiple tabs to compare different websites. They can scan full page images and not be turned off by large sections of type. The best practice for desktop users is to approach storytelling with the goal of exploration and evaluation.

A tablet offers information for browsing and then acting on the selling points. Users can scan the information, but if they are viewing the reduced website, the text will be difficult to read. The information will need to be abridged with callouts.

A mobile phone or tablet user does not need to have in-depth or complete information about a company product or service. They are looking for a fast answer, and the page needs to use brevity to encourage a visitor to choose to stay longer.

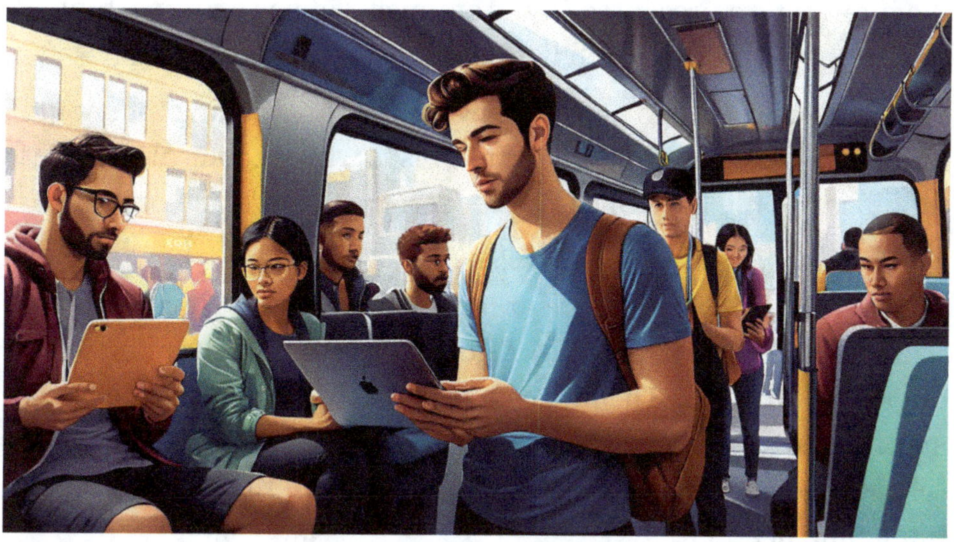

FIGURE 5.3

Everyone wants to be connected.

AI Practicum} Deep Dream Generator Prompt: Bus interior, diverse crowd with devices, young man with laptop, passengers standing, casual attire, digital illustration, vibrant colors, realistic style.

The mobile user

A mobile user usually has one task they are trying to perform. They are looking for something specific that they can make one decision about. If the mobile user has to think about the website information and what action to take, they will move on to another website.

A visitor is more likely to stay on a website designed for function and not explain in detail background information. They will scroll vertically and not horizontally. This can change on e-commerce sites, but the designer should be prepared that potential customers will not know when to scroll horizontally.

When users enter a query into the search engine and scan the results page, they compare each website based on its position and the information presented in the snippet. Time is an important concern; the clarity of each listing has to be a quick read.

When the user goes to a website, what they are looking for should immediately surface in their scan. This is why a good rule of thumb is to only have one CTA per scroll and have one primary action on a row.

Content should explain in clear language why it is relevant to the searcher and what to do next. A good practice is to summarize the offering with a link. The link can be a drop-down or the anchor to another part of the page to stop scrolling but immediately go to that solution. This type of design allows the user to establish their intent and act on it.

Link to bullets on the first and second scroll set up with minimum choices. Storytelling is a secondary solution. When designing the page, it should be solution-driven. Images, diagrams, and graphics are secondary. This is partly due to the need for faster download speeds and partly because images can distract the visitor. The options must not be camouflaged. The design is set up for one-handed use.

If the goal is to have the potential customer call or email or fill out a form, this needs to be an effortless, simple, clear action. The areas need to have large tap zones that allow for minimal precision. The user may be moving or in a moving vehicle, with bumps and turns affecting their dexterity.

ENGAGEMENT SUGGESTIONS

10 Designing tips for addressing user intent. The designers layout should encourage a visitor to act.

Time-sensitive

1. If the visitor is looking for immediate service, then the call button, the message form, or scheduling link should be on the first page and stand out.

2. Have a tracker system-automatic or manual, that keeps the customer up to date on when the team member will arrive.

Financial

3. Cost is always a concern and the design can address this pain point with pricing or ranges visible on the first page.

4. The feel of the website should subconsciously say how affordable the product or service will be for the potential customer.

Quality

5. Questions about the company or product caliber can be answered with prominently placed warranties and reviews.

6.Will the product last and does it say what

Legitimacy

7. Visitors may hesitate about an unknown company's trustworthiness but video referrals can address those concerns.

8. A successful company will focus on its history and display recognizable credentials as trust signals.

Proof-driven

9. Examples of before and after projects can demonstrate on a company's expertise.

10. A direct headline that addresses the problem with concise confidence can show they will solve the problem.

DESIGN A CAPTIVATING STORY

Besides promoting a product or service, websites are meant to build the company's credibility. If the visitor does not know about the company, the website must establish the company to be trustworthy and a solution.

Engaging design includes choosing the perfect font to communicate the message of the website. A well-trained and educated graphic designer has spent weeks, months, and even years studying typography. Understanding how an individual responds to a typeface, weight, and style is crucial to keeping visitors on the page.

Building a strong story starts with a clear statement about the product, service, or company. The visitor needs to know immediately what is being offered, if it is for them, and why it is better, and there is no reason to keep searching. Therefore, highlight the benefits and features in the story.

Use a short, strong conversion-oriented headline with a supporting subhead. If a visitor understands the website has what they need in under five seconds, they will keep reading.

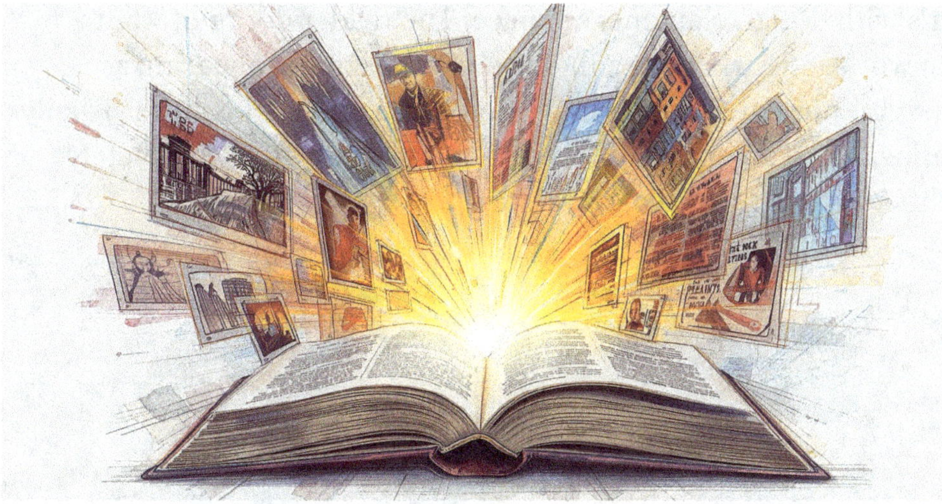

FIGURE 5.4

Develop interest by creating a story

AI Prompt} Canva Prompt: An open book looks like a monitor screen with images and words floating out. Settings: Image > Sketch-Color > 16:9 ratio.

Customers will not buy without trust. The site must have a clean layout with whitespace and the correct fonts to clarify the visual hierarchy. The content should be scannable. The mobile site must be designed and not an afterthought.

To convert a visitor into a customer, eliminate items that cause hesitation. Do not scare a visitor away with forms that pop up blocking their view, and make sure the navigation is not confusing with simple, predictable menus.

Avoid generic designs

Before anyone can dance a waltz, they must be able to move their feet in an orderly fashion that keeps a person balanced. Similarly, before anyone can design an eye-catching website, they must be able to move the elements to create an attractive order and balance.

Related items placed in close proximity to each other appear as one visual unit. Our eyes are drawn to balanced layouts, whether it's with design elements or space. The reader does not want to work at figuring out a message. Rather than appearing as several unrelated items, repetition of shapes can be more visually appealing when sized differently and placed with a completely different shape and color.

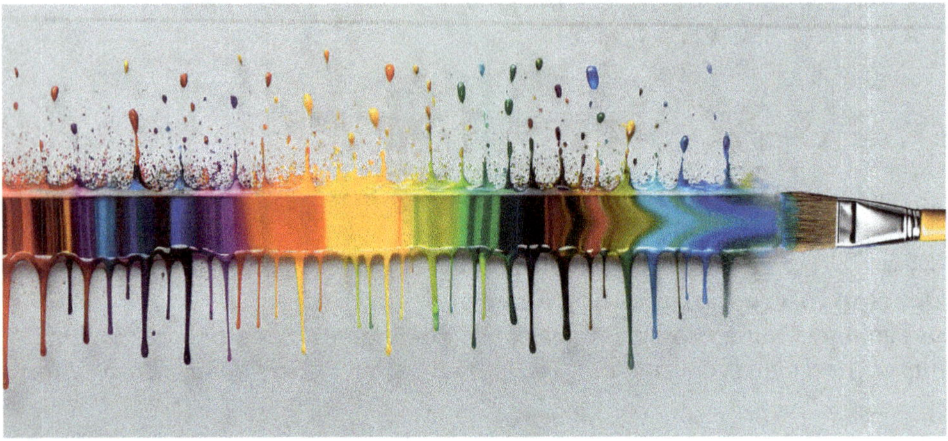

FIGURE 5.5
Color attracts.
AI Prompt} Deep Dream Generator Prompt: Paintbrush dragging along glass, creating a colorful line. Photoshop merging images.

If a creative is an artist, photographer, or designer, they know their composition does not balance when the components are not aligned. The design term is 'out of alignment,' and the solution looks at where the elements are placed on the page in relation to each other.

There are a number of basic alignments that can be used to balance the elements.

1. Centered, which is where images are centered with each other.
2. Left-aligned, which is where shapes are aligned along their left sides.
3. Right-aligned is where shapes line up by their right sides.

4. Top aligned is where the top of the images line up.
5. Bottom aligned, which is where the bottom of each image aligns with the bottom of the other images.

Most readers want an easy-to-read message that leads their eyes around the page. If the layout's alignment creates work to figure out what the website is trying to communicate, then it will lose most people.

Templates are generic answers that pretend to look attractive with old styles and techniques. Many business owners use templates for their website. They do not know enough about design to realize the template is old, overused, and does not sell the visitor.

The visual flow should lead to a strong CTA. It must be set apart with color or a button to be visible to the scanning visitor. It must be reached without scrolling and on every page.

THE TENETS OF DESIGN

Do not just use interesting images and content to sell to a visitor. Bring shapes and lines into the layout to create interest and a visual flow.

A line is an identifiable path created by a point moving in space. It is one-dimensional and can vary in width, direction, and length. Lines provide balance, texture, and direction. A reader's eye will follow a line. Vertical lines take a viewer's eye up and a horizon line draws the eye in a sideways direction.,

Lines are the second most overlooked design element. They can be expressive or define the edges of a form. Mountains and the sun can be outlined, but these lines do not exist in life. They are an element of art that is used to define space, contours, and outlines and indicate shape, mass, and volume.

Thick, thin, zigzag, diagonal, curly, curved, and spiral lines are often very expressive and can be used as textures. Their structure can convey a wide variety of messages.

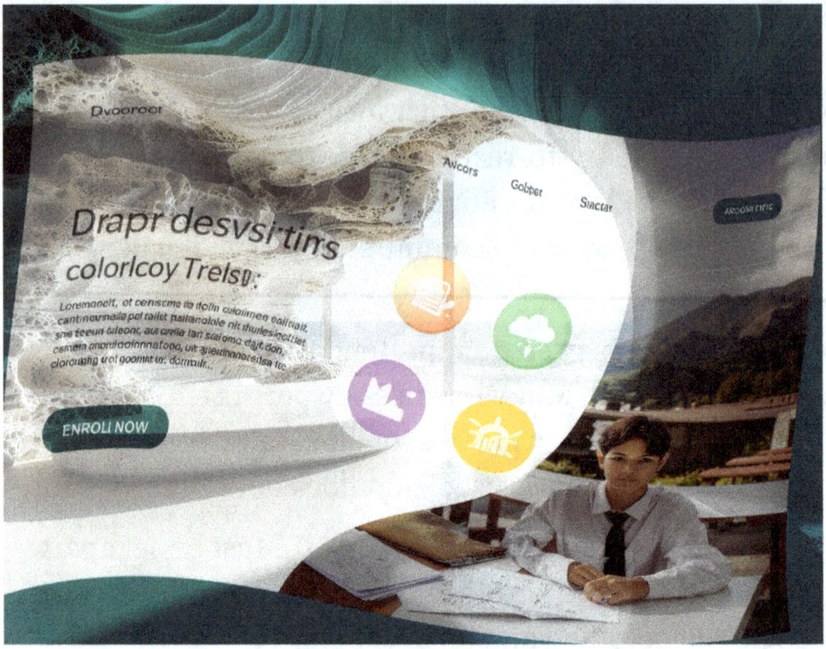

FIGURE 5.6

AI images need HI to work on the image to be interesting.
AI Practicum} Firefly Prompt 1: Website home page for a design class. | AI Practicum} Firefly Prompt 2: Webpage carved out of stone. | Combined in Photoshop online and retouched website page image, adding masks and different blends.

A line may not be there when an individual looks at something, but in their mind, we see a line. Lines can be implied. The mind will connect what is missing.

If a block of type needs to be set apart from another block, a line will not take up much space but will create a divider. In website design a line can set the navigation menu apart or the header from the rest of the page. Frequently, a line will indicate the end of the page and the beginning of a footer.

TYPOGRAPHY AND TERMS

Unlike print design, where the size of fonts is a physical measurement known as points, in web design, pixels are used.

Since pixels were the component of monitors, using pixels for font size allowed for a predictable outcome. However, the screens' physical pixel density makes the size not absolute.

For instance, the most common monitor resolution in the US has a 1920x1080 resolution, which will show fewer details, and the text will appear larger than on a newer monitor with a 3840x2160 resolution.

Use a font size for the headline that is the largest or most noticeable copy on the page. Headline and subhead fonts should be set at a minimum of 18 pixels. Body copy fonts should be 14 pixels up to 20 pixels; 16 pixels is a good size on new monitors. Do not be afraid to experiment. However, do not choose a font because it's cool or the desire to use it based on its characteristics. Choose a font it because it fits the project and communicates a subconscious message.

In the beginning of website design, the types of fonts were very limited, but now design programs automatically code the CSS on what and where to download a font if it is not on the computer. The fonts are stored on a server such as Google or Adobe, but if they fail to load, the browser looks to the basic fallback, such as Arial for sans serif or Times for serif fonts.

With literally millions of font choices, a website designer must think about the font choices and how they define the website. The impulse to stay with the same font must be ignored.

Headlines direct the audience to read first, subheads clarify or define the headline, and content or text explains the headline. The designer uses different font styles, weights, and types to set the tone of the message.

Designers use 'uppercase' for capital letters and 'lowercase' for non-capital letters. These terms originated from the cases that stored moveable type. Letters are placed along the 'baseline.' That imaginary line allows the letters to be consistently readable. Some lowercase letters, such as a 'g' or 'p,' have tails or descenders that go below the baseline. 'Leading' refers to the space between baselines. If the content has a lot of descenders, it may need space between the baselines, which is known as leading.

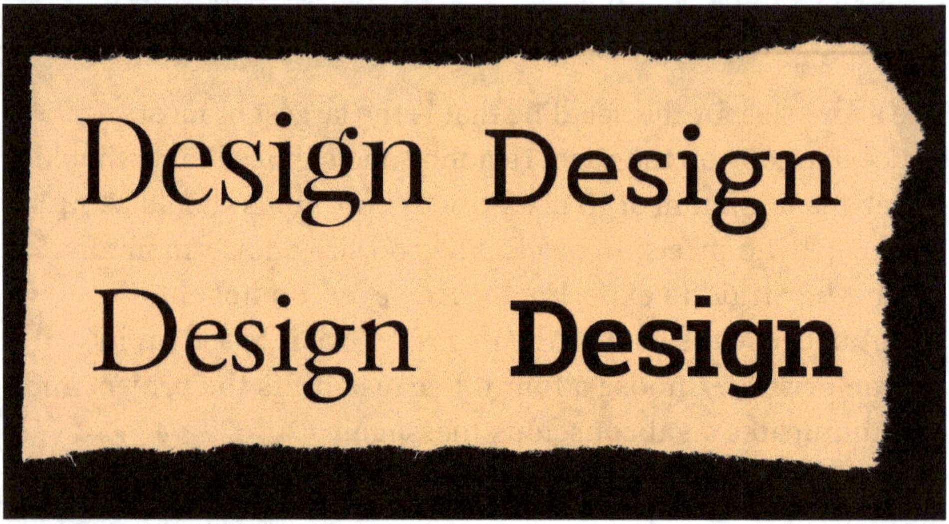

FIGURE 5.7

Fonts can imply different meanings and create different responses
Photoshop} The word "design" in multiple Serif font styles clockwise: Playfair | Belgrano | Garamond | Roboto Slab

Four Categories of fonts

It seems most of the design programs, AI or HI, break fonts down into many different categories. Knowing the qualities of the font styles allows the designer to find a look and feel of a typeface to create a planned visual response. For simplicity, there are four categories.

Serif font style

Fonts structured with little marks at the end of a character's horizontal strokes, curving lines, and added at the bottom of the vertical strokes along the baseline help with readability.

The entire serif font has thicker-to-thinner curves, horizontal strokes, and vertical lines that make up the basis of the character. Additional serifs are added to the other parts of the letter to improve readability and suggest a style to the reader.

This traditional font signals credibility and authority to a website visitor. These font are chosen to establish trust and timeliness.

The one font style that creates a natural flow between the characters, making content more readable, is serif typography. They help the eye as it scans the page due to the small additional strokes. This is the category to use for website About pages, technical or professional content, articles, and blogs.

Due to serifs' historical use since the mid-1400s, they convey a sense of timeless trustworthiness. For brand credibility, serif fonts bring character to the design. Visitors instantly feel the company is stable and the company are experts in their field. Legal firms, financial companies, and higher educational websites use the psychological tone derived from serif fonts.

A website utilizing serif fonts stands out now in the popular trend of minimalistic design that has overwhelmed internet design with sans serif fonts. Serifs add a polished sophistication to a website.

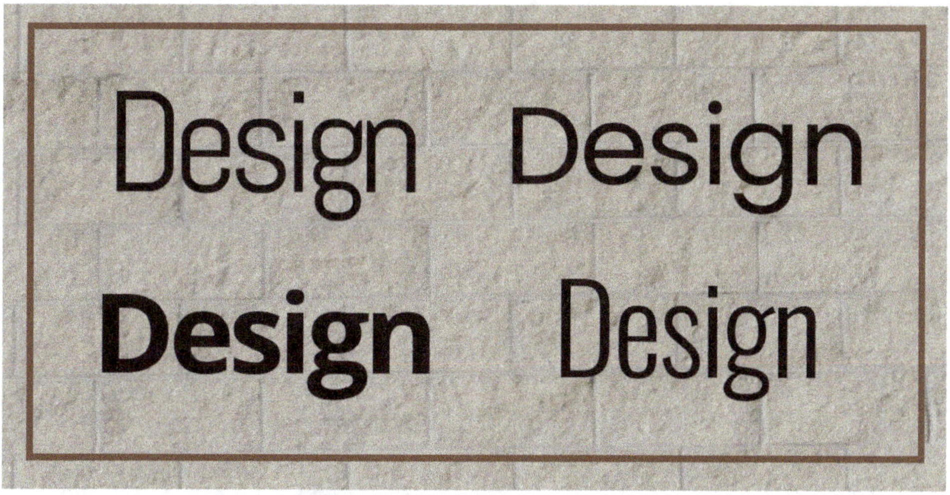

FIGURE 5.8 *Photoshop} The word "design" in multiple sans serif font styles clockwise: Abel | Poppins | Opens Sands | Oswald*

Sans serif font style

Characters with straight or blocky strokes and very little thick and thin are sans serif. Sans is of french origin and means 'without' or "absence of." They are legibly stronger as headlines and take up less width than a serif. When comparing serifs and sans serif characters at the same size, such as 72 points in height, the sans serif is usually the taller one.

Originally known as 'grotesque fonts,' Sans serif fonts were introduced in the late 1800s. At that time, sans serif was considered a modern font that people associated with a newer design for modern companies.

Now, over 125 years later, visitors who are looking for a modern product or service look for different font styles. However, it is surprising how many individuals think sans serif is a newer style than many of the modern serif options, which may seem more modern and elegant.

This currently popular font style is easy to read. Sections of content will appear cleaner with straight edged columns and with proper leading, be easy to scan.

Websites that use sans serif fonts are developing a modern, streamlined visual that creates the perception of a forward-thinking company for visitors. This contemporary font style has crisp strokes, so brands appear tech-oriented.

Using sans serif fonts can make a website appear easy to read and without clutter. Due to the numerous weight options in a sans serif font family, they can be used to create a visual hierarchy without mixing in other fonts.

Sans serif fonts help the brand appear flexible and user-friendly. Sans serif fonts create a fresh, refined design that creates the image of a forward-thinking brand.

Since sans serif fonts can be considered emotionally cold, they can be paired with script to soften the overall website design. The ornate nature of script fonts contrasts smoothly with the lack of embellishments of sans serif type styles.

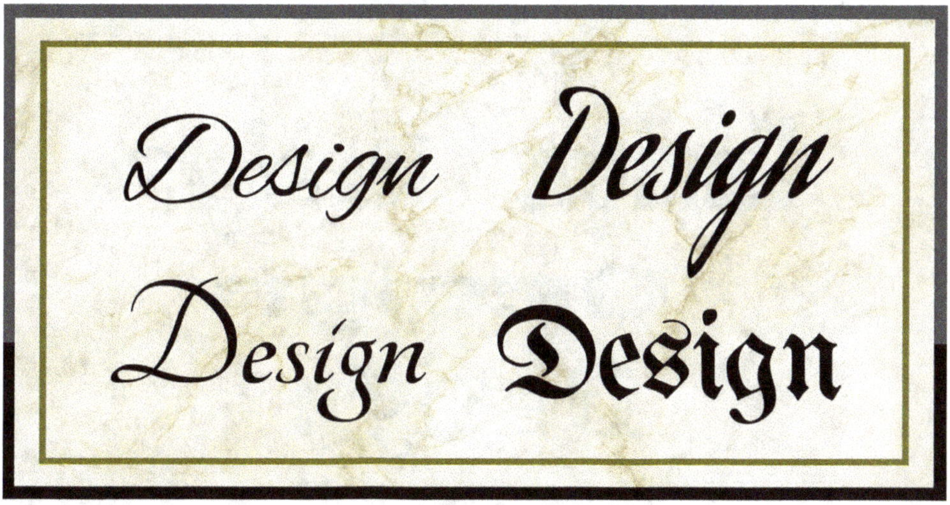

FIGURE 5.9

Photoshop} The word "design" in multiple Script font styles clockwise: Alex Brush | Aguafina | Tangerine | Unifractur Mag

Script font style

The handwritten style was the first font developed by typographers to communicate to readers. Hand printing or carving was the first option, but it is a slow method. By keeping the pen on the paper and only lifting it to start a new word, individuals could put down ideas or communications faster.

The script fonts consist of fancy letters with embellishments or resemble handwriting. This font category is perfect for elegant logos, personal headlines, and short sentences. Script fonts do not lend themselves to easily scanned paragraphs.

If a website wants to have a visual personality that is elegant, artistic, luxurious, or playful, script fonts are the more expressive font. These fonts give a brand a personal identity. For hero text, sales promotions, and warmth, the curving characters add a human touch to the brand.

However, script fonts only work for headlines and subheads. Body content needs to be readable to be memorable. Designers need to learn which script works well when combined with a specific serif or sans serif font.

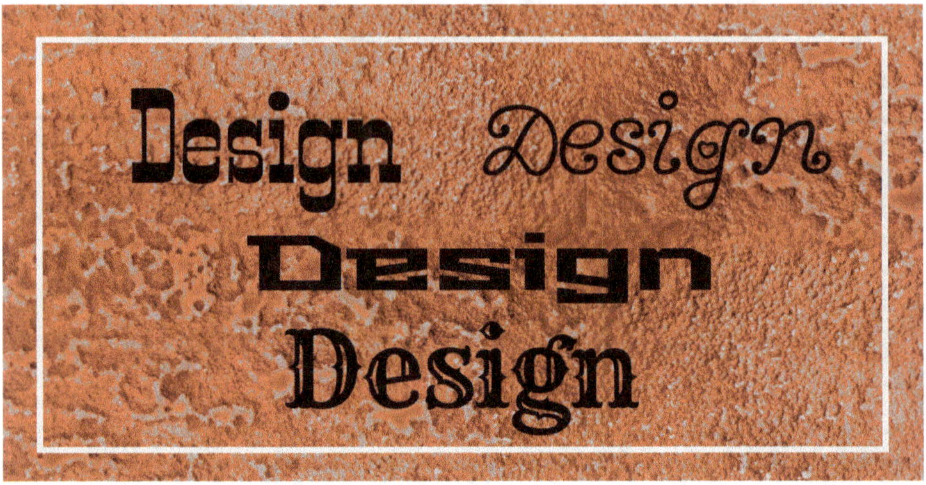

FIGURE 5.10
Photoshop} The word "design" in multiple Decorative font styles clockwise: Smokum | Bonbon | Stalinist | Rye

Decorative font style

These typefaces are basically font styles that do not fit in the other three categories. Decorative fonts can be grungy, edgy, futuristic, and old-fashioned.

The styles of these fonts are not meant to be read as a sentence but used for short words and phrases. Their nontraditional structures establish a website's approach immediately. Decorative fonts are distinct and unique. As long as they are legible, these fonts bring individuality to a company brand and memorability to a website.

Decorative fonts vary in strokes, angles, baselines, and readability. But they stand out and grab a visitor's attention. Their visual impact is unconventional and unique. The personality of a website will match the decorative headlines.

They are ideal for conveying retro and futuristic themes. Grunge, gritty, rugged decorative headline fonts can instantly strengthen a brand's visual identity without affecting the logo itself.

Entertainment companies, creative industries, restaurants, and fashion websites use decorative fonts to highlight sales promotions. They should be used as design accents and not the main fonts. Use them to break the monotony of paragraph-dense pages but never as body content.

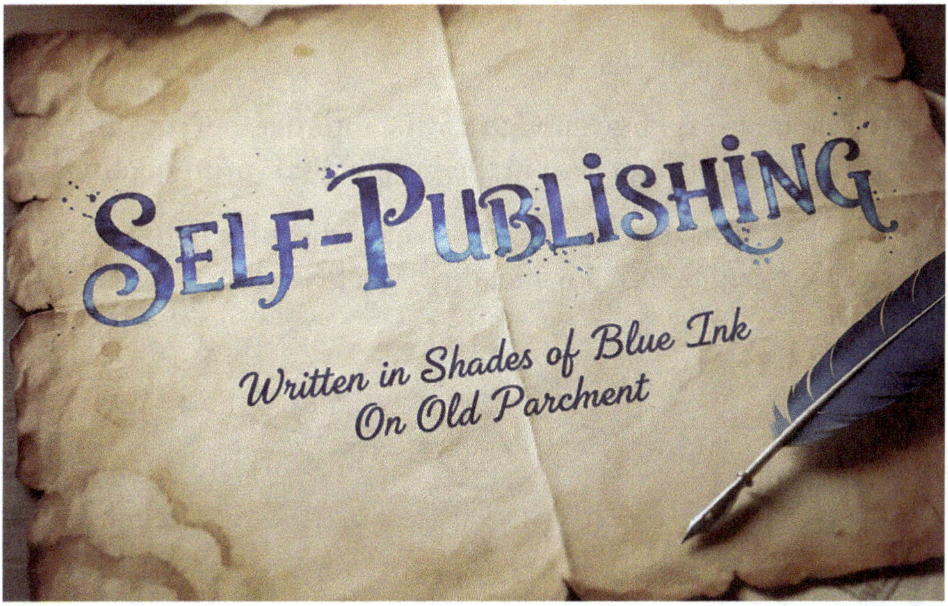

FIGURE 5.11

Stylized to interest authors

AI Practicum} Express Prompt: print 'self-publishing' written in shades of blue ink on old parchment.

Demo Adobe Express—create designed headline

This professional-grade AI design program is intuitive in its interaction and it does not have a steep learning curve. The basic features of Adobe's Express are free—for now.

1. Open up new.express.adobe.com

2. From Chapter 2, a ChatGPT headline is going to become artwork. It should be shorter so it can be easier to read.

3. Select Generate Image.

4. Choose Gemini 2.5 Flash Image model.

5. See Figure 5.10 for the prompt.

6. Select Generate.

7. The image is large enough for the internet, but for print it will need to be larger, so in the prompt add "print quality."

8. Select "edit" at the top of the page, where it can be resized and cropped before downloading as a PNG file.

The Magic of Prompts

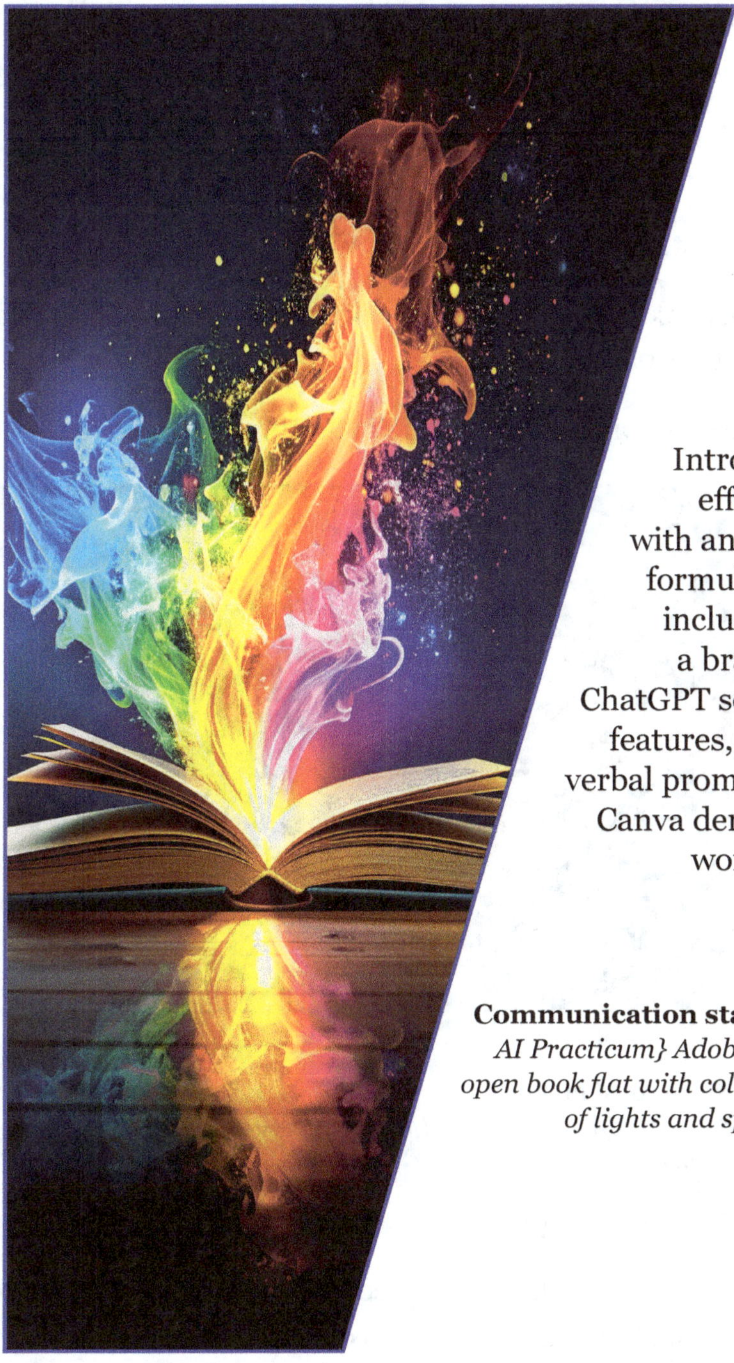

C6

OVERVIEW

Introduces crafting effective prompts with an easy-to-follow formula. The process includes developing a brand statement. ChatGPT settings, hidden features, and delivering verbal prompts are shown. Canva demo to illustrate words as artwork.

FIGURE 6.1

Communication starts with words

AI Practicum} Adobe Firefly Prompt: open book flat with color magical swirls of lights and sparkles flying out

PROFESSIONAL TERMINOLOGY

Embedded: Content, images, and videos that are added directly into a website.

Header: The top area of a website.

Landing Page: Single marketing page promoting one product or as a linked destination.

Links: Hyperlinks allows visitor to select and go to an area on a page or another page.

Prompt: Instruction to guide artificial intelligence's output.

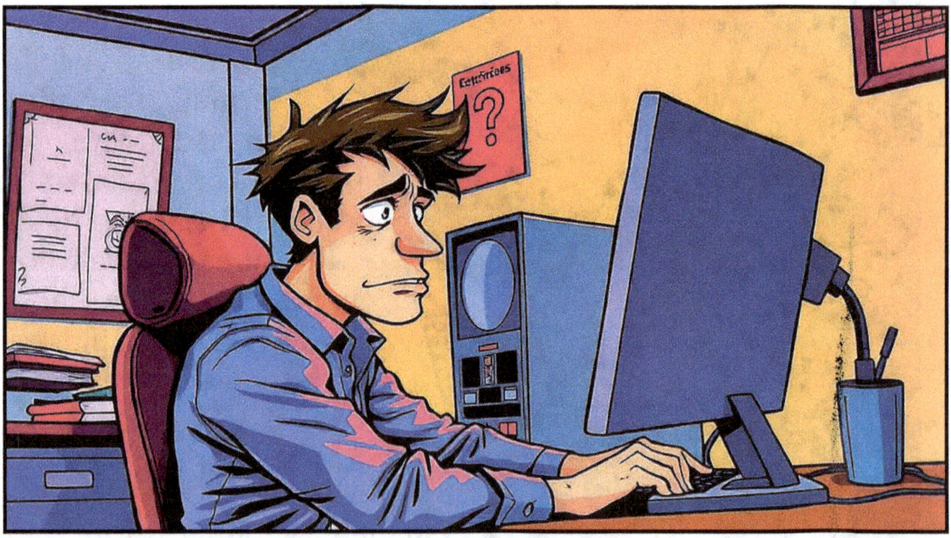

FIGURE 6.2

Not knowing the language of prompts

AI Practicum} Pixlr Prompt: Artwork of man sitting at a desk in front of a computer with a look of frustration.

BRAND STATEMENT

The brand statement should be clarified before starting to prompt AI models. This sentence is intended to direct the message of the marketing and design but is not easily constructed.

Start with a short value proposition that includes the audience and how they benefit from the product or service offered. While this message is focused on sales, it should present the company as trustworthy and committed to them.

In the next step, the company should define its unique selling point that sets it apart from the competition. The goal is to make it easy for the customer to instantly understand why they should use the company. To accomplish this, sales and marketing must know how the brand is seen by the target market.

The brand statement should define the company by communicating value and setting a tone. This public brand message will be its identity.

THE PROCESS OF PROMPTS

Prompts function as an interface between concepts and the outcomes generated by AI. There will be less frustration and more use if the time is taken to wordsmith a prompt. After all, prompting is really a conversation, not a command, since AI with natural language was based on human discourse.

Iterate = try > review > adjust > try again.

The first stage, or the establishing prompt step, is to set up the query in such a way as to not get a random structured response. If this happens, sometimes it is better to start a new query instead of spending time clarifying a non-starter. Giving it a direction to go in can be accomplished by creating a feel for the verbiage. Defining the output format and setting a limit means the AI does not have to guess. As an example, state in the prompt that it should be in paragraph form, 500 words, and include the tone, such as "friendly."

Review how the AI responded, and in the second stage add the audience and role to help with the tone. If a structured example sentence will give the AI the style and energy, for clarity. Make use of a sentence break, such as a period. Use "Make it friendlier.

In the third stage, establish if the AI's answer is going in the correct direction. Refine by using "Good start—make it..." or "Perfect—shorten to nine words."

√Add a call to action. √ Perfect—shorten to 7 words.

Give the AI a role

If too vague, AI fills gaps with guesses. EX: HVAC video 2X4. Breaking into steps (chain-of-thought) produces better results. Don't overload. Ask for revisions to improve quality AI does not know fun, so use playful as a tone, which removes guesswork. AI cannot perform human decision-making.

A common mistake to avoid is being general with the prompts or asking too many things at once. Individuals stop after the first answer, especially if they were using ambiguous terms. AI cannot judge the solution. Therefore, do not ask it to supply the 'best' answer.

Verify Information: Cite your sources

Tips on Prompts

Compound commands such as "Concisely generate..." mean keep it short. This is not the prompt if the solution should be step-by-step or detailed.

Use an example, which means AI will not have to guess at the tone with an example. Ask the AI to summarize in a format such as an essay or paragraphs. Forces AI to distill information and prioritize the most relevant details.

Prompts such as "rewrite or polish prefacing the input content" are asking for editing grammar and understanding of the provided text. If the query is asking the AI to teach, not just describe, a good lead-in is "explain for an audience in step-by-step bullets..." This approach leads AI to give clear, easy-to-follow phrases to achieve better understanding for the reader.

The 4Cs Prompt Rule

1. Clear—no ambiguity.
2. Contextual—includes background info.
3. Constrained—has limits or structure.
4. Conversational—can evolve through feedback.

Examples:

Rewrite it for college students. Make it more playful, under 50 words, for college students.

Concisely rewrite and polish it in a more professional tone for a business newsletter.

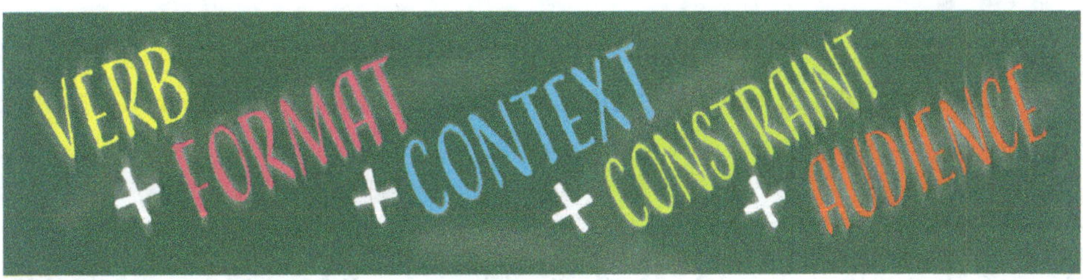

FIGURE 6.3

Prompt Formula

HI Practicum} Photoshop [Format] + [Context] + [Action Word] + [Audience]

PROMPT FORMULA FOR CONTENT

Following the formula is a type of checking off when crafting a prompt for an AI generator. This four-step process can have more directions added as a person gets experience and success. The goal and keywords can be part of the query.

[Verb]

Using an action word explains to the AI model the goal of the response

Example: Write

Write tells the AI to provide new text and not answer with a definition or research results.

Write in bullets without emojis the main areas inspected in a house by a home inspector.

Uses: Sets up for quick scans of the homepage, breaks down info into phrases instead of getting bogged down in the details, and describes main benefits of a product or service.

Options: Summarize, compare, rewrite more polished, create 5 options, or explain.

[Format]

The format sets the arrangement of the writing and indicates to the AI generator how in-depth it should be limiting the details of the response.

Example: Essay

Essays typically follow a standard structure, which makes it easier to generate content and stay on track. Allows for a deeper dive into a topic, exploring ideas, analyzing information, and providing supporting evidence.

Write a 1500-word essay about the impact of artificial intelligence on modern society.

Uses: Reports, blogs, newsletter articles, or the About Us page on a website.

Options: Sentence, phrase, paragraph, post, or website article.

[Context]

Stating the context for whom the AI is answering sets the tone, depth, and vocabulary.

Example: Marketer

By stating the context is that of a marketer, the content will sound like a person that advertises or promotes something for a company.

As a marketing expert, write a paragraph introducing a new disinfectant service.

Uses: Product descriptions, headlines,

Options: occupations like inventor, salesperson, writer, teacher, or web designer.

[Constraint]

By setting the parameters for AI using a constraint will set the length of the response in words such as "in 500 words" or uses "for a Google Post."

Example: Concise

When only a small area on the website is available, or the attention span is limited, the word "concise" helps the AI focus on brevity and clarity.

Write a concise explanation of this product for a beginner.

Uses: Contact web page, quick explanations, emails, or social media captions.

Options: Friendly, energetic, informative, or humorous.

[Audience]

AI will know to whom the content is targeting and their interests, motivations, fears, and goals by identifying the audience.

Example: Business Owners

This term tells AI to speak the language of businesspeople, such as KPIs and ROIs. It focuses on the goals of saving time, growing sales, and reducing costs—not technical details.

Write a motivational paragraph about AI adoption for small business owners.

Uses: Website Homepage content and the Services page direction.

Options: Target markets such as small business owners, customers, or college students

Instructions—Not Commands

When using AI to create content for a website, the verbiage must be understood by humans and identifiable with keywords for search engines. AI has progressed from using code to garner a response using normal conversational content.

Natural Language Processing (NLP) or Large Language Models (LLMs) are AI systems designed to understand and generate human language. They use learning methods, but NLP itself is not a learning method.

Examples of NLP tasks:

- Understanding prompts
- Translating text

• Summarizing documents

• Writing content

• Answering questions

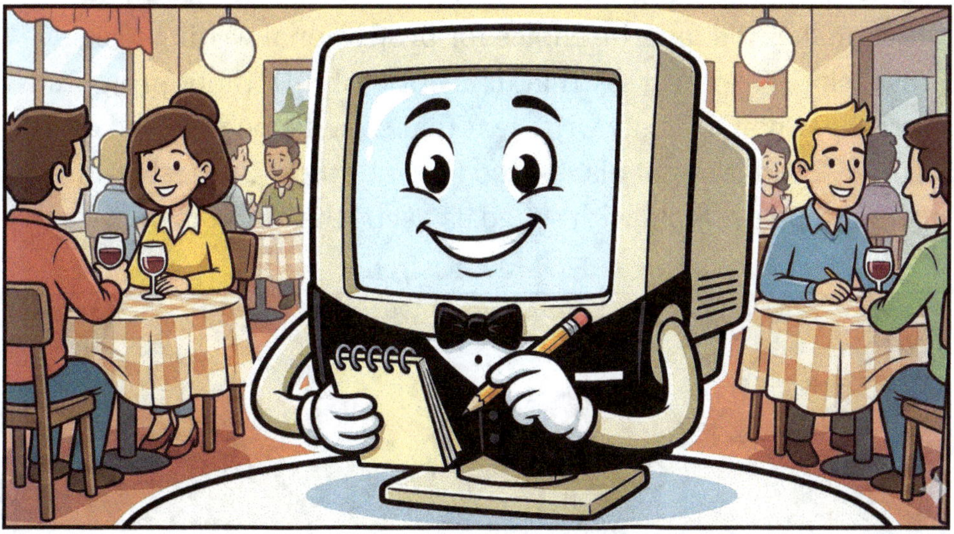

FIGURE 6.4

Prompts are instructions—not commands

AI Practicum} Gemini Prompt: Cartoon of a smiling computer dressed as a waiter, holding a notepad to write down an order.

Prompts are what the user gives the AI so it can generate a response. The model does not learn in real time from your prompts (unless specifically designed for fine-tuning or training).

CONTENT GENERATORS

There are a number of strong, solution-driven content generators. Individuals will have their favorite or may use two or three different ones depending on the outcome. They are looking for whatever they are writing. Here are brief descriptions of a few with their strengths and weaknesses.

ChatGPT is the solution with the best overall writing quality and flexibility, so it can be used for a lot of different types of content. It shows that it can think and reason well, which lets it make outputs that are both nuanced and new. It has a vast set of tools that work with images, data, and voice, so it can fit into different workflows and make designer more productive. This AI agent also creates adequate capable long-form, business, and technical content, which makes it a favorite choice for professional writing tasks. (Just ask GPT—it will say that, it is not bashful). If not prompted correctly, ChatGPT may write text that sounds too polished or "AI-like," and it might also be too long at times. Understanding how to write prompts with set goals keeps the answers on point.

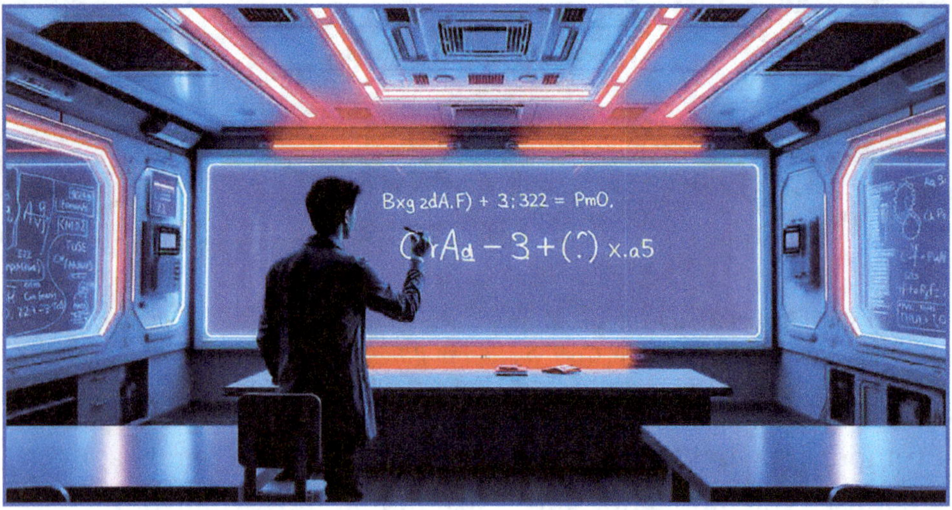

FIGURE 6.5

Magic Classroom

AI Practicum} DeepAI Prompt: Mystic futuristic classroom with a person writing a bizarre formula on a glass blue board.

Microsoft has Copilot built into Word. This AI content generator is very skilled at rewriting, summarizing, and adding to sections, and it helps a lot with formatting and structuring documents. Copilot is very helpful for reports and business documents. This AI generator works with Microsoft 365 data, such as emails, files, and notes. It is not as creative or good at telling stories as other options, and it's not the best tool for tasks that require a lot of ideas. Copilot works best with a Microsoft 365 subscription with Copilot turned on to use it.

Google Gemini is adept at remembering facts, especially when they are linked to Google Search. It is effective at providing information for content that needs a lot of research since it gives quick and clear answers, cites where it found the answers, and works well with Google Workspace. Gemini's writing is not as creative as that of other content writers and sometimes results in responses that are too cautious or general. Additionally, it doesn't have much power to shape long-form content.

Claude is very good at writing long pieces, and it often has the most "human" tone of all the AI writers. This content generator is extremely proficient at editing, rewriting, and making structured documents, and its behavior is very safe and predictable. However, it's less proficient at working with images or outside tools, it's not as good at real-time factual data, and it tends to be slower than ChatGPT on hard tasks.

QuillBot is a quality tool for rewriting, paraphrasing, and giving written content a professional finish. It is easy to use, inexpensive, and it gives the writer a great deal of control over grammar and style. It's especially helpful for students and quick changes. For social media writing and website articles, it has different voices to rewrite the same content for the different end readers. But it's not a real generative AI for long-form writing, and its style can sometimes feel mechanically rewritten, with little creativity or depth. It can be downloaded as a plugin to add to your Word and email writing.

Goblin as an AI copywriter is excellent for producing short marketing copy. It has useful templates for ads, hooks, and calls to action, and it can quickly make social media posts that are short and to the point. But it doesn't work well for long or technical writing; it often makes the same thing over and over again, and it's not very useful for anything other than marketing. It is a useful tool for breaking down tasks and creating checklists.

Grammarly is a powerful AI writer because it can fix grammar, make things clearer, and change the tone of a piece of writing while keeping the same voice. It works directly with browsers and apps, so it's great for improving drafts that are already there. It is, however, not very good at coming up with new ideas, can make writing too formal or boring, and the writer needs to pay for a premium plan to use all of its features.

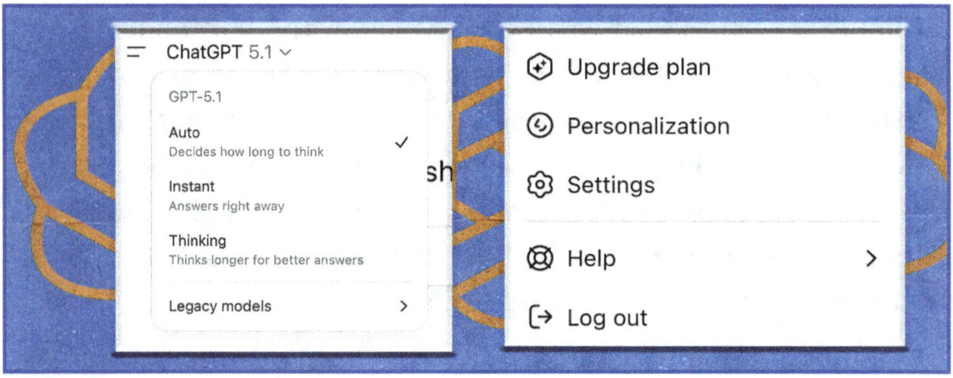

FIGURE 6.6

GPT hideaways

HI Practicum} Photoshop retouch and design of screen grabs.

GPT—TIPS AND HIDDEN ITEMS

ChatGPT 5 has hidden options that are available for solutions. Next to the icon at the top or the drop-down carrot when it is selected, options for auto, instant thinking, and legacy models. If ChatGPT is allowed to just choose the method of generation, it will pick the fastest result, which may not be the best use for specific areas of a website.

Auto Mode

This mode is the most balanced method and since it is the recommended working option, it also the default. Use it when ChatGPT should pick the best method, general use cases, and short tasks.

- Detects the complexity of your question
- Switches to Instant for short tasks
- Switches to Thinking for complex tasks

Instant Mode

This option can be used for quick definitions, simple instructions, everyday questions, short lists, and casual conversation. This is not the mode to use for complex analysis. Multi-step reasoning and writing long documents. This mode is set up to:

- Responds extremely quickly
- Gives short, direct answers
- Uses minimal reasoning
- Great for quick facts, summaries, short replies

Thinking Mode

Should be used for legal-style problem analysis, business decisions, strategic planning, long tasks, essay or manuscript writing, contracts, and proposals.

- Uses extended reasoning
- Breaks down steps
- Provides deeper analysis

- Better at logic-heavy tasks
- Can reason through multi-step problems more reliably

Select your name to see a number of options but look at the General and Personalization settings. Filling out some of them can speed up the time GPT uses to respond to your query.

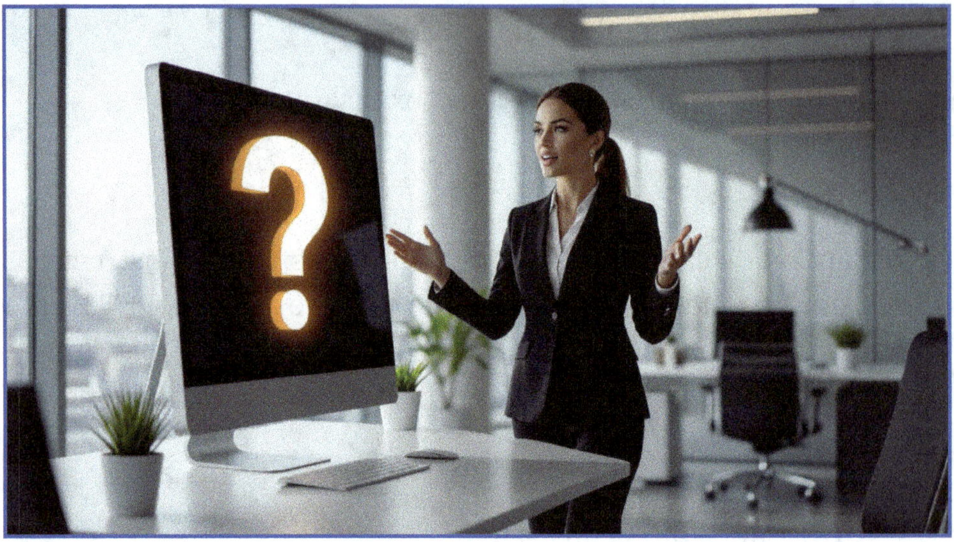

FIGURE 6.7

Speaking but not communicating

AI Practicum} Canva Prompt: A businesswoman pacing in her office with hands held up high and gesturing while she is speaking to a computer that has a big question mark coming out of the screen and big ears.

VOICE INPUT

If an user accesses ChatGPT through their mobile phone, instead of having to manually select a dropdown option, they can use certain verbal phrases. Instructions such as "start in expert mode," "use deep analysis mode," or "switch to thinking mode" should be said before a query.

At some point when accessible, the user should review what was written in the response, especially if the answer had technical terms, brand names, email addresses, and numerical information such as dates.

Verbal prompts are practical for brainstorming, creating drafts, and hands-free work. It allows for pacing in the process instead of being locked to a computer.

Think about the goal of the query and stay on subject without rambling. Filler words to make complete statements are not needed. Example: "Write concise headline for homepage aimed at new authors to encourage them to click CTA."

Use prompt blocks and pause between ideas. Speaking in clear, short sentences helps the AI model provide accurate responses. If a prompt gets off target or needs to be changed, tell the AI to "scratch that. I meant..." Add punctuation or if dictating, clarify if it should start a new paragraph or switch the format. For long prompts, end with a final phrase such as "now rewrite and polish.

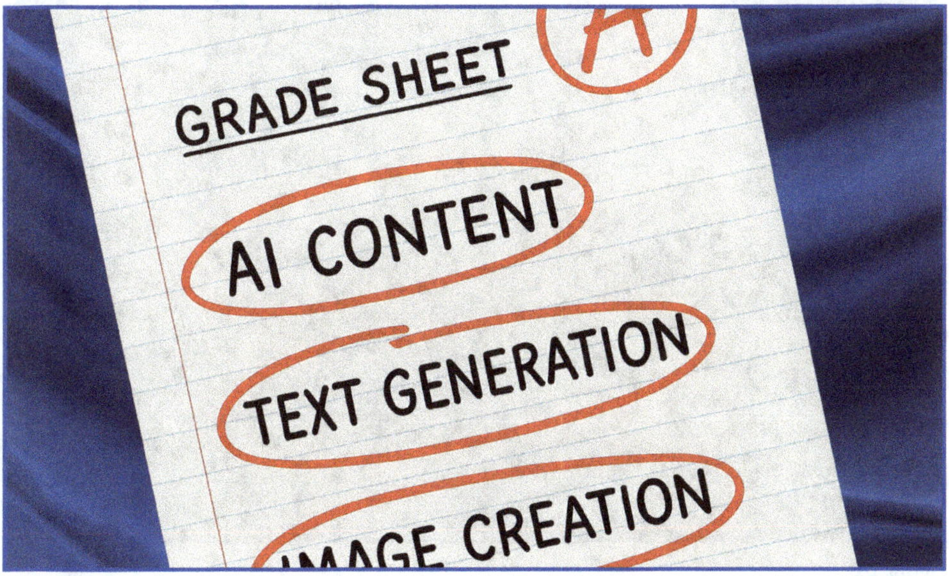

FIGURE 6.8

Testing content

AI Practicum} Canva Prompt: Image of grade sheet with AI content prompts and words circled.

TESTING CONTENT

Easy-Peasy.ai quickly checks headlines for clarity, emotion, and engagement, followed by AI-powered suggestions that are simple and likely to get clicks. It has marketing tools that are useful for landing pages, ads, and email subject lines, making it a good choice for small businesses. The platform is quick and easy to use, and headlines can be adjusted to fit the different voices of audiences.

It has a strange scoring system known only to it, and some of the suggestions resemble AI-written clickbait. Works best for general audiences instead of specific target audiences.

This tool is great for landing pages, ad headlines, email subject lines, blog posts, social media hooks, and product pages. It is useful for short, catchy headlines that are easy to edit and adapt to a marketing campaign.

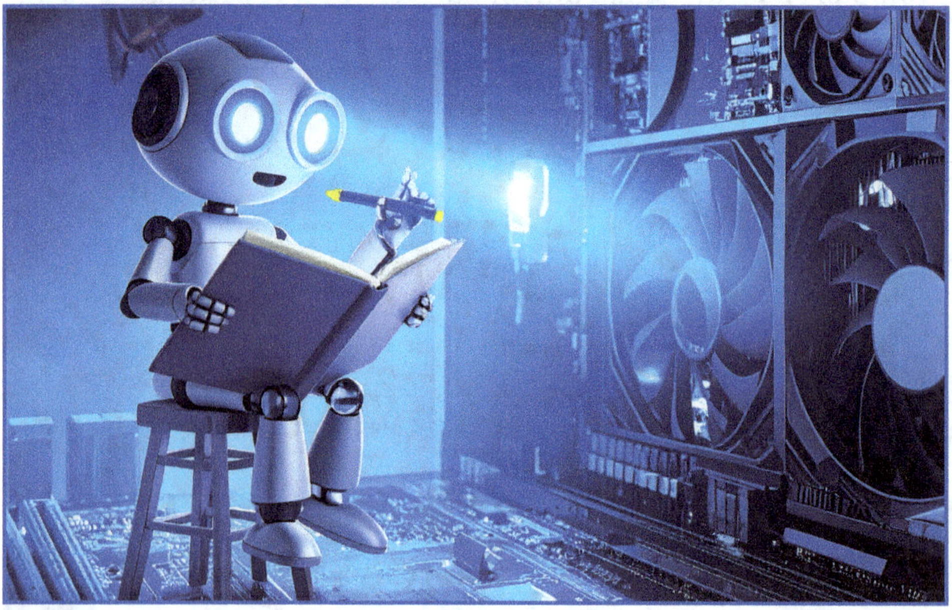

FIGURE 6.9

It's in here somewhere...

AI Practicum} Firefly Prompt: Photograph of the inside of a computer with GPU boards for walls, where a cartoon-like Chatbot is reading a through a technical book and holding a highlighter marker.

Demo Canva—create designed headline

Another popular AI design program being used by the small business community is Canva. It has a free level and does not need a great deal of studying to be able to work on its features.

1. Open up Canva.com

2. In Chapter 3, Easy Peasy created a number of alternate headlines. Since they are going to be converted from type to artwork, they will need to be shortened. By editing them to have fewer words, they will be easier for a visitor to read.

3. Select Canva-AI.

4. Input the prompt: The words "Invest Confidently" are written in shades of green ink on light yellow legal paper that has thin lines of light green.

5. Select Image > Creative > 4:3 and then the arrow icon to generate the image.

6. The image is large enough for the internet, but for print it will need to be larger, so in the prompt add "print quality."

7. Select "edit" at the top of the page, where it can be resized and cropped.

8. Choose to download the image as a PNG file.

9. It will need to be converted into an optimized JPG for the website.

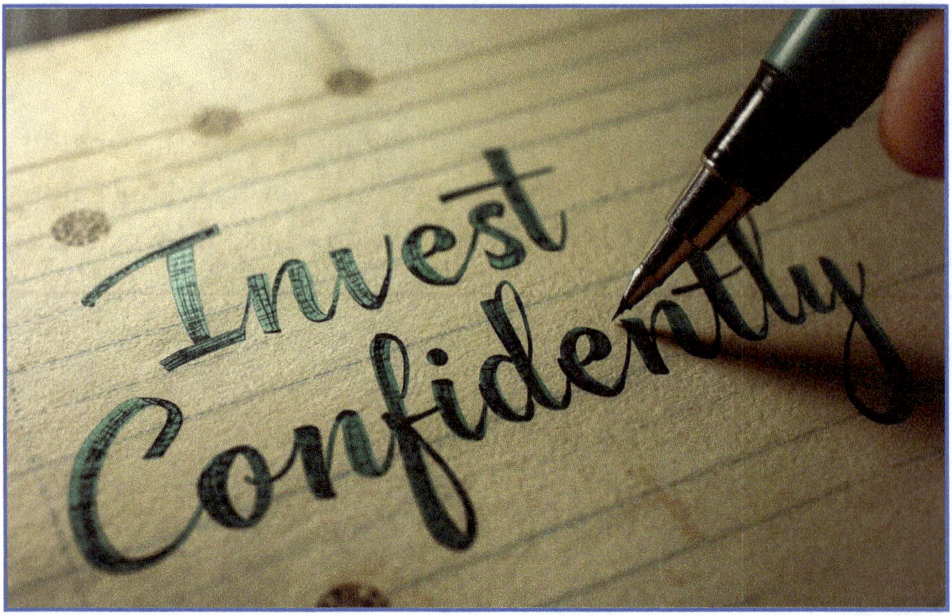

IMAGE 6.10

The website needs to grab the visitor's attention

AI Practicum} Canva Prompt: Invest Confidently written in shades of green ink on accounting paper.

Eye of the Beholder

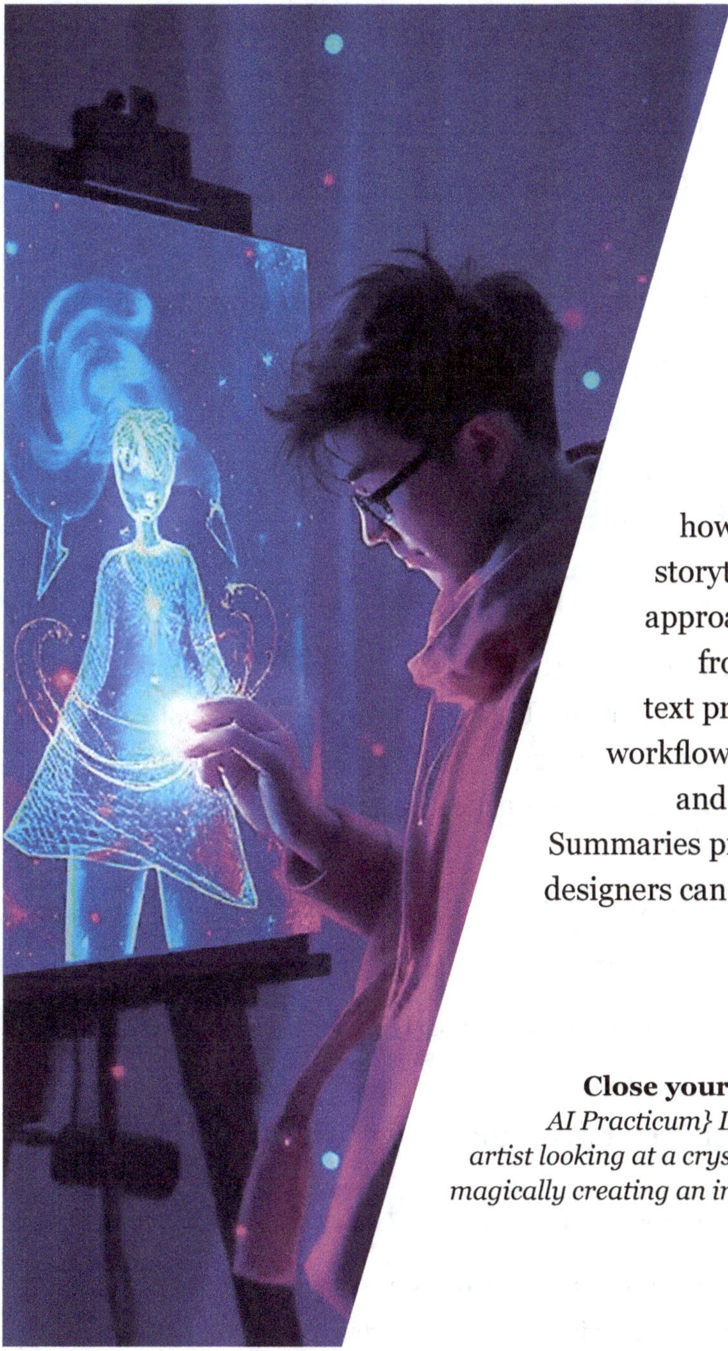

C7

OVERVIEW

Examination of how AI can improve storytelling with fresh approaches to imaging from wordsmithed text prompts. Practical workflows can streamline and boost creativity. Summaries presented of what designers can produce quickly and affordably.

FIGURE 7.1

Close your eyes and create

AI Practicum} DeepAI Prompt: An artist looking at a crystal canvas, hand is magically creating an image with swirls of dust and fireflies.

PROFESSIONAL TERMINOLOGY

Color Space: Defines the process of how colors are created for a medium.

Embedded: An image that is added directly into a website.

Favicon: A small icon showing in a browser next to a site's domain.

Hero: The large image on a website page, usually near the top

Optimize: Compressing the information in an image for faster downloading

Pixelated: A low-resolution image enlarged by stretching the pixels to fill the area.

FOCAL POINT

In visual communications, the goal is to get an individual to stop and look at the composition. Each image should tell a story with a single message and emphasize something about that image. One way to create a focal point is with cropping. Cropping an image can have many results:

- It can have more impact
- The image can be more pleasing to the eye
- Create an emotional response from viewers
- Make the image more personal to visitors
- Create a sense of tension and energy to the message

CREATE INTERESTING IMAGES

While the easy way to present an image is to drop it into a square shape, keep in mind that is what the software engineer decided is how an image should be shown. Designers are using images to create an interest in the website, and the images should be used to their full extent to grab that potential customer.

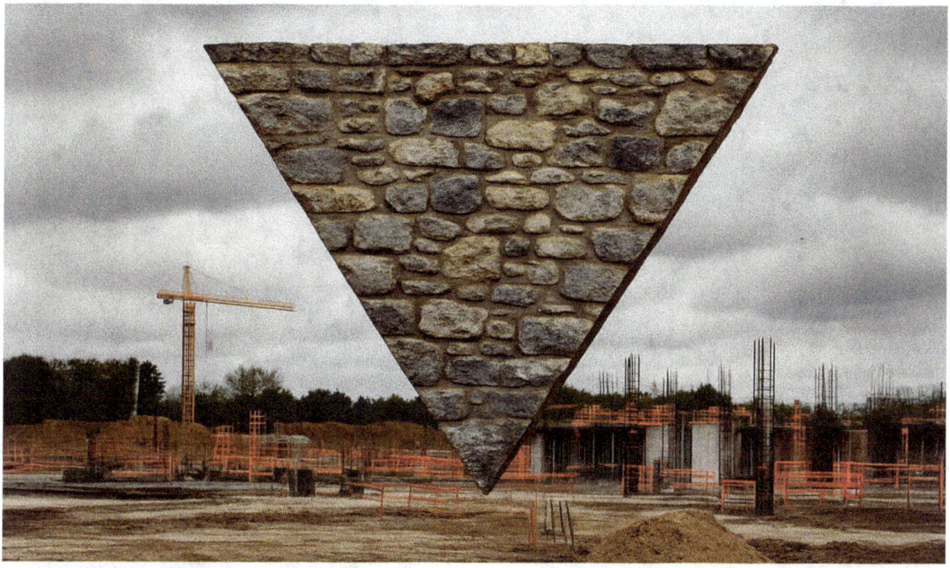

FIGURE 7.2

Show hard shapes

AI Practicum} ChatGPT Prompt: Show an image of stone wall cropped into a sharp triangle floating above a construction site in a 4 Wide x 3 Height ratio.

Each image should be approached as the element that will keep a visitor on the page. Just as the content is worked and reworked, images should have as much and more thought put into their use. The size and amount of space surrounding a picture should not be haphazard. Images can catch the viewer's eye by rotating the image. The color of the image can pull a viewer into a page. How an image is cropped can greatly improve the impact of an image.

Cropping refers to the trimming off of the areas of an image in order to produce more impact, to focus the reader, or to fit a given space. The image can be a photograph, drawing, type, sketch, doodle, shapes, or an area utilizing chiaroscuro to produce tonal lights to dark.

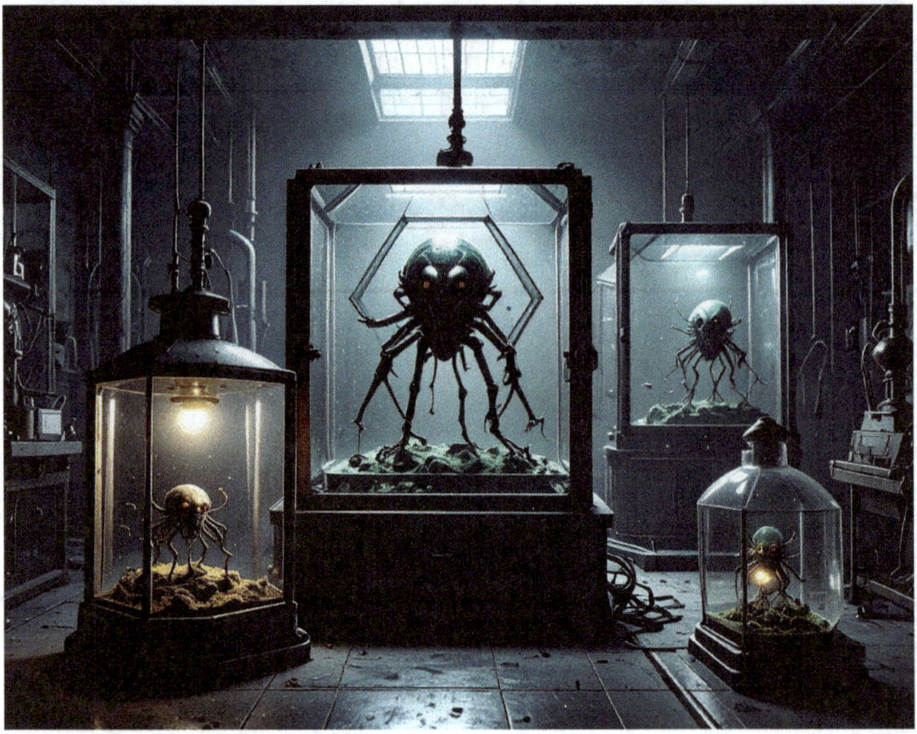

FIGURE 7.3

2-dimensional design becomes 3D

AI Practicum} Firefly Prompt: Show 5 containers with alien creature trapped in each glass polygon, that overlap to show depth, sized from small to large in laboratory eerily lit from above.

This skill requires practice and trying to look at the image after cropping as if it were the "first time." Creatively removing the uninteresting parts of an image will help the viewer immediately grab their attention.

When an area is cropped out, the image may need to be enlarged, or that part of the image may need a generative fill. Enlarging the file will cause the image to pixelate. If the image is a vector file, then that is not a concern. In the creation of an image, it is good practice to make it as large as possible. It can always be reduced in size without a loss of quality.

Cropping does not have to be done as a square or rectangle. Crop with a shape (such as an oval, circle, star, or polygon) to enhance the image.

If an image is cropped with an element extending outside of the picture shape, it will have more depth. This will present a two-dimensional image with a foreground and background.

Using different sizes will use scale for contrast and can be perceived as movement. The eye will be led around the page, which can take a visitor to the CTA.

Using an organic shape with sharp edges or curved sides can add feeling to the design. Sharp corners are perceived as modern and sleek, while rounded edges feel friendly and easy-going. Shapes, along with textures, create a flow in the design.

Designers know to use shapes that subconsciously sell a product. As an example, pillows, beds, and chairs should be in soft and round shapes. Conversely, if the product is supposed to be substantial or durable, to convey this feeling, hard and sharp shapes are used.

FIGURE 7.4

Image generators are not content generators

AI Practicum} Dall-E Prompt: In an ornate book cover design show the words Format + Role + Action Word + Context.

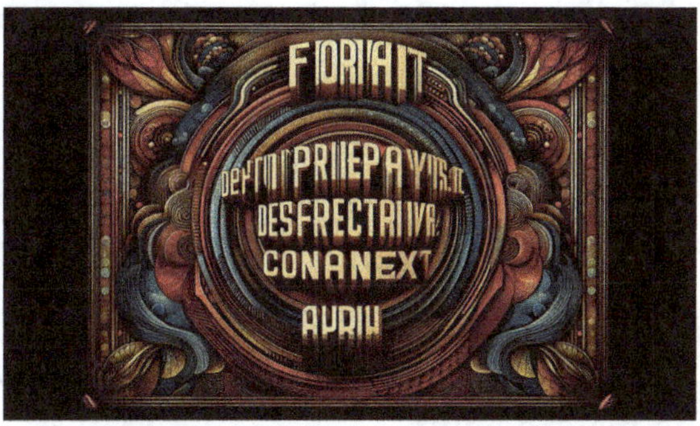

TEST THE GENERATORS

Every day new platforms to create images using AI become available. Try the free artificial intelligence generators while free use is available. AI generators will soon turn to free trial models or only be available with limited features.

It also seems that there are new AI generator partnerships to save on costs occurring, such as Google Gemini with Adobe AI generators. As with any mass-produced product or service, there has been extensive research into what price point users are willing to pay for additional features.

As expected, users want the freemium versions, but some users recognize the value of AI and will pay for additional features. In less than a year AI has grown from a fun activity to a necessary tool. Online surveys have found that in March of 2025, only 8% of the recipients would pay for additional features.[1]

In September of the same year, 40% of the users in an AI survey said they already subscribe to an AI generator.[2]

7 VISUAL IMAGING AI GENERATORS

There are a number of AI image tools and generators available for free or monthly subscriptions. Many designers use 20+ based on the look and quality they are after. Users should test the following AI generators to see which ones are easy to use and deliver the results they want to use on websites.

Each content and image generator has pros and cons. The main differences were which generators can produce images for print production. The image can be scaled larger but gets pixelated and loses details to look out of focus. An enlarged image will appear degraded and will reflect on the quality of the print design.

Most image-focused generators are not adept at including words in the images. Even if the words are spelled out in the prompt, the image will have typographical errors or the word will not be recognizable.

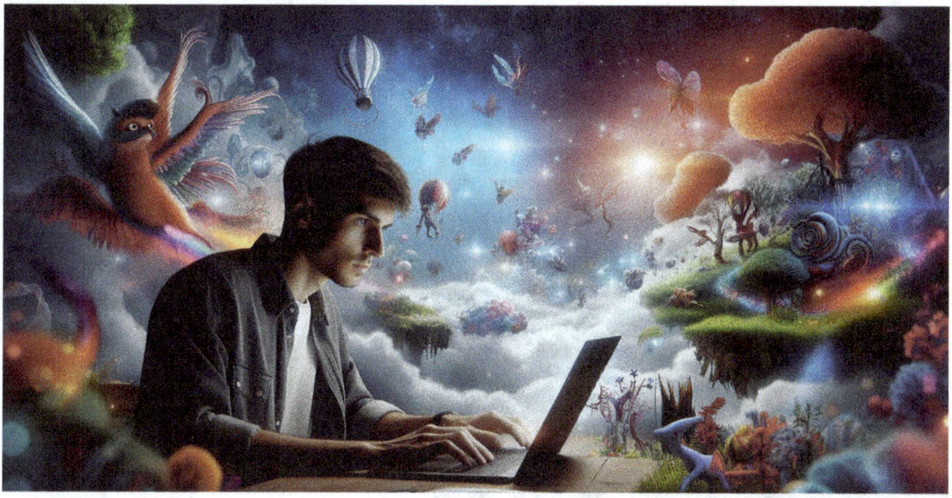

FIGURE 7.5

AI starts with HI

AI Practicum} Creator Prompt: Show a graphic designer working on creating a website surrounded by a fantasy world.

Creator from Microsoft

Microsoft's Bing Image Creator can generate intricate images with a resolution for the internet that are over 24 inches wide, but for printing, the image would convert to approximately 6 inches x 3.5 inches. It has a seamless animation option that provides 10 free files for quick results with a subscription, but after that it will take hours to create.

Website:	bing.com/images/create
Max image size:	1792 x 1024 pixels
Image features	Seamless editing with Microsoft Designer, creative & flexible images
Subscription p/m:	Included with Microsoft subscription
Notes:	Does not fill the space very well and has a slow response. Provided four almost identical options.

Table 7.1 | Creator image creation parameters.

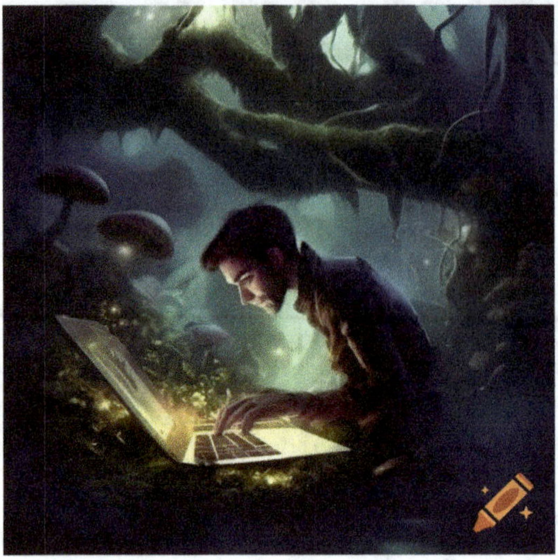

FIGURE 7.6

AI can be dark or interesting based on instructions

AI Practicum} Craiyon Prompt: Show a graphic designer working on creating a website surrounded by a fantasy world.

Craiyon

Numerous image creations, easy prompting, and fast results are features that make this AI generator preferred almost as much as Firefly. However, the quality and resolution of the images are low, there are minimal editing tools, and, as in many free AI generators, the prompter needs to count eyes, fingers, hands, and heads before downloading.

Website:	craiyon.com/en
Max image size:	512 x 512 pixels
Image features	Strong flat art and cartoon images
Subscription p/m:	Free with ads; Plans start at $10, with the pro level at $20
Notes:	Not ideal for adding space for content or headlines

Table 7.2 | Craiyon image creation parameters.

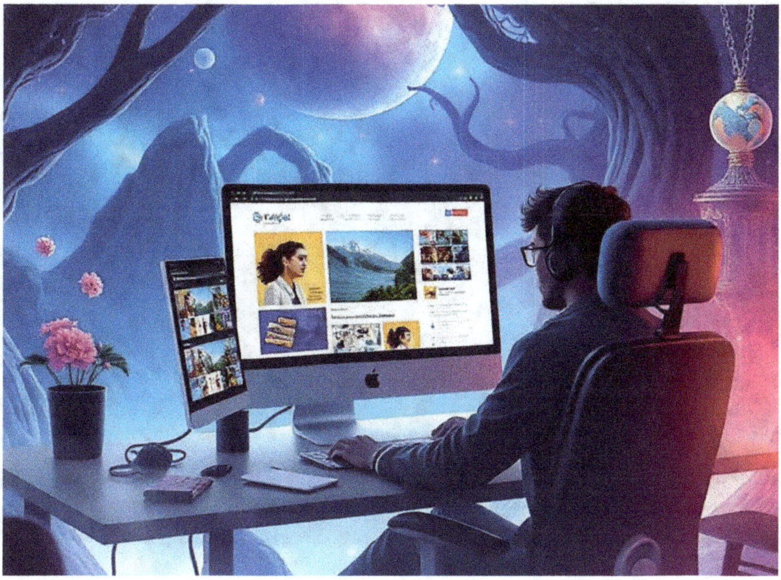

FIGURE 7.7
HI assists AI generate images
AI Practicum} DeepAI Prompt: Show a graphic designer working on creating a website surrounded by a fantasy world.

DeepAI

One of the easiest and most beginner-friendly AI generators. For developers, it does work well with AAPI integration. The free version has limited controls and has ads; there is only one option per prompt, and many times the generation takes a lot of time.

Website:	deepai.org
Max image size:	1024x1024 pixels
Image features	Image enhancer, great a fantasy creations
Subscription p/m:	Free level with Pro at $5
Notes:	Adding space for content or headlines is difficult

Table 7.3 | DeepAI image creation parameters.

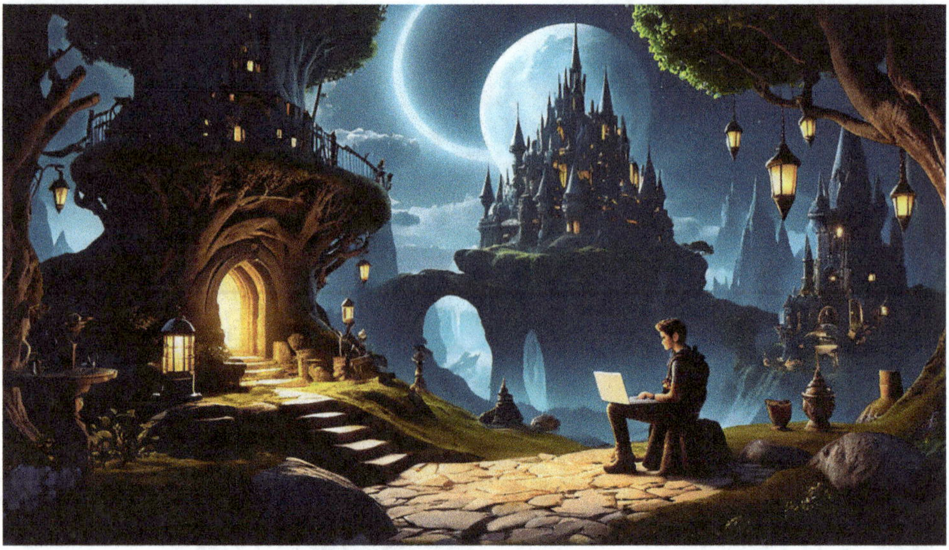

FIGURE 7.8

AI opens imaginative world of design

AI Practicum} DeepDream Prompt: Show a graphic designer working on creating a website surrounded by a fantasy world.

DeepDream

Generates different, surreal, and artistic images that are fun and Generates different, surreal, and artistic images that are fun and whimsical. A good experimental AI that will change up the look on any website. Not the best for commercial imagery—very limited customization in styles, but an interesting artistic tool.

Website:	DeepDreamGenerator.com/Generate.
Max image size:	1920x1080 pixels.
Image features	Artistic, surreal, and illustrative, but weak mainstream or realism.
Subscription p/m:	Very limited free features. Plans start at $9.
Notes:	Needs a number of prompts to get to a usable solution.

Table 7.4 | DeepDream image creation parameters.

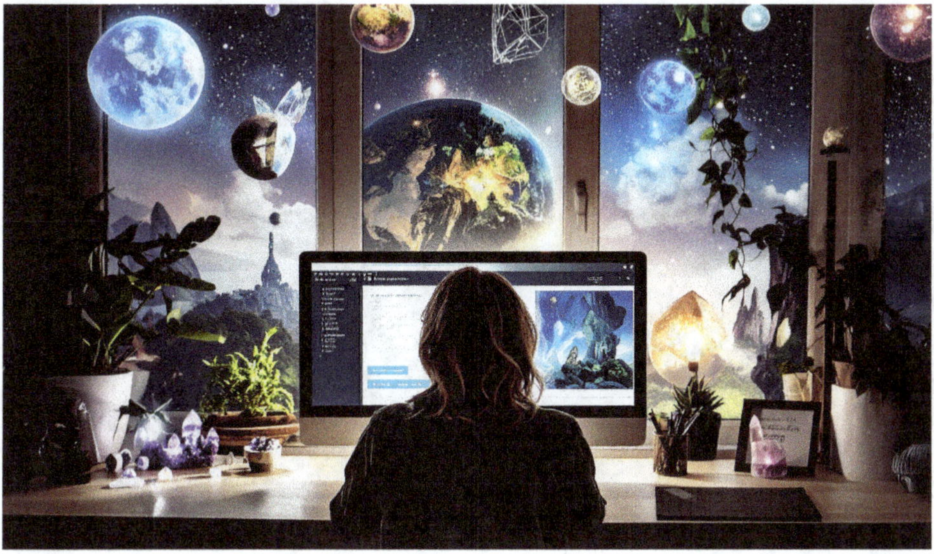

FIGURE 7.9

Creativity is not replace by AI

AI Practicum} Firefly Prompt: Show a graphic designer working on creating a website surrounded by a fantasy world.

Firefly from Adobe

Firefly is one of the best image generators available for personal and professional use; it is not too expensive, but it is no longer free. It works seamlessly with Adobe's Creative Suite and includes an online version of Photoshop. This Photoshop version is not as robust as the desktop software but includes many of the editing features an average designer would need.

Website:	Firefly.adobe.com
Max image size:	2048 x 2048 pixels
Image features	Image enhancer, high-quality professional images
Subscription p/m:	Starts at $10
Notes:	Longer prompts produce better results, and there are multiple options of image generators to use.

Table 7.5 | Firefly image creation parameters.

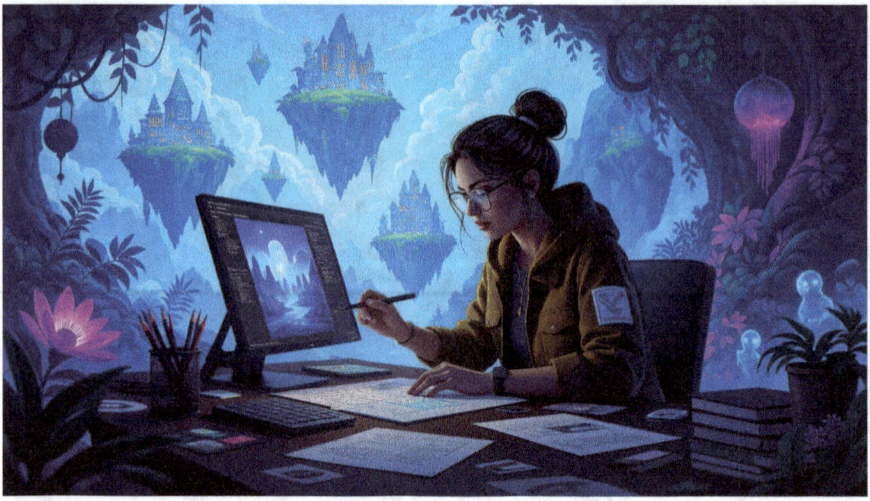

FIGURE 7.10

Have a plan but it can change

AI Practicum} NightCafe Prompt: Show a graphic designer working on creating a website surrounded by a fantasy world.

NightCafe

This strong AI generator is very popular for images that are different and eye-catching. The tools are a little difficult, and image options are not as robust as some of the paid subscription generators; some results require credits.

Website:	creator.nightcafe.studio
Max image size:	1800x1200 pixels
Image features	Creative style based on provided library of images
Subscription p/m:	Starts at $10
Notes:	Shorter prompts produce good results, with strong color and different ideas.

Table 7.6 | NightCafe image creation parameters.

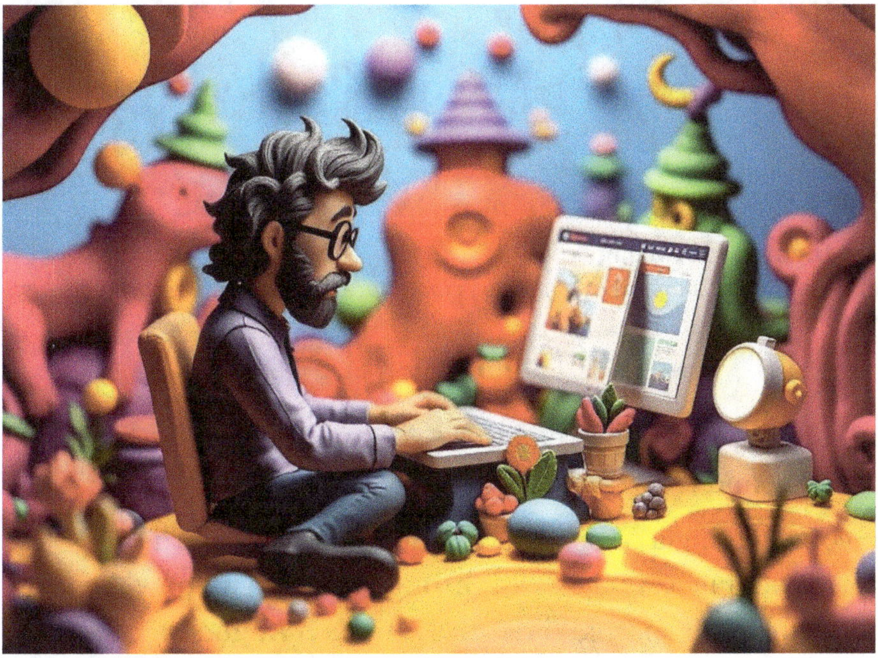

FIGURE 7.11

A nod to Mr. Clokey

AI Practicum} Pixlr Prompt: Show a graphic designer working on creating a website surrounded by a fantasy world.

Pixlr

After Firefly and Night Café, Pixlr is one of the more flexible AI generators. Numerous options, styles, and formats are presented.

Website:	pixlr.com/image-generator/
Max image size:	1800x1200 pixels
Image features	Numerous options from art style, color and lighting.
Subscription p/m:	Free plan requires registering, starts at $10
Notes:	Multiple options of the same concept provided,

Table 7.7 | Pixlr image creation parameters.

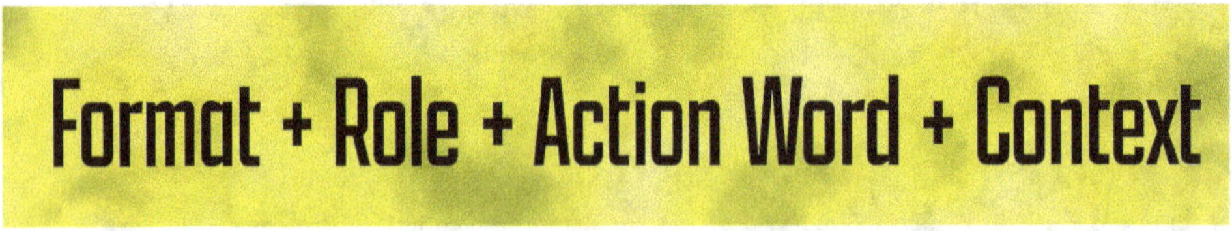

FIGURE 7.12

Prompt formula for images

HI Practicum} Photoshop created words, cloud background with high-pass filter.

PROMPT EXAMPLES

Before starting a prompt, read this section. Here are five tips to save on time and frustration.

When constructing a query, there is no one way to word the prompts. Looking at Images 7-5 through 7-10 shows how the same prompt can be interpreted differently by each AI generator. The AI neither knows the best solution nor can it judge what the best solution would be for a circumstance. These clear guidelines for composing prompts work well with image generators.

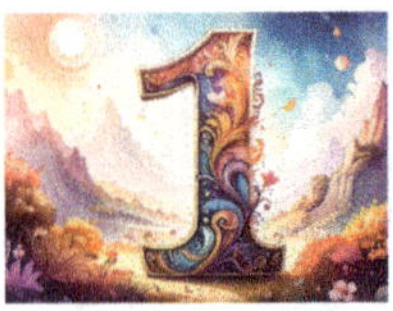

Clarify the style. Use art/design history terminology; approaches have changed over the centuries. Terms such as "brutalist, "and "minimalist" are new, while "Glasgow," "constructivism," and "art deco" are from the 1900s, and "art nouveau" from the late 1800s gives AI a timeframe and the viewer a sense of history without wasting words.

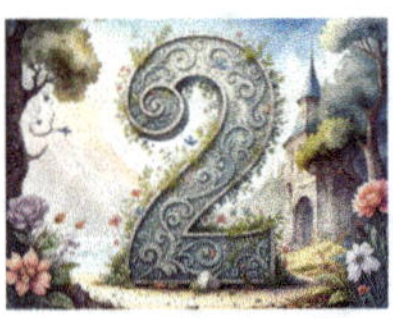

Characterize the image's lighting, colors, and tone. Try "a traditional lawyers' office made with rich wood and leather with amber lighting that projects experience and trust." For a modern office, use adjectives like "a modern attorney's office with clean lines, abundant light, and use of cool tones to imply competence and success."

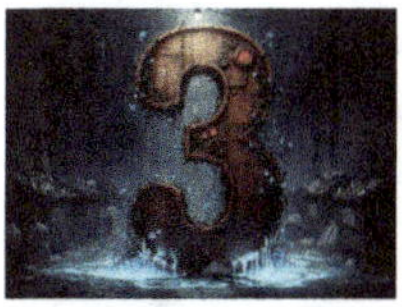

Describe the subject as a person, place, thing, or concept. Use clear terms, such as “a gathering of artists” or “one student raising a hand to immediately communicate if it is a singular subject or multiple.

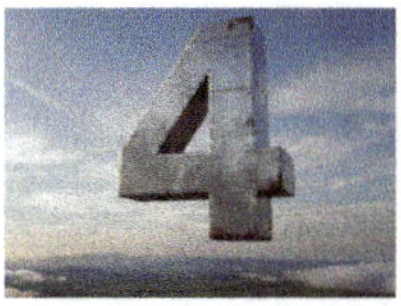

Set the point of view to guide the AI, such as a close-up or overhead, along with the format of square, rectangle, or circle, and pinpoint the focus as centered or off to the left.

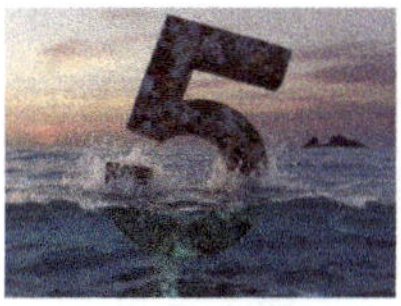

End with constraints such as do not use cliches and have an area for a little or a lot of type. If it is a hero image, instruct the AI to “allow for an H1 headline across the bottom of the image.”

At this point the prompt is getting word-heavy. AI does not care about grammar but does need words to be spelled correctly. Use phrases that can be broken with commas or as run-on sentences.

Grammar is needed if describing a relationship between images. See Figure 7.3 and compare to Figure 7.13. Both prompts have similar adjectives but with different results from Firefly.

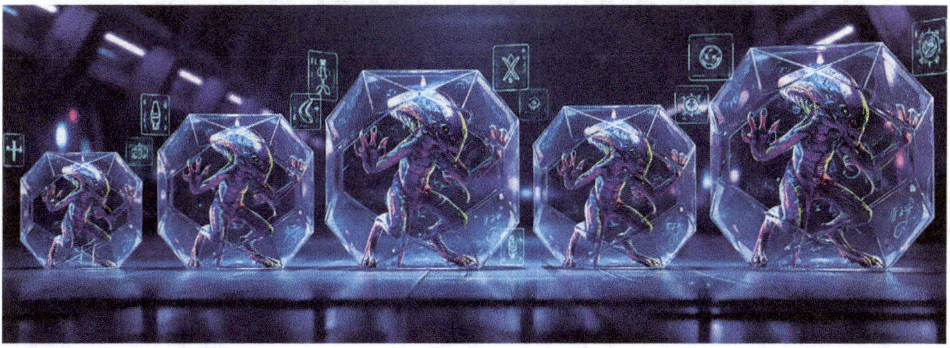

FIGURE 7.18

Alternate 2-dimensional design becomes 3D
AI Practicum} Firefly Prompt: Show 5 of the same images that go from small to large and rotate with an alien creatures.

Demo Firefly – creating images

Firefly has many image enhancement options. It also has different AI generators within Firefly to use depending on the desired outcome.

1. Create an account on Adobe Firefly with an email or by signing in with an established Google or Apple account.
2. In the prompt field select Image; in the dropdown menu select Firefly Image 4. Click on the More icon.
3. Google Gemini 3 Nano Banana may create a better solution but only one solution is provided. Firefly Image 4 generates four options which can all be downloaded at hi-resolution.
4. Open the side menu to reveal many more editing options.
5. Choose Landscape from the General Settings on the left. Note there are more options here than in the Google option.
6. Under Composition and Styles, an image can be uploaded for reference, or look through the gallery to give the AI a direction.
7. Numerous effects are available in the different categories.
8. Below the "Effects" are color and tone, lighting, and camera angle. Select "Shot from below."
9. In the prompt window in the lower right is the letter T and some stars—click on this prompt feature and turn on suggestions and enter the prompt.
10. At the end of the prompt, place the cursor and delete to make the prompt short. Suggestions will appear; select one.
11. Select generate.
12. Choose one of the images and download it.

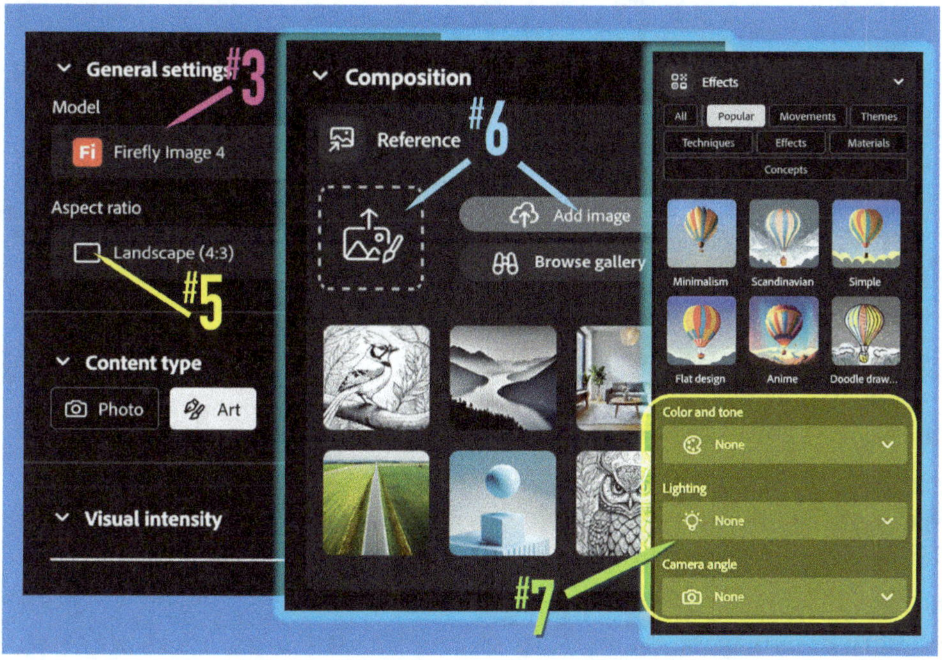

FIGURE 7.19

Control panels in Firefly

HI Practicum} In Photoshop created bright colored numbers that corresponded with the instructions in the Demo. Colors had to be saturated for CMYK printing and used high-pass filter for contrast. Outer tight glow added for the panels to pull them out and contrast with the other menus.

REFERENCES

1. Rapoza, J. (2025, May 7). Only 8% of Americans would pay extra for AI. ZDNET-Aberdeen Research. https://www.zdnet.com/article/only-8-of-americans-would-pay-extra-for-ai-according-to-zdnet-aberdeen-research/

2. (2025, September 25). In the gen AI economy, consumers want innovation they can trust. Tech, Media, and Telecom, (Deloitte's sixth Connected Consumer study). https://www.deloitte.com/us/en/insights/industry/telecommunications/connectivity-mobile-trends-survey.html insets

INSETS

FIGURE 7.13

Clarify the style

AI Practicum} Firefly Prompt: An elaborate fantasy like numeral 1.

FIGURE 7.14

Characterize the image

AI Practicum} Firefly Prompt: A adventurous ornate numeral 2

FIGURE 7.15

Describe the subject

AI Practicum} Firefly Prompt: A lit retrofitted numeral 3 in a dark alley.

FIGURE 7.16

Set the point of view

AI Practicum} Firefly Prompt: Create a numeral 4 floating tin the sky.

FIGURE 7.17

End with constraints

AI Practicum} Firefly Prompt: The numeral 5 shooting out of the ocean

24-Hour Salesman

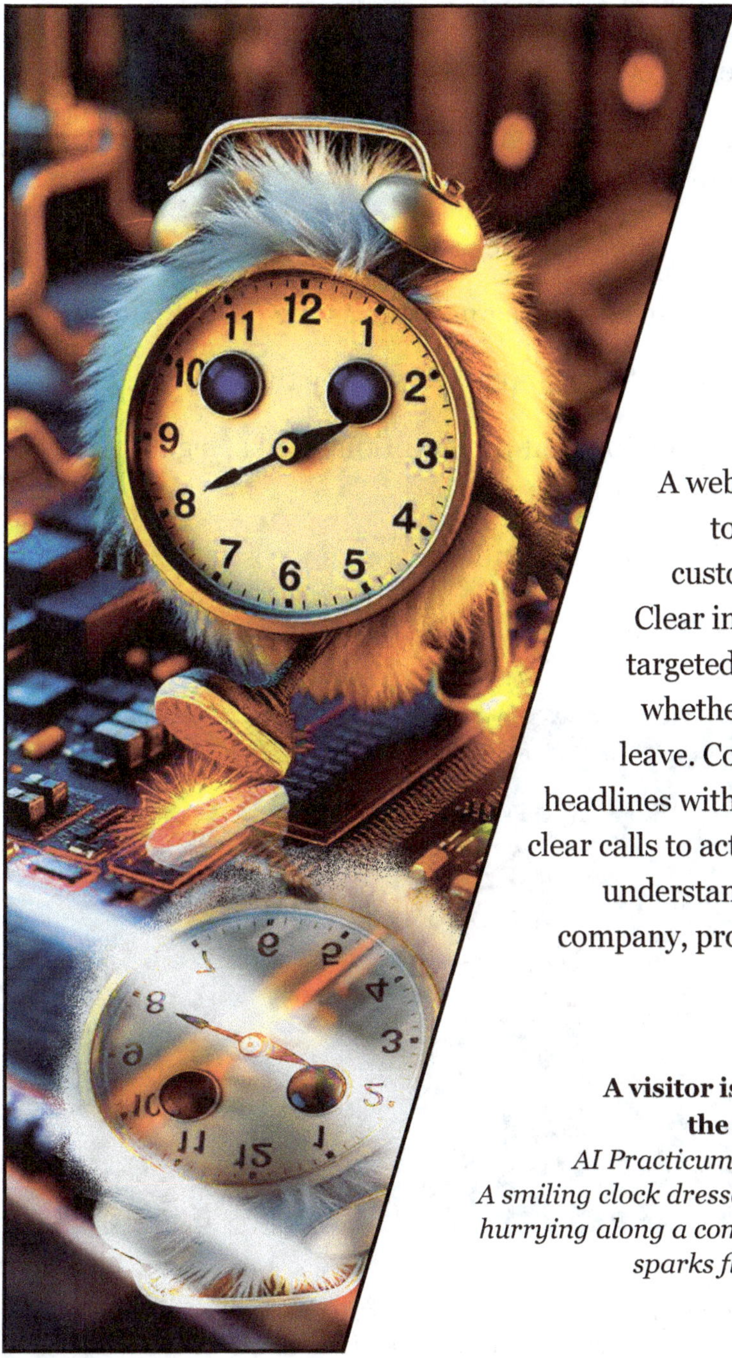

C8

OVERVIEW

A website has seconds to grab a potential customer's attention. Clear information and a targeted headline decide whether visitors stay or leave. Conversion-driven headlines with real photos and clear calls to action help visitors understand and act on the company, product, or service.

FIGURE 8.1

A visitor is on the page and the clock is running.

AI Practicum} DeepAI Prompt: A smiling clock dressed like a salesman hurrying along a computer board with sparks flying from its feet.

PROFESSIONAL TERMINOLOGY

B2B: An acronym for business-to-business that is used for specifying the target market.

Caret: A small inverted two-sided isosceles triangular arrow used to indicate a dropdown.

Chevron: Two or three UI stacked carets.

Child page: Subpage on the same topic as the parent page.

Dropdown: A term for the area revealed by the inverted caret.

Footer: Bottom section that has additional links, legal information and website site map.

Navigation: Links to pages and items on a website.

Parent Page: Main page that can lead to child pages that expand on the subject.

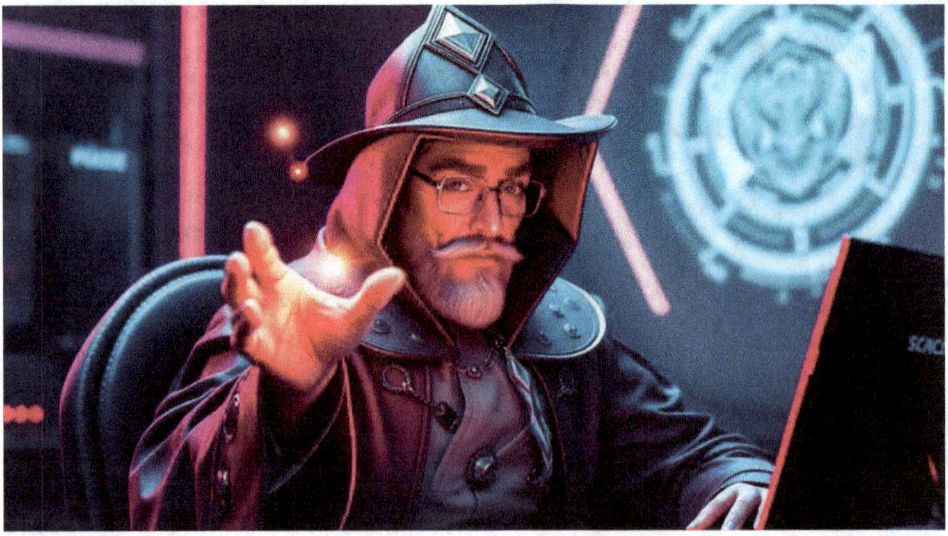

FIGURE 8.2

Is it science or magic?

AI Practicum} DeepAI Prompt: A magician dressed in a futuristic robe and diamond hat casting a spell on a computer.

LITERALLY SECONDS

When a potential customer visits a site, it has seconds to create visitor interest, followed by desire from a potential customer to stay and see more. The fundamentals of design, such as flowing space, attractive colors, simple readability, fast load time, image attraction, and scale to create a visual flow, have been worked and adjusted and readjusted to appeal to the visitor. Now it is up to a headline to make a visitor want to read on down the page. It is the major aspect of a website and must be the focus.

First impressions make individuals leave a website often before reading a single sentence. They conclude that a page feels confusing, outdated, or untrustworthy. A weak or unclear first impression undermines trust, even if the product or service is strong. Visitors arrive with a goal, and if a website does not show it, they will search elsewhere.

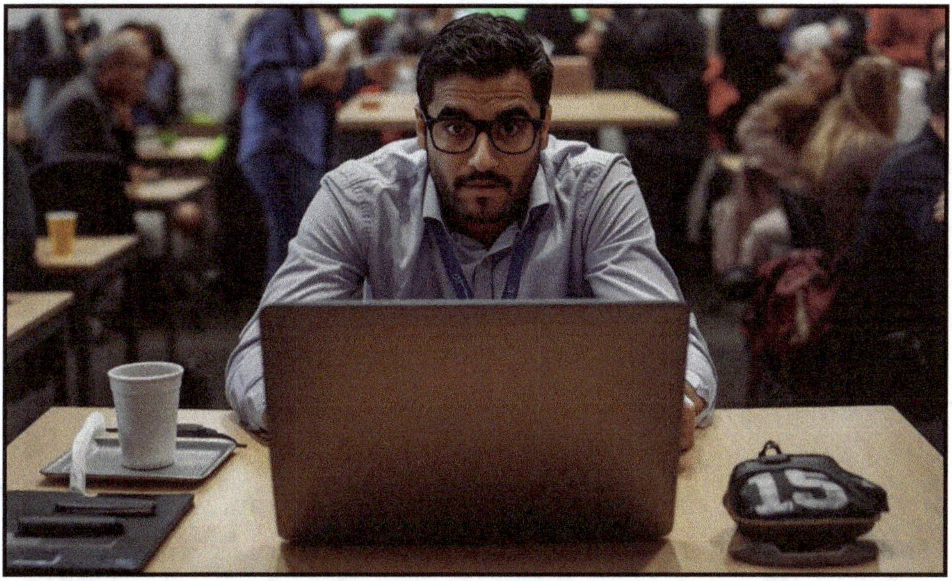

FIGURE 8.3

Clarity is in the eye of the designer

AI Practicum} Canva Prompt: Person using a computer in an office break room that has people laughing, eating.

The message must have clarity, structure, and contrast. The communication will be organized without ambiguity, setting up the tone to be warm and trustworthy. This voice must coincide with the images of what is being sold.

Statistics play a large role in deciding a website's success. Google ranks a website in search results by the amount of traffic to a website. It also follows how long the traffic stays and how they exit. The average visitor will decide in less than five seconds if the content they are searching for is on that webpage. Since this is the first time they have visited the site, these individuals are classified as unique visitors.

The first metric for deciding if a website is successful is to have a unique visitor stay 30-60 seconds. The second metric is to count how many selected the CTA. The third metric is to know if a visitor returned. All of these revolve around the content and how quickly it conveys the message to the user.

GTM OVERVIEW

The go-to-market (GTM) expression refers to the complete marketing package for a company, product, or service. It encompasses how a business is presented, positioned, and delivered to customers. Consider it a comprehensive plan that communicates what is being sold, who the offering serves, and how the plan persuades customers to choose the company, product, or service.

A go-to-market offering brings together the company, product, or service with a clearly defined target audience and a compelling value proposition that explains the problem it solves and why it matters.

This strategy is shaped by intentional positioning and messaging, reinforced by strategic pricing and packaging. The plan includes delivery through the distribution channels where customers are most likely to discover, evaluate, and engage with it.

The GTM identifies the ideal customer and explains why they should buy the company, product, or service. Establishing a GTM will minimize costs, reduce waste, and mitigate risks compared to relying on instinct-driven marketing, sales, and design decisions. In the quest to build brand awareness and excitement for an offering, the GTM serves as the broad strategy.

Rather than focusing solely on the product or service itself, a GTM strategy emphasizes how customers understand, experience, and adopt it. The GTM aligns marketing, sales, design, and strategy into one coherent market entry or growth plan.

START WITH THE HEADLINE

The web searcher will glance at the hero image, space, and the heaviness of text blocks but ultimately gauge the site by its main headline. The intent of the front-page headline is to influence a visitor's behavior. There are two basic approaches to creating an attention-grabbing headline: persuasion and inspiration. Both types must tell visitors why the website deserves their time. When constructing a headline, the copywriter knows it must be conversion-focused.

The shorter the headline, the better, but to stand out and grab a guest, usually six to nine words are needed. It should contain adjectives, adverbs, nouns, and verbs. The headline is made up of common and uncommon words, power words, and emotional words. Using the word "you" helps make the headline personal.

When developing headlines, a website writer must first understand the varieties and names of the numerous approaches. Determining the approach is dictated by the type of seller, which is the company, product, or service being presented. Since the website is the medium, the target market should be somewhat tech-savvy. Establishing the goal of the CTA can involve an action such as clicking a button or filling out a short form. Lesser considerations are urgency, budget, data, and resources.

HEADLINE TYPE	MESSAGE	TARGET AUDIENCE
Consumer	Benefits of using the company, product, or service.	Customers, retail shoppers, individuals based on income.
Business-to-business	Focus on business interests such as saving time and reducing costs.	Retailers, wholesalers, producers of services and/or products
Public relations	Establishing reputation, quality, reliability, or affordability.	Broad market based on needs and income.
Groups and institutions	Raise awareness of issues, influence ideas, affect legislation, alter perceptions.	Consumers, voters, legislators
Political	Show common beliefs, family, friendly.	Voters, sponsors, social groups, and fundraising

Table 8.1 Headline types by audience.

An example of consumer headlines is "We Guarantee Quality Service Every Time." This wording is letting the consumer know the business can be trusted and is professional.

A similar example but for business-to-business is "We get your service problem resolved the first time and fast." This wording appeals to most business owners' concern with speed (related to keeping sales) and quality.

Public relations headlines should not be a hard sell but aimed at establishing a reputation.

Government, social institutions, and civic groups websites to disseminate information to its members and citizens.

Political headlines are ultimately directed at voters but include sponsors, social groups, and fundraising. Advertising to acquire cash and resources is inherent in any campaign.

Persuasion

Writing a persuasive headline is a technique to manipulate a consumer's objectivity. By creating a need or focusing on an established concern, the headline should interest the target market in seven words or less. This approach is a hypeline. It is not ashamed to sell what a company is offering. It is unmistakably benefit-driven.

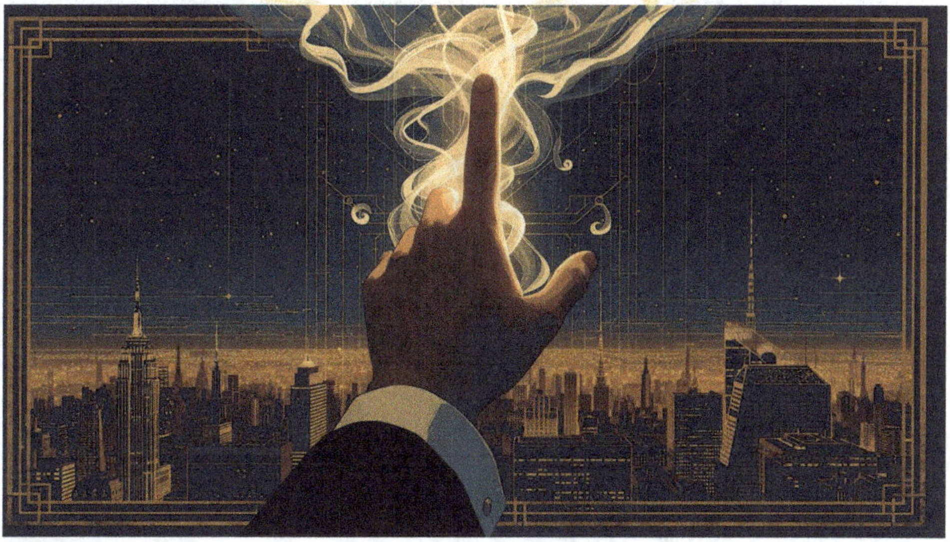

FIGURE 8.4

We want you.

AI Practicum} Firefly Prompt: Art deco styled image with glowing smoke around a hand floating above a city with the forefinger pointing out toward the viewer.

Dropping the price

The most effective manipulation tool to get a customer's interest. Promotions such as "buy one get one free" are in the same group. It must create a sense of urgency by being a short-term proposition.

Fear

Motivates individuals to move away from something harmful. An example is the headline about drugs: this is your brain [shows eggs in a pan], this is your brain on drugs [shows the eggs frying in the pan].

Aspirational

Tempts society toward something desirable. "In six weeks you can be rich selling real estate" is an example.

Peer pressure

This concept ranges from a celebrity endorsement to a doctor telling you how much you need the product. The concept is to show an influencer endorsing the company's goods or service.

Inspirational

Inspirational headlines are non-promotional and define the brand. They make people feel something, want something, or identify with something, and that makes them think of a better version of themselves.

Innovation and trustworthiness are two inspirational approaches companies use to evoke inspirational emotions. These headlines are effective as subtle sells.

Innovation

Claimed by many advertisers but really only proven by a few companies. True innovation changes the course of society or industries, such as how iTunes changed the way we listen to and purchase music. Many ads will claim their product is innovative and revolutionary, but few really are life changers.

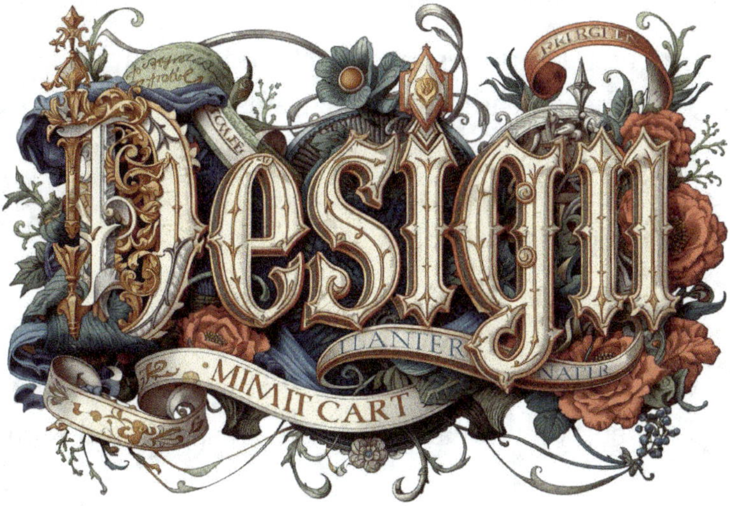

FIGURE 8.5

Pretty Design is attractive but needs more

AI Practicum} Midjourney Prompt: The word "design" in a decorative calligraphic font.

Trustworthiness

This needs to be authentic and believable. The website design should not be filled with fluff and elaborate images. It needs strong, statement oriented content.

Usually, the message is from an industry leader who must have a vision that the consumer agrees with and will follow. An example would be IBM's "Let's put smart to work." The headline is straightforward and principle-based to signal ethics as a priority and not a hypeline.

Customers look at the website for trust signals:

- Real testimonials with names and locations,
- Guarantees that state 100% satisfaction,
- Social media reviews,
- Backlinks from companies such as the Better Business Bureau.

Encouraging A Customer

Conversion-driven headlines are structured to clearly lead to an action or goal. These headlines are benefit-driven and action-oriented—exactly what boosts conversions. Marketing classes are devoted to defining the multitude of sales strategies. Here are five of the many effective approaches.

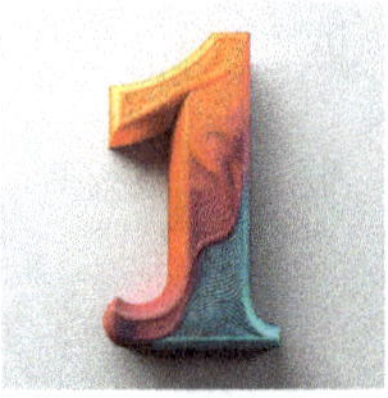

Value Proposition Headline
Structured to explain what is offered and who is served with an emphasis on speed and reliability.

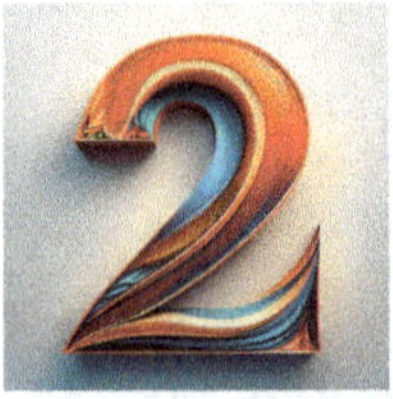

Benefit-Driven Headline
Explains what the customer gains by choosing the website's product, service, or company.

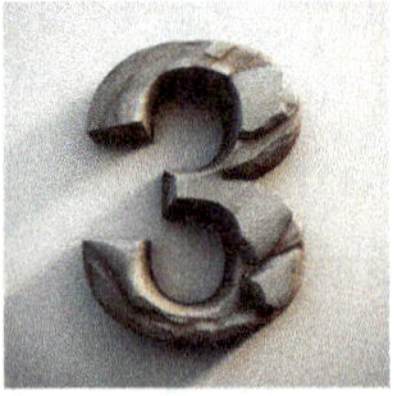

Trust-Building Headline
Guarantees quality products or services by showing how the company stands behind its offerings, which builds confidence.

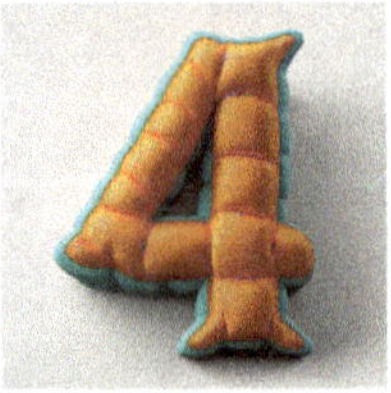

Urgency & Action Headline
Creates an impression of limited time and products. Encourages the customer to act now and not to wait.

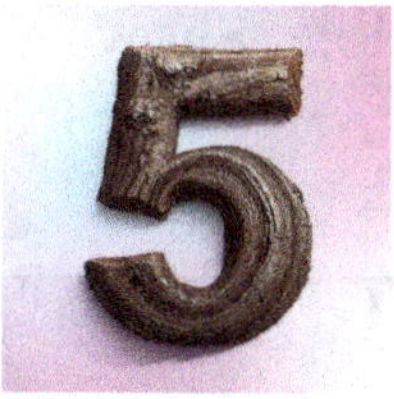

Problem=Solution Headline
Prioritizes dependable results from a local expert to take the stress and wasted time out of a solution.

CREDIBILITY IN IMAGES

Real photos can increase conversions since they show context instantly: the company, the product, and the team. The website establishes interaction with the user through psychology that visual proof lowers hesitation and makes conversion feel like the logical next step.

Original photos signal that a business is real and established. Visitors are more likely to trust a company when they see actual people, locations, or work—not generic stock imagery.

Seeing real outcomes reassures visitors that expectations will match reality, making them more comfortable taking action. People connect more easily with real faces and environments. This subtle familiarity increases confidence and makes a company feel approachable.

Stock photos are interchangeable. Real photos make a website distinct, memorable, and harder to confuse with competitors.

Clutter, poor contrast, or dense text increases mental effort. A clean structure lowers cognitive load and makes engagement feel easy. Good first impressions encourage longer sessions with deeper dives into the website pages and, hopefully, repeat visits.

AI-generated photos can help attention and clarity, but they don't prove reality. Generated images should be used to explain ideas and workflows and to set a company tone.

For new companies without visual assets, AI images can supplement real photography. However, AI should not be used completely and should be replaced as quickly as possible. Show the city in the background of images.

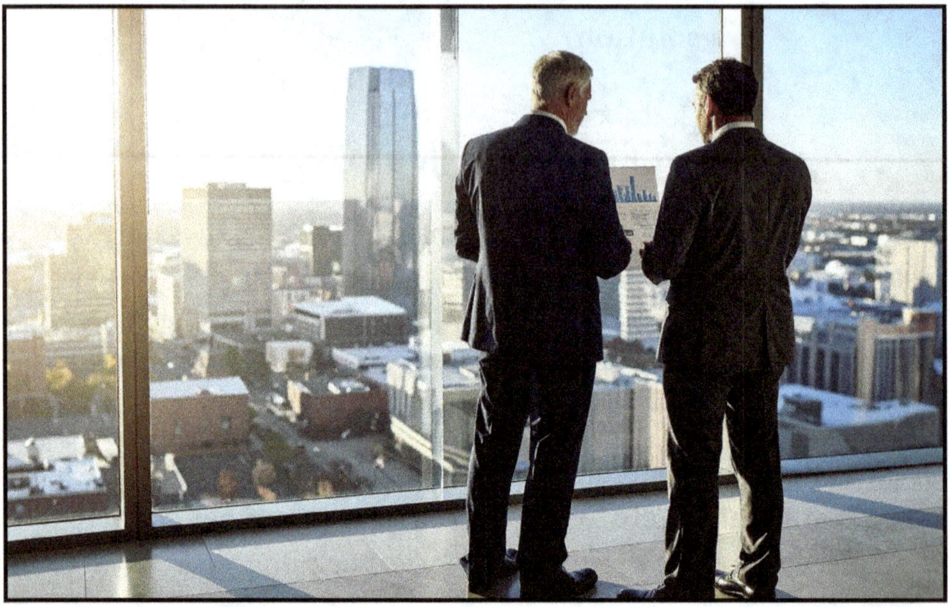

FIGURE 8.11

Businessmen with the Oklahoma City cityscape showing in the windows.

AI Practicum} Firefly Prompt: wide-angle view of the backs of businessmen meeting in a room, with a large window showing a view of the Oklahoma City skyline at sunset.

EVERYTHING LEADS TO THE CTA

It is obvious, but the calls to action should move visitors to act. However, these buttons or short phrases only show the customer where to start the process. All the elements prior to the CTA are what really convert the visitor. Make sure the CTA is short and clear. "Buy Now" is scary for some customers because they may want to know more information, such as the cost and when it will be delivered. "Buy Now" implies if they select that button, the product will be bought and paid for in an instant.

Contact forms, maps, and click-to-call buttons must not block the website page that the visitor is trying to read. It has become popular for contractor-type websites to have a pop-up page to schedule a meeting to go over the project. The visitor cannot see the content or be persuaded to use the contractor because of the pop-up. The old adage, "Do not put the cart before the home page," is a good one to follow.

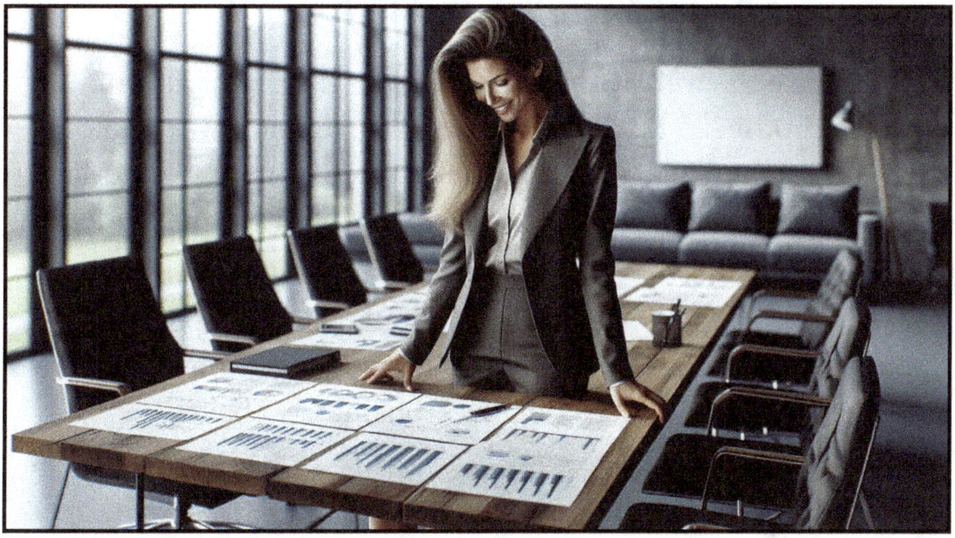

FIGURE 8.12

The GTM is deep.

AI Practicum} Express Prompt: Middle-aged businesswoman standing in a conference room looking down and smiling at marketing and sales reports covering an old big table.

Note: Person is coming out of the table. It is the artist's responsibility to exam images for three eyes, three fingers, missing ears, extra hands bloating around a body.

Creating lead magnets and opt-ins

Patience requires a long sell. Salespeople do not like this since they want to get the sale and move on with their commission. Companies like this approach since it creates long-term customers.

Simple short contact forms work well. Have certain fields required and use a SPAM filter. If they want to be called, have a few options so the saleswoman does not spend a day constantly trying to reach the interested shopper. If the visitor wants more information, make sure to include their name so the salesman can use it in the email or text reply. Make sure the visitor agrees to receiving a phone call, text, or email as part of the form.

IT IS BUILT—HERE THEY COME... MAYBE

Just because the website has everything a visitor could want to find does not mean they will become a customer. If the choice is using a company they have heard about or a company that they have not known about, the visitor will go with the known identity.

Marketing and salespeople should be in civic organizations and networking groups. They need to not only build a reputation and develop referrals but also belong to organizations that have websites that link to their members' business websites.

Websites do not convert customers by themselves. The company must use other means to advertise and promote itself.

Small business owners may not have a marketing team ready to develop a marketing plan. In this case, explore AI for decision-making and successful promotions. When prompting ChatGPT or Gemini, assign a business scenario along with the name, product, and goal. If it is not a new company, AI will find a lot of details it needs on the internet.

When prompting AI to create and plan a marketing campaign, explain assumptions, target the general market, and supply the price points. Instruct GPT to develop the plan for the website, social media, and ads, and think about direct mail. Emails are overwhelming potential customers so much that they have either deleted them without opening or just let the email program store them.

As with any marketing strategy, follow up with an analysis of the plan and evaluate what worked well and what did not. A different AI may work better for the company on the next plan. Use the analysis to adjust and change content on the website.

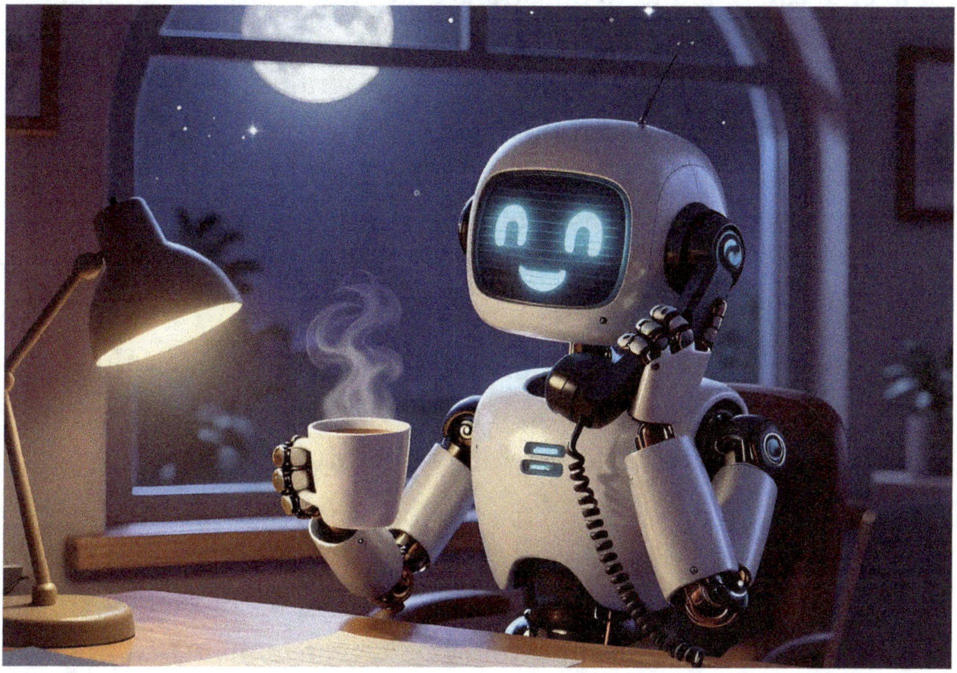

FIGURE 8.9

What I want to know is who decided these hours?

AI Practicum} Nightcafe Prompt: A chatbot drinking coffee and talking on the phone sitting at a desk with a window showing the moon and stars.

CHATBOT-24 HOUR ANSWERS

Customer service can be frustrating for the business owner and the customer. The number of employees dedicated to answering the phones or web contacts has become time-consuming. Written correspondence may not be clear and concise. Responders tend to use canned answers that frustrate the sender.

The common question of asking the status of their order has been resolved. Tracking software options now allow customers to find out where the order is at in the process without contacting an agent. However, many other questions, especially technical ones, take time to resolve for people, while artificial intelligence is already set up to retrieve the answers.

AI agents can respond to questions quicker and provide options in seconds. It can handle a higher volume of interactions at the same time since the data is already programmed into it. This collaborative model is not replacing customer service. AI agents allow humans to focus on the complex issues and answer frequently asked questions about the order. Consider having a chatbot that can answer visitors' questions instead of them leaving and looking for an answer on the website.

Presently, chatbots are programmed with set questions and answers. This takes one or more employees hours to complete. AI can create the files to upload with a structured prompt.

To save time, companies can use options such as Voiceflow, Botpress, ManyChat, Intercom, and ChatGPT to generate a structured data file in JSON, CSV, and TXT to program the AI chatbot. An example prompt would be "Create a plain text file of 21 pairs of FAQs with short answers about a certain product or service."

The AI customer bots can take files with hundreds of questions and answers. There are conversational AI agent platforms that can have the technical data uploaded as files and retrieve the best answers based on the parameters of the questions. Some AI options are Intercom, Zendesk, Ada, and Aisera.

SMALL BUSINESSES WEBSITE MISTAKES

Nonprofessional copywriters do not understand the basics of constructing headlines. For example, their headlines are too wordy. Visitors decide if a webpage deserves more attention by scanning the first and last three words of a headline.

The goal of the site may be to get a visitor to call and buy a service, but in the long term the website is part of a plan to build a visual identity of the brand. To achieve this branding, consistent, clear sales language must be used across the campaign. The logo needs to be on each header and footer along with the contact telephone. The website should be using the brand's color palettes and fonts.

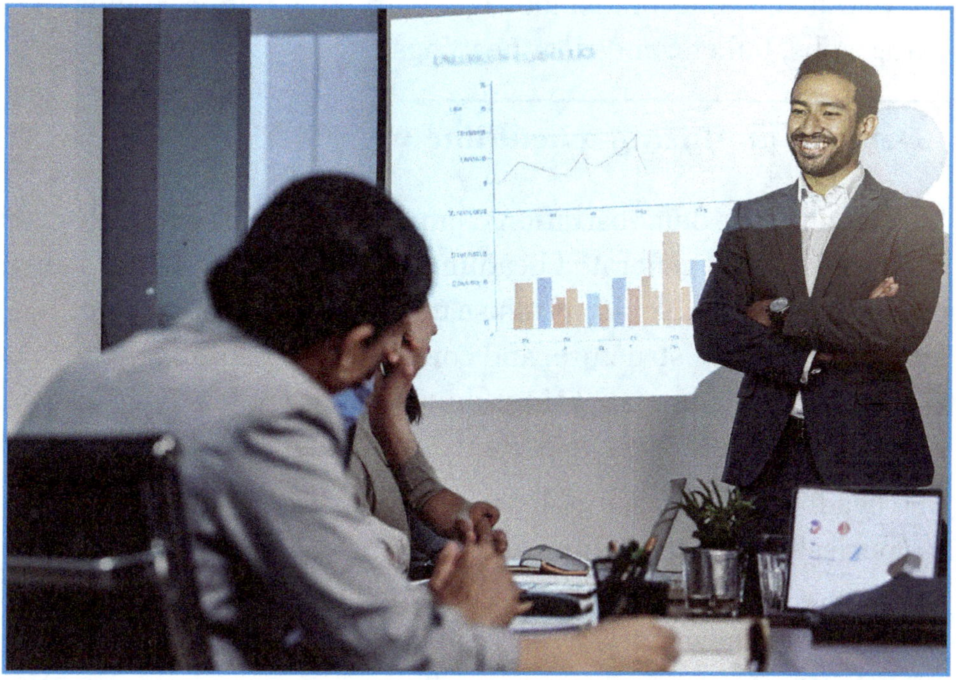

FIGURE 8.14

"The website will be designed my way—don't waste time figuring the customer's needs"

AI Practicum} Firefly Prompt: Meeting room with a business man standing in front of a screen, arms crossed, and smiling at the board member who look frustrated.

Small businesses and most designers want to start the website layout immediately. They only focus on one message sell...sell... sell. This may be the goal but not the message a visitor wants to see.

The website should focus on what the business does in a clear headline that has been analyzed for engagement. This may take a number of tries to finally write a headline that encourages the visitor to keep reading.

Designing based on the owner's opinion ignores the potential customer. The owner should take the time to research customer questions and pain points to trigger a decision.

Most visitors do not want to find a website filled with text. They scan and walls of text look like marketing fluff. Use short paragraphs, bullets, and clear headings.

Demo of analyzing a headline

In Chapter 3 the demonstration compared a human written headline to an AI generated headline. This demonstration a deep dive into using both options to use methodical process create headlines. Clarity, structure, and contrast are AI strengths that when edited by a human, bring a humanist approach—voice, warmth, judgment, lived experience, and intention.

The headlines have been constructed and patiently adjusted to concisely interest a visitor to read more. However, will it be effective? One way to check is to use analyzers for the visitor and for search results. The scores are based on a possible 100 percentage points.

To analyze the effectiveness on a website visitor, Sharethrough, IsItWP Headline Analyzer, and AI-powered Analyzer are free and include a score and suggestions. Jasper AI, Frase, and Headline Analyzer Studio Pro are paid versions.

Headline for engaging a visitor

After writing and rewriting, a lengthy headline was created: "We get your HVAC service problem resolved the first time and fast." It is personal, using 'we' and 'your,' and addresses their concerns. It is HEO, also know as Human Engagement Optimized.

Go to 'headlines.sharethrough.com' and paste the headline into the field. Select 'Other' and then the analyze button. It scores a 68, which is better than the optional headlines Sharethrough AI supplied. They were longer and do not score high enough to use.

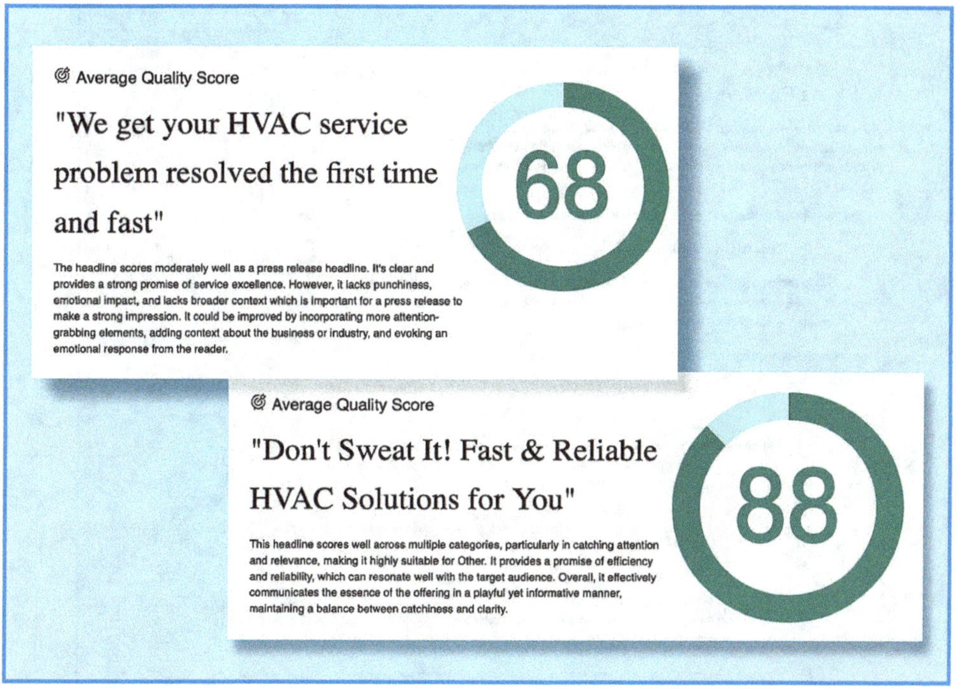

FIGURE 8.15

Sharethrough Headline Analyzer results

HI Practicum} Photoshop rebuilt Screen Grabs to be readable.

On Sharethrough analysis, a good score is between 60 to 80. The target is between 78 and 92.

At 'aminstitute.com/process/headline.cgi,' the free service scored the same headline at 36.6. The scale is 0-100, so for human engagement, the Advanced Market Institute graded the emotional appeal to be low. Analyzing the headline, it scored even lower with a 25.

Going back to Sharethrough, the AI suggested the headline, "Our Rapid and Reliable Service Redefines Excellence in Your

Industry." When analyzed, it scored 68 and had too many words.

Finally, a winner on Sharethrough in a clever rewrite, "Don't Sweat It! Fast and reliable HVAC solutions for you" scored high with an 88.

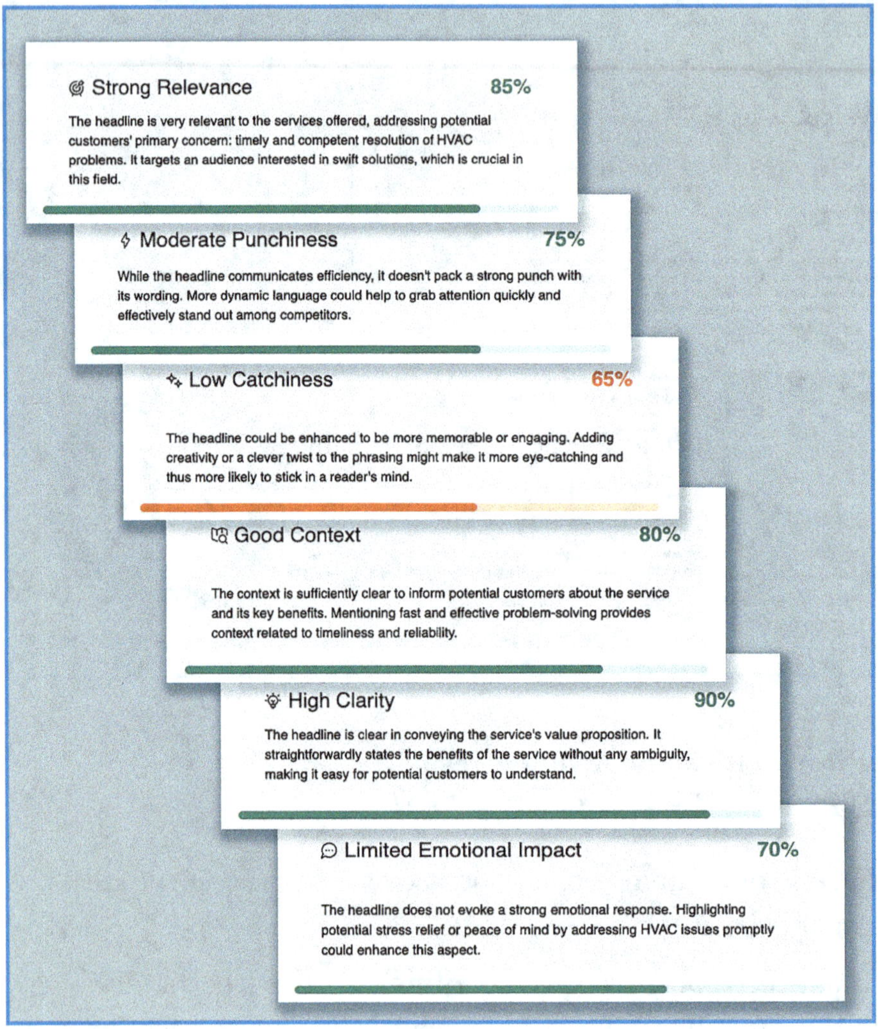

FIGURE 8.16

Sharethrough Headline Analyzer results.

HI Practicum} Photoshop rebuilt Screen Grabs to be readable.

Headlines for SEO

Use analyzers to test headlines that a search engine shows in the results. These headlines can be used in snippets or also on the website page. Search Engine Optimization (SEO) needs to always be a part of creating content.

Instead of rewriting a new headline, use the previous headline "We get your HVAC problem resolved the first time and fast."

Go to 'Aiseo.com/headline-analyzer' and paste the headline into the field. Select the analyze button. It scores a 72, which is good for SEO, but it should be improved.

It was revised and shortened to "Quickly solving your HVAC problem the first time." This headline scores an 88. Adding an emotional word could make it score higher, but it would be longer, and nothing seemed to read as well.

At 'isitwp.com/headline-analyzer,' it scores a low 48 and explains what it needs to have more impact.

CONCLUSION

Many times a headline works well to engage a visitor and it scores a 78 on Sharethrough but the same headline in AIOSEO will score low around a 48.

The dilemma is which way to go. If it does not show up well in search results, users will not select the website to check out. If the headline engages them, when they go to the website, the same headline will lose them. The solution is to have two headlines: one for SEO, which is entered in the backend (see Chapter 11), but a different one is used on the actual webpage (see Chapter 9). Choose an AI tool that can also be used to check internet marketing, such as email subject lines, YouTube titles, and social media headlines.

To save on the frustration of rewording the headline, it may save time to use a copywriter. They will provide alternate options and H2 ans H3 headlines for the rest of the page. A marketing copywriter will communicate the correct tone and the nuances for a target market.

INSETS

FIGURE 8.6

Type of Headline: Value Proposition
AI Practicum} Express Prompt: 3D number 1 made up of clay with textures.

FIGURE 8.7

Type of Headline: Value Proposition
AI Practicum} Express Prompt: 3D number 2 router wood with painted streaks.

FIGURE 8.8

Type of Headline: Trust Building
AI Practicum} Express Prompt: 3D number 3 made up of unpolished marble.

FIGURE 8.9

Type of Headline: Urgency and Action
AI Practicum} Express Prompt: 3D number 4 made to look like a cuffed soft pillow.

FIGURE 8.10

Type of Headline: Problem=Solution
AI Practicum} Express Prompt: 3D number 5 made up tree bark textures.

AI and HI Web Design

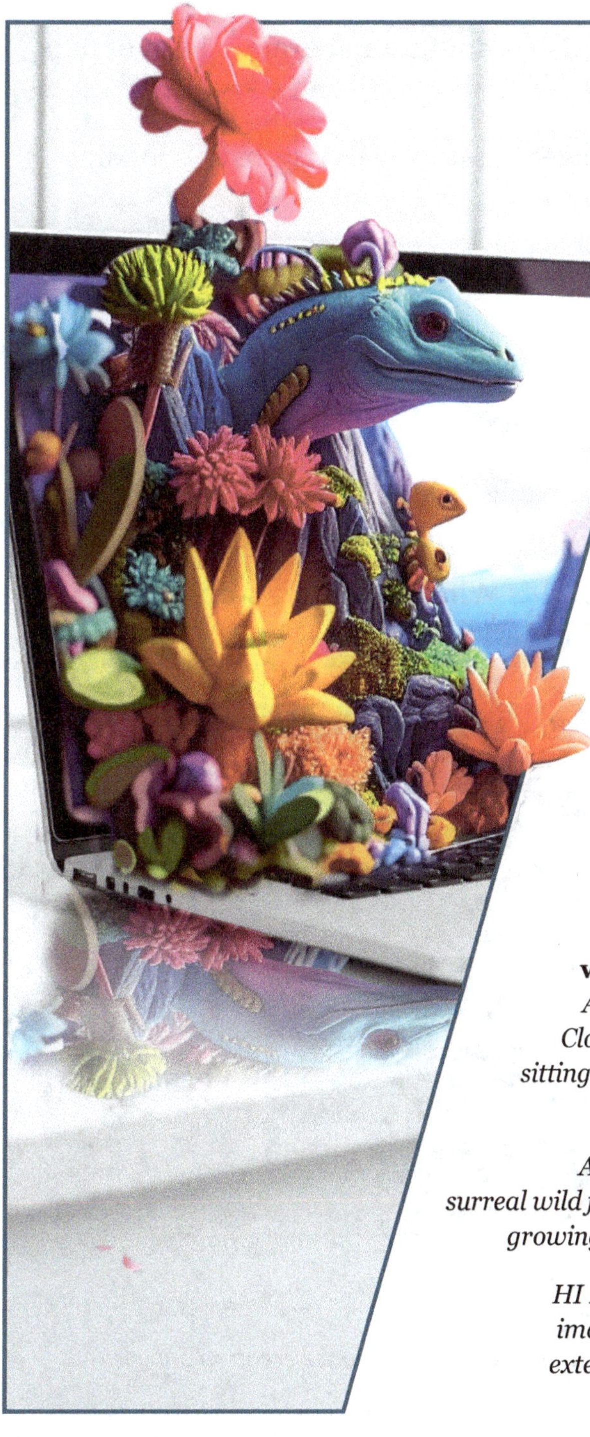

C9

OVERVIEW

Artificial intelligence streamlines and enhances the website design process. Recommendations on how to use AI to accelerate website development and elevate the quality of modern web design to avoid clutter.

Figure 9.1

Using Human Ingenuity with Artificial Intelligence.

AI Practicum 1} Express Prompt: Closeup photograph of open laptop sitting on a white desk in a white room vertical format.

AI Practicum 2} Express Prompt: surreal wild futuristic wildlife and vegetation growing out of a laptop vertical format.

HI Practicum} Photoshop: Melded images together, added reflection, extended top and bottom of image.

PROFESSIONAL TERMINOLOGY

Analytics: The methodical computational examination of data or statistics.

Cache: Temporary storage that improves a website's loading speed on future visits.

KPIs: Key Performance Indicators: Used to measure the success of a website's goals.

Royalty Free: Stock images that are paid for once and can be used without additional fees.

Stock Photos: Paid for or open-source images to use on a website.

WYSIWYG: What You See Is What You Get is software that generates the code for the design.

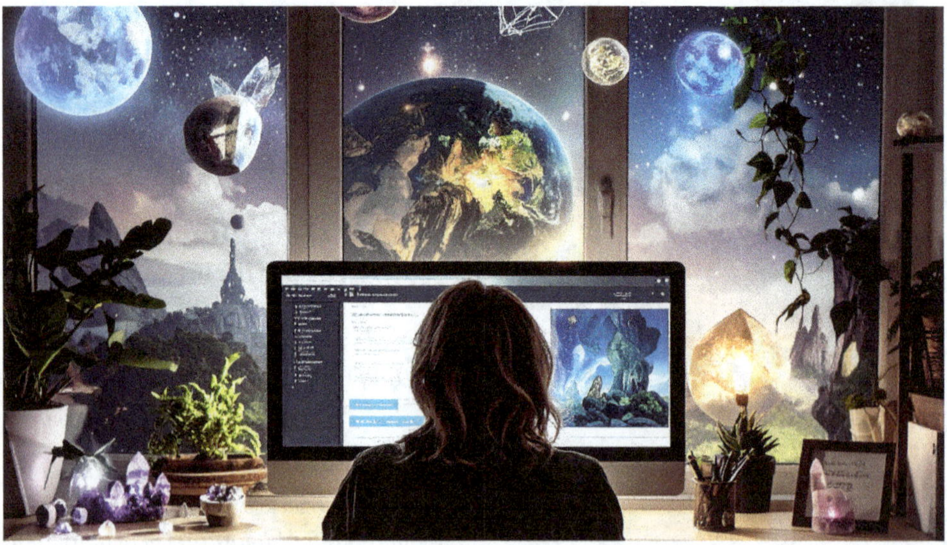

Figure 9.2

Don't stop in the middle of a creative idea.

AI Practicum} Firefly Prompt: Show a graphic designer creating a website.

START AT THE BEGINNING

The previous chapters covered content to engage visitors, analyze content, create images, and edit these images. Most designers immediately start laying out the website visually. The problem with this approach is that the designer is constantly stopping to create the content, create the images, optimize the images, and place them. This process slows the creative flow to almost a complete stop. The designer loses track of ideas, concepts, and spur-of-the-moment decisions.

The most effective approach for designing a website is to complete all the preliminary preparations in advance. Ensure the images are the correct size, optimized as the best file type, and in the correct RGB color. Prepare and test the headlines in advance. Ensure the body content is written and edited for placement.

Before the elements can be compiled. The website plan with a strategy needs to be in place. This approach necessitates having the website's overall look roughly laid out. There are five general website layouts (see Chapter 12). Visitors may recognize the layout from previously viewed websites, and determine what type of business they are viewing. The designer's challenge is to first of all decide on the layout and then make it different enough to be memorable.

Based on the layout approach, headlines can be generated, the amount of content can be written to fit the layout, and the type of images can be created, sized, and optimized. The images will need to have text that describes the image and captions for visually impaired viewers and search robots.

If the designer gets all this setup process ready, the creative is not interrupted. The focus will be on creating what the visitor needs to see in a visual flow. It is fairly easy to know when looking at a website if the designer created it on the fly or planned it all out.

Do not bypass the hard work required to have a website that will attract a visitor and produce interest in the website.

Building a website is similar to building a house. There has to be a plan; the elements are gathered, and then it is built from the foundation up. A general contractor cannot start without a plan. This process means a house can be built in 90 days instead of 90 months.

Get organized.

Set up a spreadsheet with a tab for login credentials and addresses of hosting, domain, website, and plugins such as Divi with renewal dates. On another spreadsheet, use the free AI assistant 'Goblin. tools' to set up a checklist and schedule. On another tab, set up the status of each page and have a general breakdown. Do not get bogged down in the details.

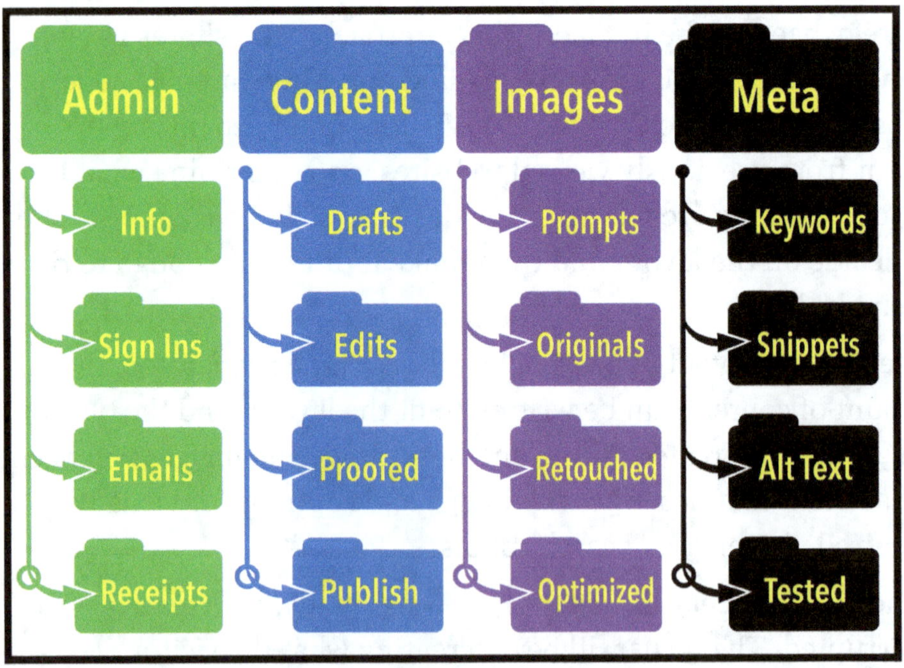

Figure 9.3
HI Practicum} Photoshop: Show folders as parents with subfolders.

On the computer, have a parent folder to hold all the elements needed for the website. Within this folder, set up folders as shown in Figure 9.3 to house the different elements for the website: admin, content, images, and meta.

For the types of content, have subfolders labeled from the draft stage through to the final content ready to publish (see Figure 9.3). Include a reference list for content of descriptive words and verbs that need to be changed out.

Save another spreadsheet for word replacements into the edits folder. Each table heading an easily understood label and the list below should have options to replace the overused terms words.

Visitors will get tired of reading the same repetitive words not only in different paragraphs but also on the different pages. Try not to keep repeating the exact keywords on every page. In another tab, have the keywords used to replace the average nouns, verbs, etc.

Along with that file, add a separate tab for the meta information. This will make the process faster by copying and pasting. Meta should include page content, image alternate text, keyword-laden search engine content, and snippets. In a new folder, label images, and within it have original, retouched, and converted images. This way, it is easy to just drag and drop and keep designing. Name image files to match key search terms.

AI ASSISTANCE IN WEBSITE DEVELOPMENT

Human ingenuity can plan and strategize the website, but the assistance of artificial intelligence can save time and improve strategies. Use AI to generate a structure after being given details. These tools can analyze a competitor's site for not just layout but also keywords. It can also create a sitemap, which is an outline-type blueprint of each parent page and the subsequent child pages.

The GTM should start with why the company, product, or brand will be attractive to customers. This draft statement will take HI, Human Ingenuity. While this concept may seem obvious, stating it in a clear and concise statement can be difficult. The idea should be understandable to every team member. Then choose an AI agent to help develop the GTM and compare the capabilities, features, and key benefits of each.

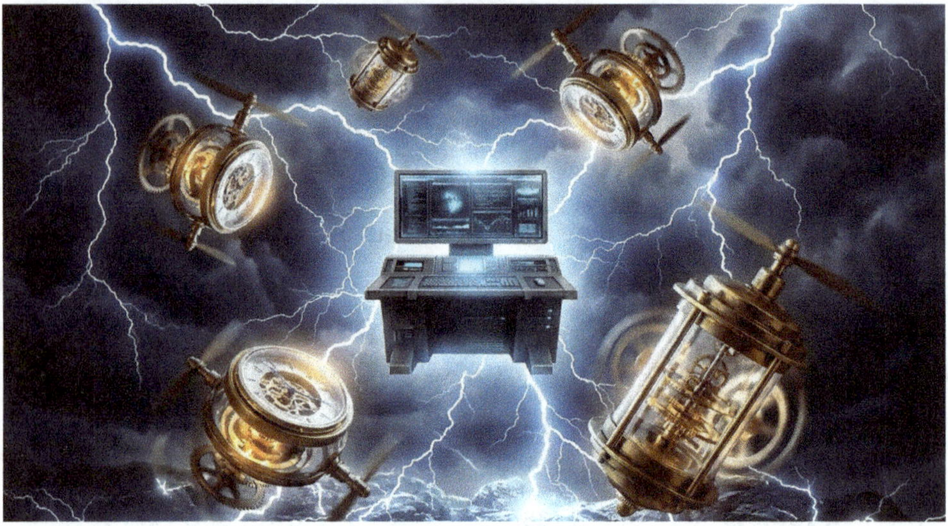

Figure 9.4
Time flies when having adversity
AI Practicum} Gemini 'Thinking' Prompt: Propelled futuristic clocks spinning around a computer in a lightning storm 4x3 ratio hi resolution for printing.

AI tools to help with establishing the website structure and sitemap are VentureKit, UpMetrics, and Jasper IQ. These agents can generate complete business strategies, including business plans, strategies, forecasts, and audience research.

AI planning agents that generate visual structures of a website are Relume, which is the most widely used planning AI agent; Octopus, which can build a visual sitemap and the parent-to-child page hierarchy; and Modulify, which analyzes the prompt and will generate sections for pages based on the logic of the prompt. These AI agents do not rely on templates but generate based on the information provided.

AI website builders are assistants that help in speeding up the development of the elements. They understand color, provide images, and create a design that goes with the value proposition.

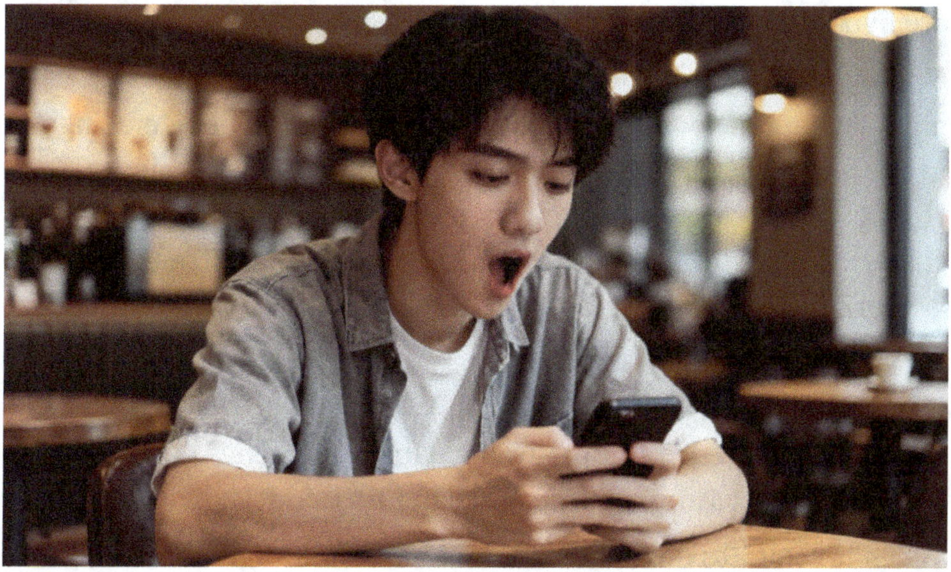

Figure 9.5

Patience is not a virtue of potential visitors

AI Practicum} PicsArt Prompt: A GenZ staring at his mobile phone yawning in a coffee shop.

When processing the images, AI tools can save time by resizing and optimizing the images that are generated. These tools for post-processing turn the AI-generated images into faster downloads when a visitor accesses a website. Pictures, especially hero images due to their size, with long loading speeds will cause a visitor to leave rather than wait for the website to load. Part of every website image workflow is to convert the image to the best 'optimized' file before placement. Three free tools to use for optimizing an image for the website: Squoosh by Google, Adobe Express, and Canva.

AI behavioral analytical tools are available after the website is up to see where users clicked or scrolled on each page of the website. Microsoft Clarity is available with Copilot to summarize viewer interactions. Hotjar can integrate data with visitor feedback. For online stores and e-commerce, Mouseflow finds where the visitors are bypassing pages and CTAs.

Not long ago, SEO included adding keywords and phrases into metadata and into the website content. Now with Google using AI in the form of its trademarked Search Generative Experience™, Hookwords are used to connect with a searcher's intent. Two strong AI tools for this part of SEO are Semrush AI Toolkit and WriterZen. AI agents that can also assist with keywords, snippets, and the overall SEO of the website are Surfer SEO and Frase.

Rank Math and AIOSEO work with WordPress to detail what elements are needed to rank well in Google searches. These plugins use a scoring method and can link to the Google Toolkit.

When it comes to design creativity, that is a human quality. Use AI for technical and repetitive tasks, which will allow a designer to tell the story.

AI WEBSITE DESIGN GENERATORS

Some AI agents, such as Adobe Express and Canva, can design sections of a website with content and images that are downloaded and then uploaded to the CMS. Both are geared toward non-technical website designers. They are professional grade but work on the fly instead of studying a book. These AI-assisted design tools are a good way to save time and come with the needed software as part of the subscriptions.

However, sometimes it is easier to build the site with human skills. For more control, easier edits, and no wasted time trying numerous prompts, use a design platform such as Divi or Elementor, which have AI assistance and are better in the long run.

There are many purchasing plans. If the website design is a practice run just to learn how to design a website, there is a plan for that. If the plan is to create an active, live, fully functional site for a business, choose a plan for that. Any popular design platform will have numerous videos and content answers for nearly all problems or questions.

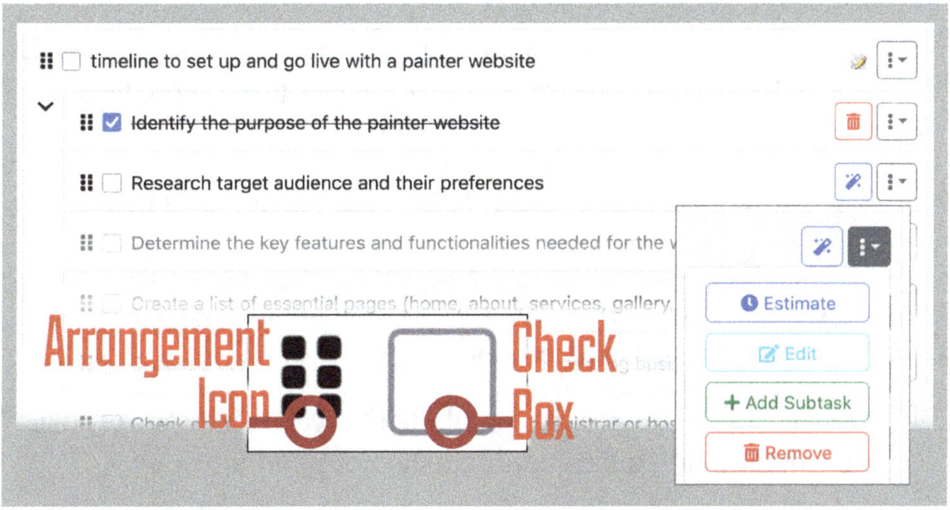

Figure 9.6

HI Practicum} Photoshop: Closeup of Goblin MagicToDo tools from screen grabs, unsharpen, add type markings.

Demo Goblin for a checklist

Goblin offers a free AI used by educators to set up class schedules and anyone to help break down large projects into tasks. It reduces the overwhelmed feeling when faced with a massive project, especially for the first time. It can bring a focus to manageable tasks and even estimate the time an individual should spend on each item.

1. Go to Goblin.tools > MagicToDo
2. Describe the website starting with the prompt: simple timeline to set up and go live with a website but add some specifics such as the type of website. Narrow it down to general descriptions, such as whether it is a business or a service website, an online store or a nonprofit, a portfolio, or a public relations brand. Select the large plus sign.
3. On the right, select the magic wand, which will break down the item. Once it has done that, select the caret to see the tasks.
4. Under the caret, note the six dots—the arrangement icon. Use the cursor to select the dots to move the tasks into a different order.
5. Next to the arrangement icon is a checkbox that, if selected, marks off the tasks as finished.
6. On the right side are three dots with a caret. The dropdown options include deleting any tasks not needed.
7. Add any steps or edit the names.
8. Estimate the time for all the tasks or just individual tasks.
9. Go live with the website.

TIP ON GENERATING IMAGES

Do not give up on a good idea. If there is a need for a specific image to create a tone or interest, keep editing the prompt. See Figures 9.7 thru 9.9 and how adjusting the words and finally restarting produced stronger options.

- Try another version from the beginning so the AI image

generator starts with a clean instruction.

- Expand the information on the prompt.
- Start over with a new prompt but upload one of the prompt' image that was close to the solution as a reference.

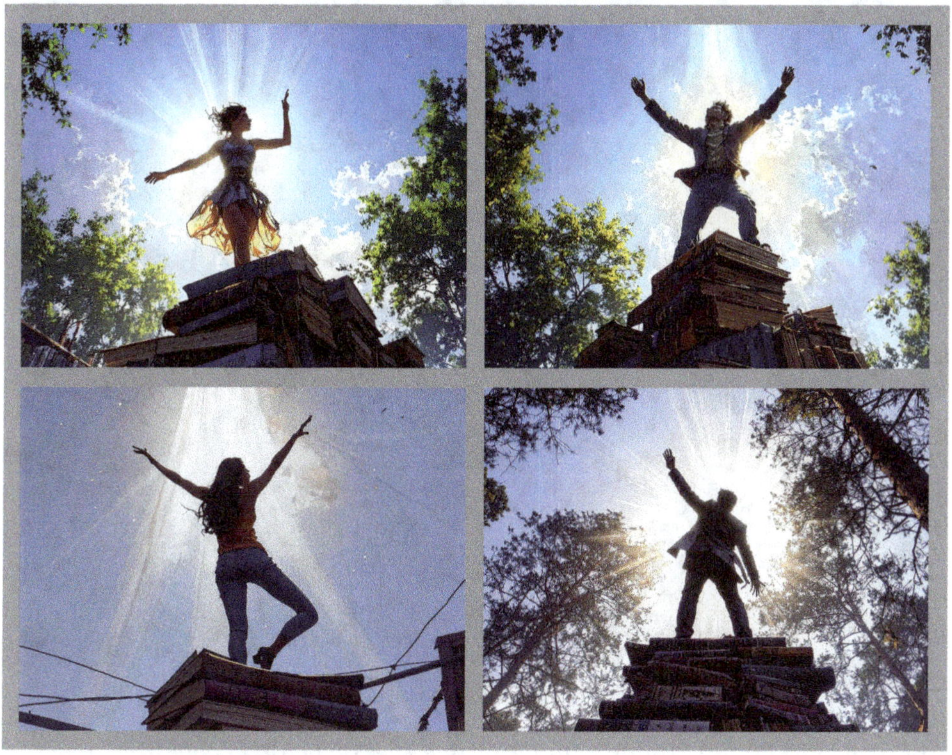

Figure 9.7

Different concepts from similar prompts for a publishing website. *AI Practicum} Firefly Prompt: Author standing on books in a park, arms raised, backlit from sun, fill to see details.*

LIST OF IMAGES TO CREATE AND OPTIMIZE.

When it comes to images, the options of size are numerous. This is where the GTM and brand statement will guide the designer on the layout method to follow. See Chapter 12, the section on Five Website Formats, and the section on Images Defined for more details on site layouts and the art of hero images. The website will need the following images, which can be photographs, drawings, cartoons, illustrations, and videos.

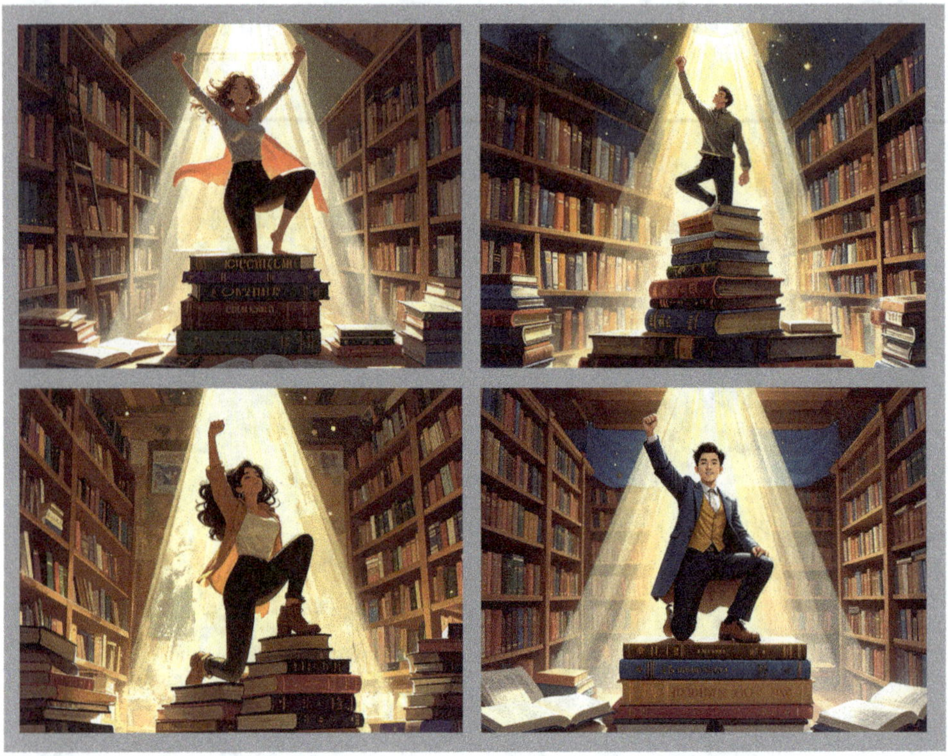

Figure 9.8

AI Practicum} Firefly Prompt: Author on one knee on books in bookstore, one arm raised in winner pose.

SIZING RECOMMENDATIONS FOR HERO IMAGES

Decide now whether to use type on the image or outside of it. The image will need to be retouched with lighter or darker areas if it has type to increase legibility.

The image is sized for impact and the content should match the tone and subject of the hero image. Use only one hero at the top of these pages.

HERO TYPES	FORMAT SIZES	OPTIMUM FILE SIZE
Cover	1920×1080 pixels 1440 x 1080 pixels	Less than 400KB Less than 300KB
Splash	1920×720 pixels 1440 x 1080 pixels	Less than 300KB Less than 300KB
Window	1080×1080 pixels 1080×800 pixels	Less than 200KB Less than 200KB
Landscape	1440 x 800 pixels	Less than 250KB
Banner	1520 x 500 pixels	Less than 200KB

Table 9.1 | Sizing and file size for Hero images.

Home Page

Immediately explains the website to the visitor. Should demonstrate the brand, service, or product to engage the viewer.

About Us Page

This image can be a team photo or show equipment and vehicles.

Services Page

Illustrates the company process, but the subject should add information about the company.

Contact Page

Many times a map or another 'About 'Us'-styled image.

IMAGE TYPES	FORMAT SIZES	OPTIMUM FILE SIZE
Feature	1200 x 600 pixels 1440 x 1080 pixels	Less than 200KB Less than 160KB
Sectional	450 x 300 pixels 350 x 250 pixels	Less than 50KB Less than 40KB
Insets	500 x 300 pixels	Less than 15KB
Thumbnail	150 x 150 pixels	Less than 10KB
Favicon	512 x 512 pixels	Less than 80KB
Logo	250 x 250 pixels	Less than 25KB

Table 9.2 | Sizing and file size for non hero images.

SIZING RECOMMENDATIONS FOR OTHER IMAGES

Supporting Images

The workhorses of a website are the supporting images that explain and present the company, product, or service. If a large *Cover Hero* is used, that file size impacts the number of other supporting images that can be used.

Feature

Use in place of hero images to make each page different to the visitor. This type of visual is medium to large in size and is used to highlight a specific section of the website. The picture is adjacent to headings and content. The page can have more than one feature image, such as showing different views of a product. They can depict services, company equipment, or personnel.

Features can be placed across the page or on the right or left of the hero section. Plan on showing at least one feature image on these pages: About Us, Services, and Sub-pages.

Sectional

Images are usually the width of the section column. Keep the images simple for readability and the files small by optimizing for quick downloads. Can be photos, graphics, or background gradations or solid colors. They complement the content, telling the visitor why they want to stay on the page, but do not dominate the page. They are an element of the visual flow and are used extensively by e-commerce and articles.

Use for testimonials, catalogs, news articles, sidebars, and dividers for scrolling breaks. Visually support a content block and rarely just float on a page. They are smaller than half the page width and many times are based on the width of the columns on the page.

Thumbnail

Small postage stamp-sized images or icons that will link to another page or area that expands on the brief information on the parent page. Sometimes they are repeated to create texture, and they can serve as place markers to be clicked on as a link.

Favicon

An icon that can be associated with the brand label. It is at the top of the browser windows and tabs before the URL. It is also positioned by the website name in bookmarks lists.

OPTIONAL PICTURES AND GRAPHICS.

If the website is not going to be heavy with picture files, then consider adding a background image to the page headers.

Type readability is the number one requirement. The second requirement is that the section image add to the story. CTA buttons, icons for services, and footer graphics can be created to keep the visitor interested.

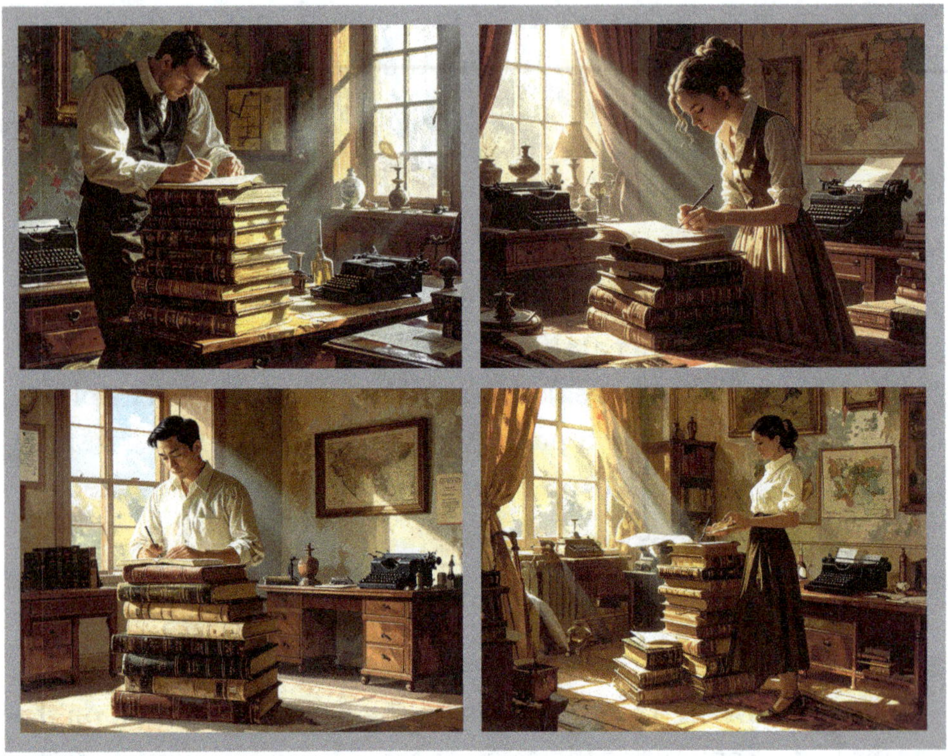

Figure 9.9

AI Practicum} Firefly Prompt: Restart. Earth-tone illustration of author by a stack of books signing one opened book, office life, old days, retro tone.

IMAGE TOTAL SIZES

The need for speed cannot be overemphasized. If the page is slow to load, it will chase away customers and Google search bots. One of the key search results factors is page speed. Optimization of images is a fine line between quality and capacity. Because smaller images load faster, do not rely on the design platform to decide the file size. AI cannot make these decisions; it takes an unbiased eye to judge the line.

A rule of thumb is to keep the total of the image sizes under 1.5 MB per page. If the visitors live in an area with less tech speed, that count should be much less.

The type of file also affects the file size. PNGs, which can be transparent, have more details and are larger than JPG files. GIFs can be rasterized to have less color information and be quite small. It all comes down to how much visual information is needed to show a quality image.

If a product image will need to be enlarged to show details by the potential customer, it needs to be larger than sectionals. The size will be based on the popup frame.

IMAGE META DATA

When an image file is saved, use a descriptive name that goes with the page. These Hookwords should be aimed at users searching for answers to their queries. When Google bots crawl a website, they cannot see the images. The bots can read the file names and will index the images based on those names and the meta data. Establish a file naming convention to always use. This process will save time later changing everything.

Do not use spaces between words since some web servers can have errors. Best practices is to avoid spaces and use hyphens or underscores between words. Do not use punctuation except before the type of file such as ".png" or ".jpg" in the names and keep the character count below 60. Do not use search terms that are not describing the image since this practice can be marked as keyword stuffing.

This backend verbiage includes alternate text, file name, description of the image, and a caption for the search bots and the visually impaired users. These text fields are prime areas to use detailed terms to assist in SEO. The Alternate Text is one of the strongest SEO signals for bots to understand an image and should not be left blank but poor terminology can be worse.

If it is a graphic element purely for decoration or a visual break, no alternate text is needed. If a video is placed on a webpage, have the script words spelled out nearby.

Alt text + Captions + Nearby content = Help bots understand images

When creating an image such as the home Page Hero, do not embed the type. Google bots have a difficult time making out the words. Instead have them float over the image in a text box.

All Together Now

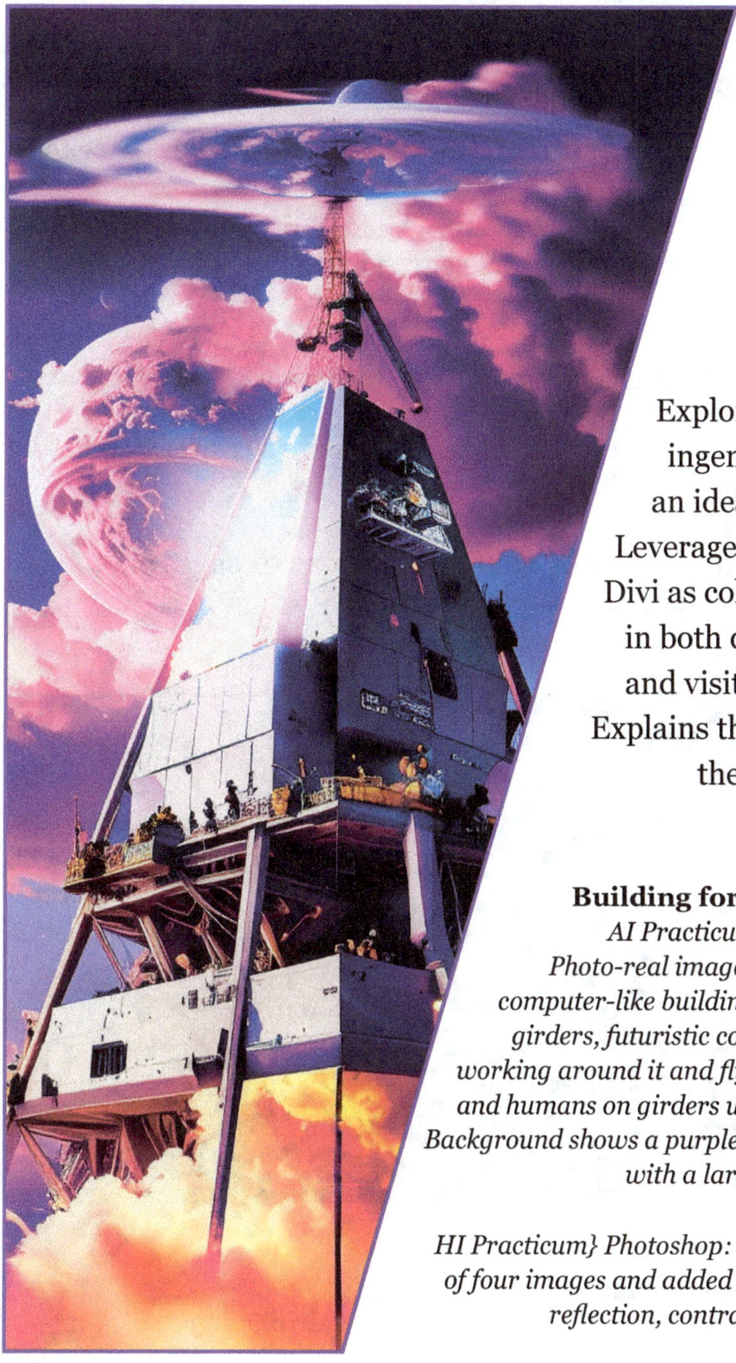

C10

OVERVIEW

Explores ways human ingenuity transforms an idea into a website. Leverage WordPress and Divi as collaborative tools in both design efficiency and visitor engagement. Explains the basic setup of the admin sidebar.

FIGURE 10.1

Building for the future now

AI Practicum} Firefly Prompt: Photo-real image of a 3-story metal computer-like building made out of steel girders, futuristic construction vehicles working around it and flying cranes, robots and humans on girders using welding tools. Background shows a purple starry space night with a large 2-ringed planet.

HI Practicum} Photoshop: HI combined parts of four images and added motion, highlights, reflection, contrast, and saturation.

PROFESSIONAL TERMINOLOGY

Human Ingenuity: The ability to create an original, clever, or inventive concept or idea.

Keyword: A word or phrase users type into search engines to find information.

Search Bar: Field area visitors search a website for specific information.

Sidebar: A callout area that features topics on a website.

Snippet: An extract that describes a website's content and purpose.

Submenu: Housing links or hidden options to pages or sections on a website.

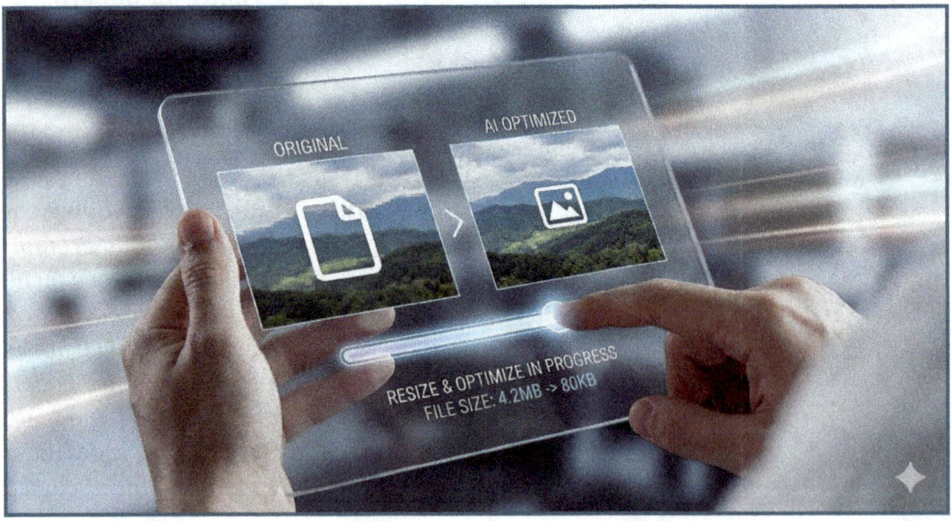

FIGURE 10.2

Resize and optimize images.

AI Practicum} Gemini Prompt: Generate an image illustrating a futuristic AI interface working on a photo optimization task.

TEMPLATE OR FREESTYLE

Decide on what program will be used to design the website. As mentioned previously, coding to build a website is not a desirable software solution. Since the end result is a visual experience, it makes sense to use a system that shows you the design as you work.

The advantage of template-based content management systems is the speed at which a site can go live. The disadvantage is the lack of customization to be unique and how visitors judge the template. Many templates look very old.

A freestyle option allows the designer to start with a blank slate but bring in template sections to customize. This approach takes longer to publish but shows the visitor a new visual, which may make it more memorable.

User-friendly WordPress does not require knowledge of coding, but it allows for it if the webmaster wants to add or adjust the code. It has templates that beginners can start to use and the ability to start with a blank screen. It is open-source software that can be customized for us to you and has community support, and then if you have questions or problems, you can ask and get answers. Designers use a strong design plug-in, such as Divi from Elegant Themes or Elementor. Both structures are CMS with WYSIWYG, which means what you see is what you get. They have built-in options to convert a desktop site to mobile and tablet sites fairly easily.

Sometimes security is an issue, but you can add plug-ins to improve that concern. Approximately 25% of all websites are built with WordPress, which is the program this book will use to show the basics on how to design a website. For a more in-depth study, online videos and books are available.

WP can be an impactful and memorable visual website since it allows for builder platforms. Popular theme builders that can be nested in WP are Elementor and Elegant Themes' Divi, which have numerous online tutorials and videos. Divi has an affordable price and updates without additional fees, and it is the design program utilized by this book.

PROS AND CONS FOR SMALL BUSINESSES

WP is a strong platform for beginning web designers to understand how to set up the different elements, place and adjust the website settings, and customize the appearance. As a business grows, the website can scale with it. It can be visually attractive to potential customers and easily optimized for search engines.

Maintenance and updates will be required to avoid security and design issues. It will require some technical skills and understanding of verbiage. The main negative is that since it was open source, it has been continuously added onto, and it can get cumbersome on the backend to do some of the simplest revisions. It needs a strong hosting service to keep the website fast for a good user experience.

Since WP has been available as an open-source platform, it has a large user community to assist with problems and directions. The main cost is hosting with an SSL and the domain. An additional cost is a theme builder. Functionality such as password-protected areas, e-commerce, information areas for articles, and custom plugins are easily uploaded and activated into the platform.

While the SEO is built into WP, plugins such as Rank Math and AIOSEO have better results and are more thorough. AIOSEO includes a Google integration, and Site Kit by Google can be uploaded.

Web designers need to keep the plethora of plugin options to a minimum and delete any not used before the site goes live. Bloating and conflicts can occur with too many active plugins.

SET UP THE SITE FOR DESIGN

Due to its popularity and easy-to-learn interaction, WordPress (WP) is going to be used but only as a system to house Divi from Elegant Themes. WP is a free website management system that has a large community to answer questions and supply plugins. Most of the plugins have free versions, and the best features then require a subscription. The downside of WP is it must be constantly updated for security since hackers target it. If the images are not optimized but WP is allowed to do it, the website will be bloated and very slow when visitors try to move from page to page.

If time to conduct vital maintenance is an issue for the website owner, most hosting plans include a managed WordPress hosting plan. Many of the plugins, PHP, and WP versions will be automatically updated. Always check to make sure the plan automatically backs up the website in case a new version causes problems. Then the old version can be substituted until the problems are solved.

A number of website design options are available for a designer to use that do not require understanding and writing code. Most of these platforms follow comparable methods and avenues to create a website in real time.

Choosing a website hosting plan that appeals to the designer requires research of the features included and not included. The process can go in three directions.

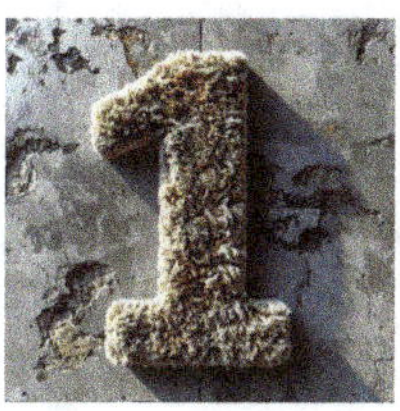

Register a domain name. Choose a hosting provider. Select a WordPress hosting plan. After setting up the plan, it will need to have the design platform, such as Elementor or Divi, installed.

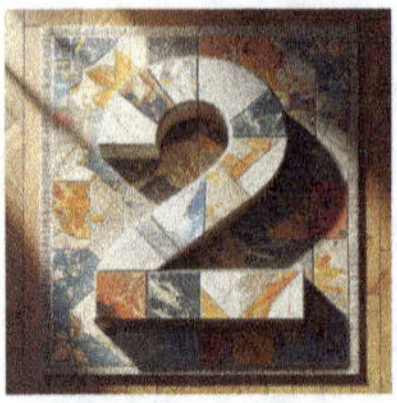

Nearly the same as Option 1. The difference is registering the domain with the same hosting company. This way the DNS is already set up and does not need to be edited to direct it to the website.

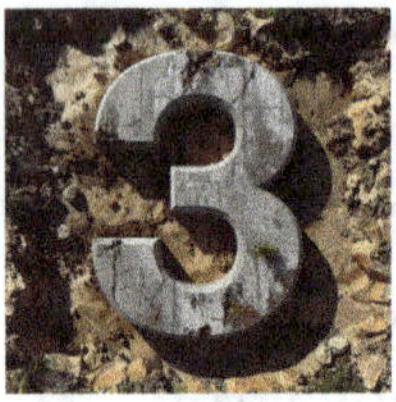

An all-in-one method. Have it all set up by the platform company. Purchase the domain and WP Hosting, which includes the designing platform, such as Elementor or Divi.

Companies that offer affordable plans and completely load for WP and the design platform enable the designer to start laying out the site. If the platform needs to be uploaded, a zipped file should be available when signing up for that program.

As an example, for Divi in a separate tab or window, go to Elegant Themes at <elegantthemes.com> and sign up. Download the Divi theme file. But leave it zipped. Copy the Divi username and API key. Then use those to set the WP up for Divi after uploading the Divi file into the themes. In the hosted account, upload Divi into Appearance > Theme.

Load Divi

This book is not a manual on Divi. This book covers the basics to get a design started. Take 30 minutes to get acquainted with Divi through their tutorial articles and videos. Learn the basics and understand what each popup editor is used to edit and create parts for a website. Learn how to pull up the text box, how to upload an image, and how to add descriptions to the image.

Sign in through the hosting account or through a browser with the URL <domain.com/wp-login.php>. The extension may not be ".com" and needs to be replaced.

Go to Appearance>Themes, and at the top of the page select 'Add Theme.' Load the Divi zipped file. It is available after signing up as a download. Do not unzip it. Select 'Install Now' and then select 'Activate." In the pop-up menu, input the username and license number. Most likely it will need to be updated to a newer version. Follow the prompts to add the username and license key.

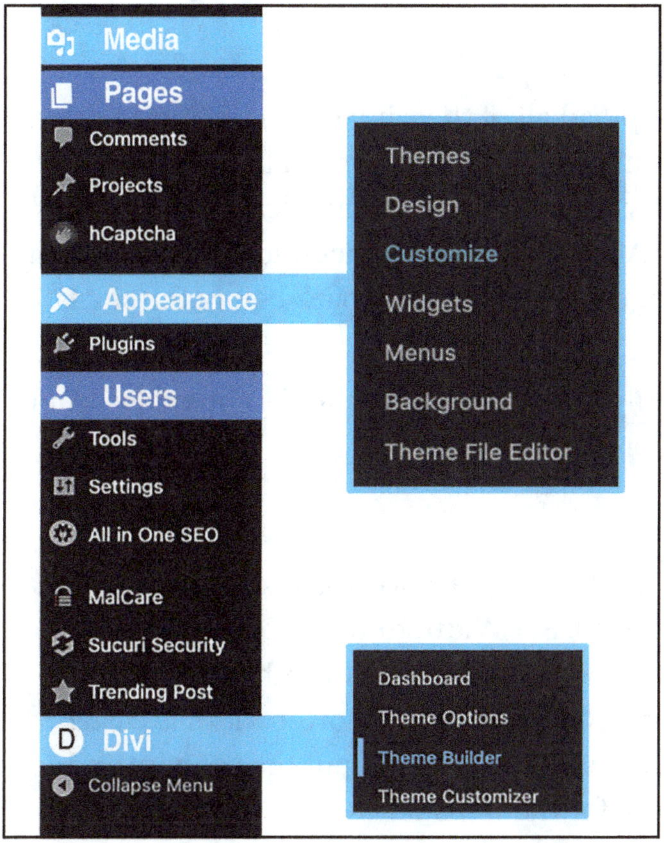

FIGURE 10.6

WP Backend Admin Sidebar

HI Practicum} Photoshop: Use screengrabs to highlight five main areas for beginners to start using WordPress with the Divi option.

Admin steps

Over time a designer will use all of these backend controls to set up articles under posts, adjust settings for plugins, and many more details. For now, in the Admin Sidebar, concentrate on these five control menus: Users, Media, Appearance, Pages, and Divi.

Check the 'Users' section to make sure there is a profile for the designer and an administrator if that is two different people. During setup, the host will automatically add the overall administrator. For ease of logging in, add the username and 16-character password to be used by the designer.

Two ways to load images

Some designers will upload all of their images to the media area and enter all the alternate metadata. Others will upload as they need them in case they need to resize or find ideas that will work better in the layouts. At this point it is difficult to stop and add the metadata, so the designer will need to go back before the site is live to add it.

Make sure to delete any unused images, graphics, or videos from the media library before going live.

Site appearance

In the Admin sidebar, select Appearance > Customize > General Settings > Layout Settings. Set Width to 1080. Designers have preferred sizes, but for the first time, use a width of 1080 pixels. Instead of going 1920 pixels, the shorter width is easier to translate into a mobile website later. Input the primary and secondary colors to use for the website.

By setting up a theme in WP appearance, pages will automatically be consistent with fonts, sizes, colors, and the appearance of links. Divi integrates Google Fonts, which allows the designer to use the same look and feel across multimedia marketing.

At fonts.google.com, select these fonts or other available families and paste in content with headlines. That way, before making a decision, the designer will know which fonts to use.

Continue in 'General Settings' to 'Site Identity' to add in the name, tagline, and a square site icon. To save any changes, select Publish at the top of this sidebar. Go to 'Typography' and change body text to 16 pixels and 1.7 line height. Make the header text size 36 pixels with 1.3 line height.

Select the 'Header' and 'Body' fonts and weights. Have all the text colors black, #000000. Leave the link as blue. The 'X' on the left closes Appearances and returns to the backend after publishing.

From the Admin sidebar, in 'Pages,' add Home, About Us, Services, Info, and Contact Us. Select 'Publish' twice each time and move out of each page by selecting the WP icon.

Go to back to General Settings > Appearance > Menus, and under Menu structure, enter the name 'Home.' After saving the menu, add all the pages except for 'Home'; it may be necessary to drag each page using the cursor to place the correct order. 'Display Location' as secondary and save. Create a new menu named 'Primary,' but this time add all of the pages. The display location is Primary Menu. Always save before leaving any editing or action.

Through other customizing options, the designer may want to turn off the search feature, disable footer credits, social icons, etc. Go to Homepage settings and set the Homepage as a static page and select the HOME page.

THE GOAL IS CONVERSION

For a website to convert visitors into customers, it must inspire confidence and make the action easy to understand. Design for a clear message. The motivation to make an action possible is based on the written content without ambiguity, which will lead to a decision.

Divi provides a number of layouts for nearly all types of industries. For beginners, sometimes it is easier to start with a template and change out colors and fonts and images. Once they understand how it all works, then it is easier to start with Canvas.

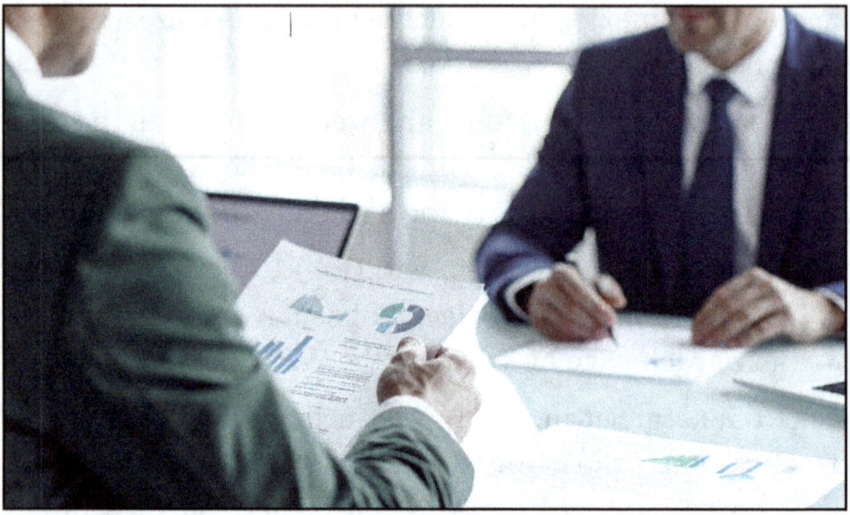

FIGURE 10.7

Data shows the success or failure

AI Practicum} Firefly Prompt: Close-up green-tone image with view from behind of businessmen working with data results.

The ultimate goal is conversion, and engaging fonts will boost those rates. Based on the brand proposition, decide on a serif or sans serif type that has numerous weights to choose from for the content subjects and uses.

If the same font is always used, subconsciously, the website will feel boring. Finds fonts that work well together. For example, Playfair is an elegant serif with a condensed character width, which allows for more information, making it more gentle on the eyes. It can be contrasted with sans serifs such as Raleway or Roboto.

Fonts should be divided into headline and body content. Consider how easily the fonts can be read, what tone they convey, and if they fit the brand message. As an example, Montserrat is a strong geometric sans serif, strong for headlines, and works well for tech brands and corporate companies. Playfair is readable as a headline but not as small text. Its elegance is a great choice for creative and lifestyle companies. Modern sans serifs such as Poppins and Nunito are modern sans serifs with a business feel and complement serif or sans serif body text.

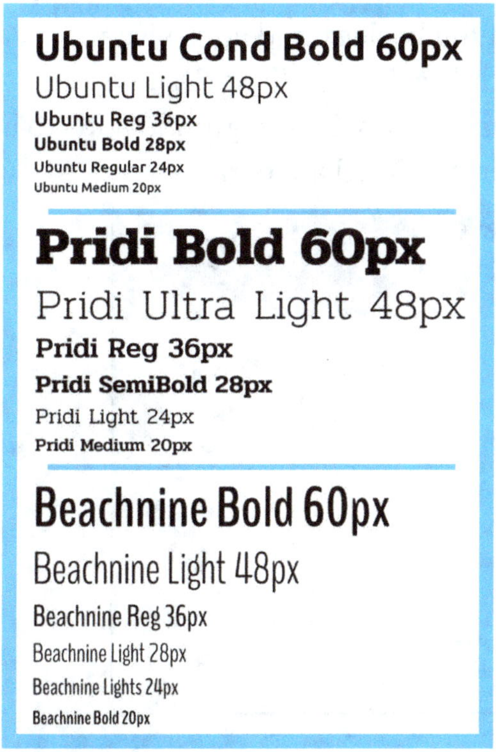

FIGURE 10.8

Three similar fonts that appeal differently to viewers.

Set up color palettes for fonts, dividers, backgrounds, and rollover items. Look over the images that are going to be and make some notes on the main colors used. Decide which colors from the hero images to use on a page and which color will create contrast and complement the images as backgrounds and for the type.

IT'S DESIGN TIME

Finally, the big moment is here. The images are ready, the content is proofed, the headlines are tested, and the structure has been defined. To start and get a feel for Divi, we will create a small but important header with the company brand, menu, and tagline.

Images can be used for backgrounds, but the type must be readable, which means good photos with great contrast are not good backgrounds. Graphics with very little contrast are the best option. For modern design, a muted background adds visual interest without overwhelming the navigation links. Usually, headers are a solid color and using a graphic background adds to a feeling of a modern brand and professional appearance

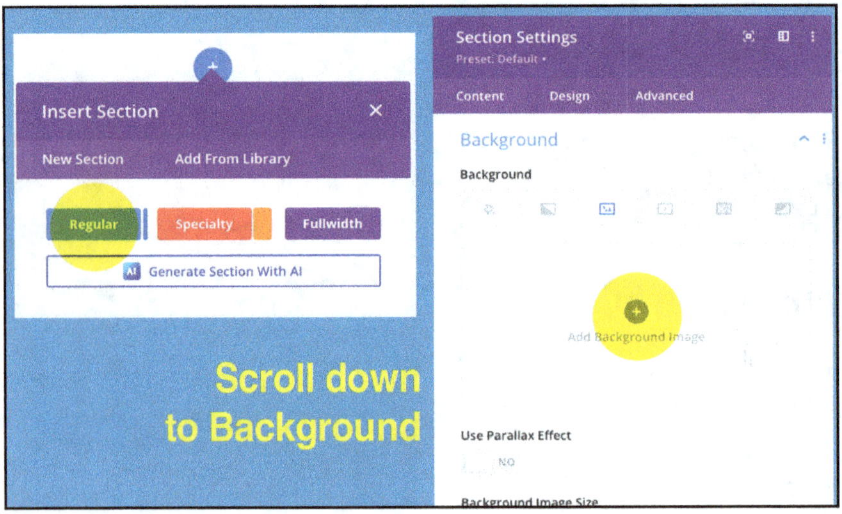

FIGURE 10.9

Divi modules used to start Header Template.

Demo on setting up the header

Using a blank canvas in Divi instead of a premade layout or template gives the designer more control and cleaner outcomes. For brand-driven and conversion-focused sites, it gives the layout key advantages over the "template look" since it is easier to match a brand style than edit presets.

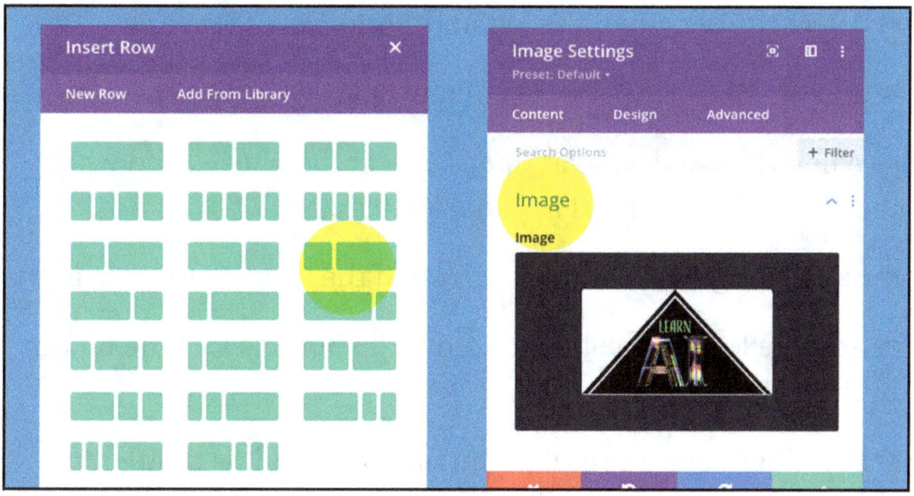

FIGURE 10.10

Divi boxes to start designing the Header
HI Practicum} Photoshop: Screen grabs of rows and image modules.

The designer set the sections, rows, and modules without fighting a preexisting layout. Templates try to provide all the options a page may need, which can affect the first impression by a visitor. The designer will have to take the time to delete unneeded modules.

From a performance perspective, there will be fewer modules, and the design can have key-words that do not look stuffed into the format. The placement is dictated by the visual flow and not preset by a template.

After initial setup, new pages will develop quicker since the designer can reuse established colors, space, and font families. There will be consistency across the website in look and tone.

Templates are focused on supplying a fast way to populate a website. They are affordable since they do not require an outside source to build them. A framed design will give the business owner an internet presence.

➡On the left side near the bottom, go to Divi > Theme Builder > Add New Template > Build New Template.

➡Choose All pages for now. It can be changed later to specific pages and posts.

➡Select the pencil on the left and Build New Template.

➡Choose All Pages in Use On Menu, followed by Create Template.

➡When the blank canvas opens, select the blue +, and when the Insert Section pops up, choose Regular.

➡Select the green +, and an option in the window (Figure 10.7).

➡Add the logo in the left box from the options and the menu in the right box.

➡Divi does have a preset menu module, but it is limited to the logo and navigation. For visitors and Google, it is better to build the header, adding a telephone number and tagline.

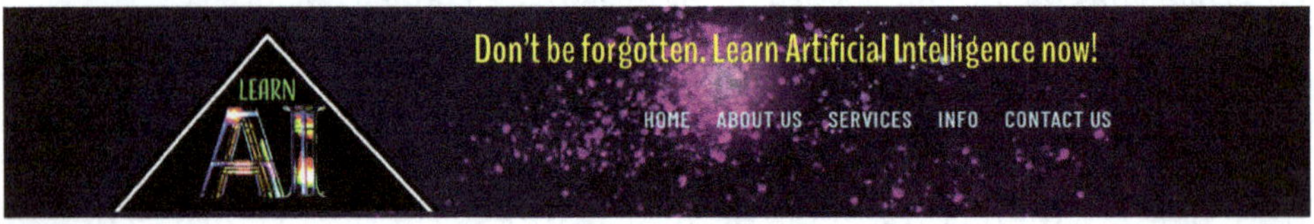

FIGURE 10.11
Final Header

Using Monster Insights, which is a free headline analyzer, the brand message is "Don't be forgotten. Learn Artificial Intelligence now!" It scored a 92! It was set in Benchnine as an H2, 36px, #fff600 which is a medium yellow with some red.

Since the page will have almost all white backgrounds, the header needs more than a solid color. A muted futuristic background was created that extended the logo background. The JPG specs were 1600 x 380 pixels optimized to 74 KB. The logo needed a transparent background with PNG specs of 300 x 170 pixels at 35 KB. These file sizes are part of the total when a page is visited.

Metadata can be added when the images are uploaded. In the right sidebar, fields are available to add descriptions. The file name can be changed here without losing the file.

The menu module was set with the primary setting under content, and in design, it was white for text color and an electric blue active color.

Adjust for mobile layout by selecting the thin vertical phone icon and making all adjustments. Test in another browser and on a mobile phone.

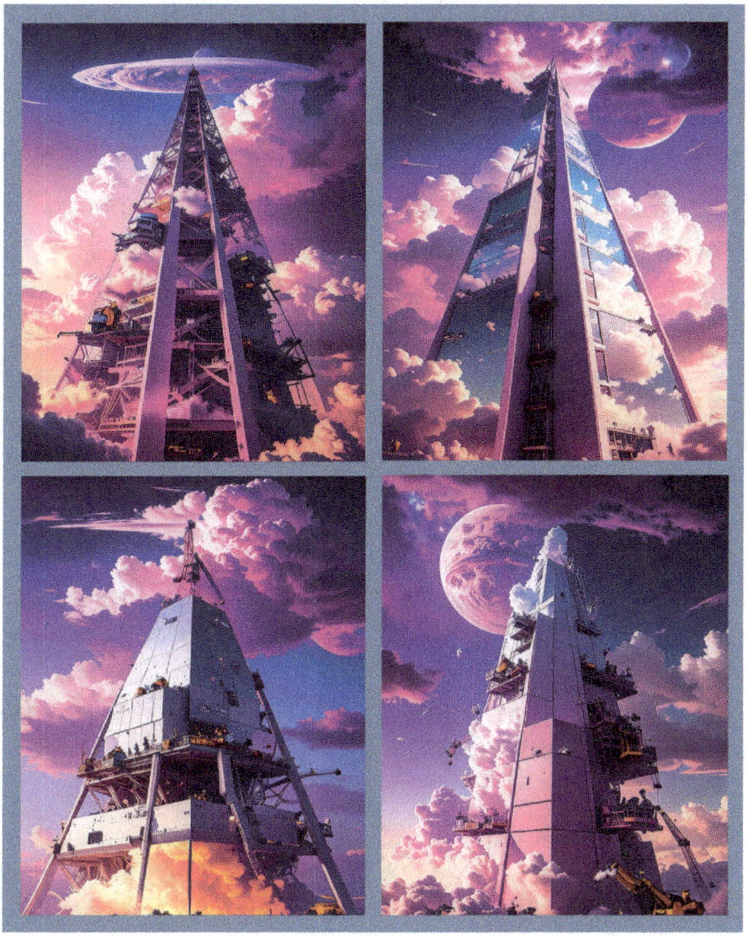

FIGURE 10.12

Impactful storytelling image enhanced by Human Ingenuity.
HI Practicum} Photoshop: Parts of four images combined, saturation, contrast.

With this basic understanding, apply the skills learned from watching Divi tutorials and videos to fill out the rest of the website. In the above example the page Services would later be changed to Classes, and another link would be added for Online Seminars. Only on the Contact page was the number displayed since the business was set up to teach and not verbally take information on the phone. This process would delete most non-tech students who may struggle with learning online and would be better off attending an in-person class.

For non-online educational sites, it is best to have the telephone number in the header, footer, and middle of the page. Marketing stresses the need to make contact easy and not a treasure hunt to find out how to connect.

INSETS

FIGURE 10.3

Set in stone

AI Practicum} Express Prompt: Photo real 3D image of the number 1 with carpet texture set into worn, damaged concrete.

FIGURE 10.4

AI Practicum} Express Prompt: Photo real 3D image of the number 2 with tile texture on a colorful rug with fringed edge layed out on a bleached pine floor.

FIGURE 10.5

AI Practicum} Express Prompt: Photo real 3D image of the number 3 with worn concrete texture on a dried crusty mud floor.

Start Your Search Engines

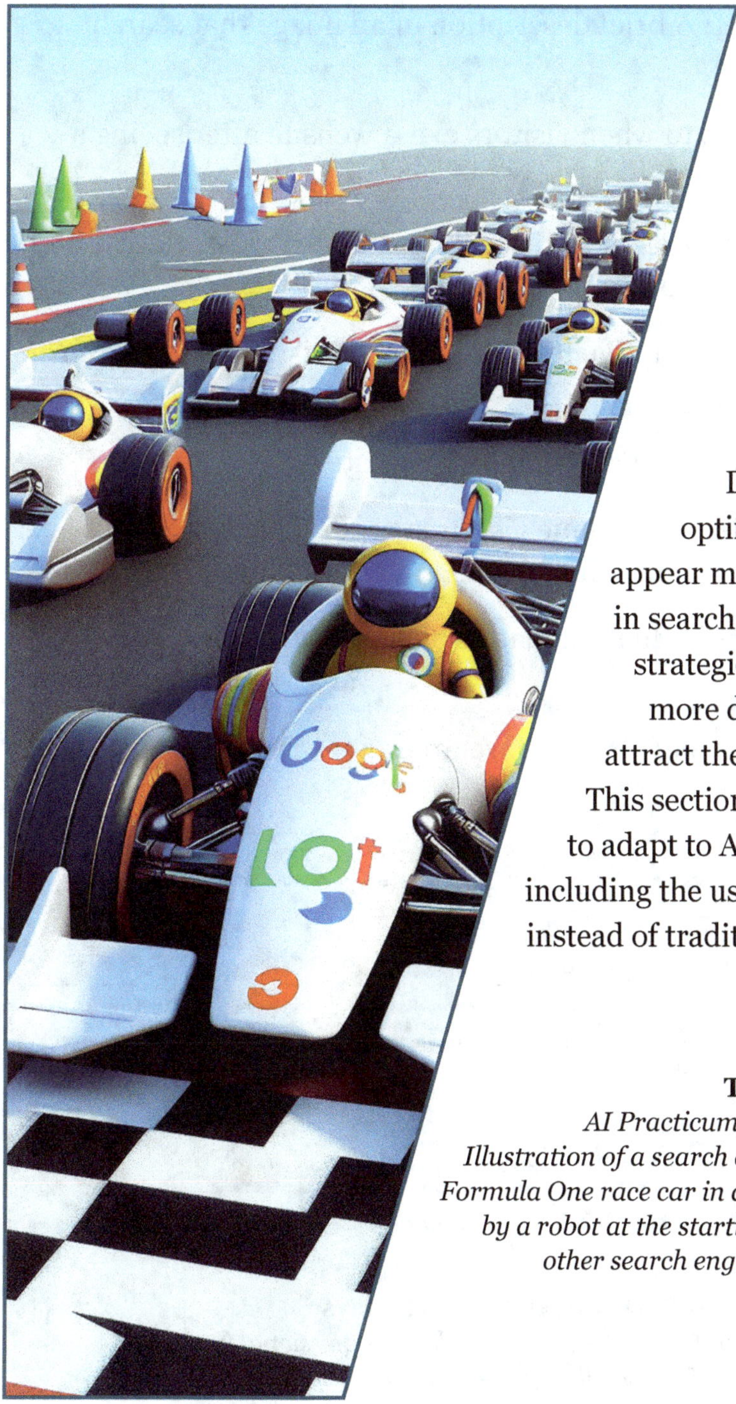

C11

OVERVIEW

Describes how to optimize websites to appear more prominently in search results. Concise strategies make content more discoverable and attract the right audience. This section identifies ways to adapt to AI search results, including the use of Hookwords instead of traditional keywords.

FIGURE 11.1

The starting line

AI Practicum} Creator Prompt: Illustration of a search engine similar to a Formula One race car in appearance driven by a robot at the starting line of multiple other search engine-type race cars.

PROFESSIONAL TERMINOLOGY

Alternate Text: A brief description of an image that search engines utilize.

Bounce: Refers to when visitors exit a website after seeing a single page.

Hookwords: Words or phrases that establish trust, clarity, and relevance to visitors.

Meta: Short descriptive text for potential visitors and search engine robots.

Traffic: Total number of visitors that enter a website.

User: Considered a unique visitor, an individual who looks at a website one or more times.

Visitor: An individual that lands on a website.

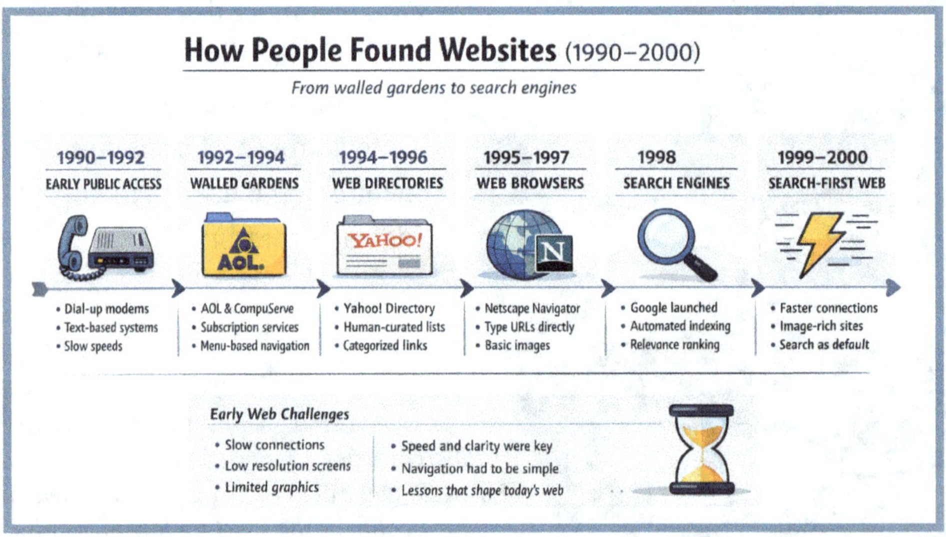

FIGURE 11.2

How People Found Websites in the early days

AI Practicum} ChatGPT Prompt: Create a clean, professional horizontal infographic timeline. From walled gardens to search engines.

A VERY BRIEF HISTORY OF THE INTERNET

Search results have grown from very basic lists to complex, secretive algorithmic descriptions displayed on pages, in maps, and in paid advertising. If a designer understands the origins and history of websites, they can understand the function of Hookwords, establishing trust and engagement with the visitor in relation to search engine optimization.

When the Internet first became accessible to the public in the early 1990s, it was difficult to use. To identify a website required a closed subscription-based system, also known as walled gardens, such as AOL and CompuServe, which required a computer connected to a dial-up modem to access the internet. These gardens and later directories, such as Yahoo and DMOZ, displayed communities and storefronts within the system's directory. AOL listed this content with links to take a user to certain companies and news sources around the world. The locations had to be bookmarked since a URL was difficult to input.

These website lists were information-oriented and did not include many images. AOL worked on curating lists of what people think and not what computers provided. AOL provided common categories such as news, weather, and sports, along with short descriptions to tell the user what was in each site. To surf the web took time and patience due to the speed of a phone line. An option to speed up the download time was to turn off the design and any images.

Netscape and other browsers made it somewhat easier to locate a website if the user knew the URL. Google started off as a doctoral thesis by two students at Stanford University. Their work proposed that robots could search the internet, record websites, and list them so that information seekers could easily find the sites with answers to their queries.

From that rudimentary start, Google was developed to provide relevant and related search results. Developers quickly learned to build websites for consumers by using specific search terms to be found on the rapidly expanding internet. Companies realized the value of being found, indexed, and listed by Google bots. Online shopping became a prime market and a new income source.

The search experts at Google had to develop a list of rules on website development to combat marketing methods to falsely rank websites in searches. These standards became known as Best Practices in optimizing websites for indexing by robots. This SEO approach became synonymous with search results, but it is actually two separate building and continuous actions.

Marketing to the internet user went from a small part of the campaign plan to a major tactic. However, for a potential customer to choose a company, product, or service, trust and recognition are essential. Brand strategy added a new method of promotion on a new medium.

Slow speeds, low screen resolutions, and limited image quality strongly influenced early web design. The ability to stream information with faster connections allowed for engaging website designs with larger quality images and content.

A handheld pocket sized computer telephone revolutionized the use of the internet. The use of scientific knowledge changed from an informational tool into a source for news, communication, shopping, social interaction, and entertainment. Websites became major income producers, and the focus of technology in less than two decades. Artificial intelligence is the next stage of the internet evolution and website should be optimized for this development.

START WITH RESEARCH

Before starting the design of a website, the business owner and marketer should begin the steps to develop search engine-optimized Hookwords and content. Establish the words or phrases customers use to find answers, narrow the list to the top ten used by the competition, and add terms that explain why this website is superior to the competition.

Before listing the Hookwords, a marketer will start with HI, human ingenuity, to develop a short list of five questions. Create a test survey and refine it to make it functional based on clarity and speed. The questions will need to be structured so the respondent is not spending a lot of time thinking of the answer.

While open-ended questions have higher-quality answers, multiple choice is perceived as faster for the respondent. Research the questions to ask by speaking to company employees, salespersons, customer support agents, and the customers. Questions should focus on high-value Hookwords in their phrasing. Always use natural language, not business terms, because those words are what will be used to identify the company to potential customers.

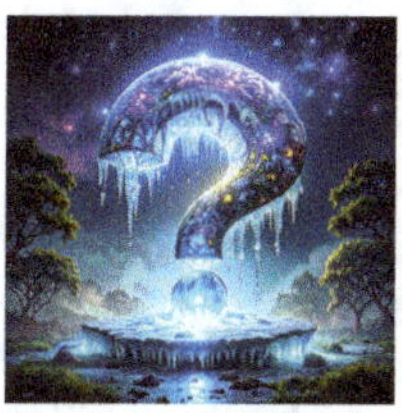

Ask: **"How did you search for this (fill in the offering here)?**
Small businesses should always ask callers where they found out about the company, as this information can help determine what to include and what to prioritize on the website for future campaigns.

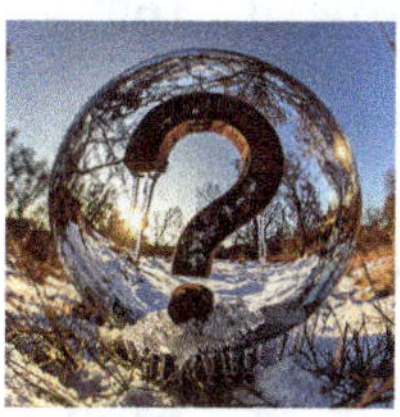

Ask: **What alternative did you research and compare to the (fill in the offering here)?**
This question is a great way to discover how the competitors' marketing is interesting to the potential customer. Try to discover the competition's names or what attracted the respondent.

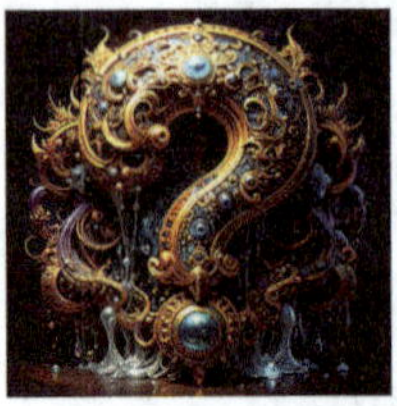

Ask: **What was special about (fill in the offering here) that made you consider us?** The value proposition created before starting the marketing can be tested, rewritten, and improved based on these answers. See what 'trust' differentiators are signaled by the marketing.

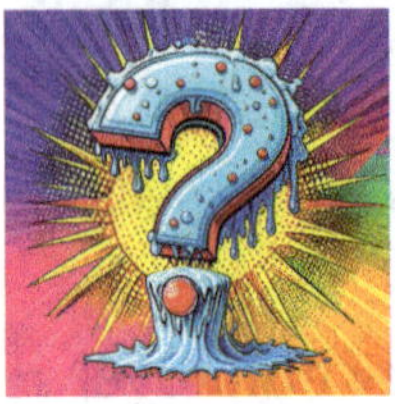

Ask: **How would you refer (fill in the brand name here) to a friend or family member?** Note how their description structure is usually not a compound sentence. Clarify any metaphors and non-technical wording.

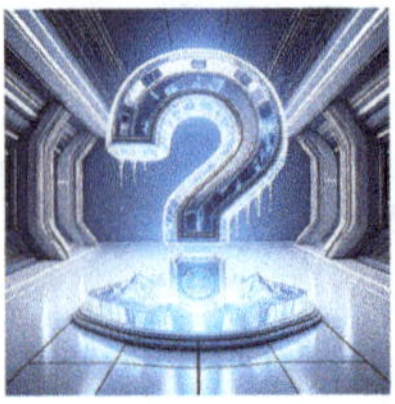

Ask: **Were you trying to find a solution for a problem or need with (fill in the offering here)?** In marketing, these are known as pain points, and they can pinpoint frustration or strong emotional feelings to use in headlines and hook words.

After the research, consider breaking the answers into stacks. These are categories, such as problems, solutions, comparisons, outcomes, and trust. Make sure the phrases are noted exactly as they were told. Results can be inputted in ChatGPT to find out the most common phrases and words. Use another AI, such as Gemini, to create an H1 headline, followed by the next most popular response terms for the H2 and H3 subheads. Tweak and refine the hookword phrases with HI and test.

In addition to the obvious visual responsibilities, a designer needs to organize the information to help with the structure of the website. Hookwords cannot be stuck into content to make it nonsensical or foreign. Visitors will not understand the content, and Google will know the website owners are trying to stuff the website with Hookwords. If a hookword is repeated more than three times on a page, Google may judge it to be poor content and list it lower in searches.

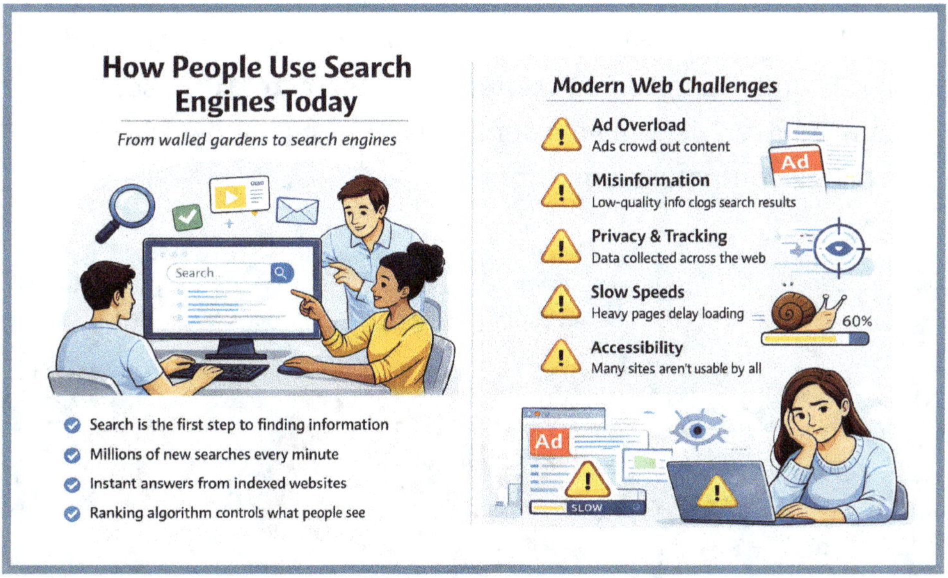

FIGURE 11.8

Searches and Challenges

AI Practicum} ChatGPT Prompt: Split screen, on the left an illustration of people using a search engine together at a computer. On the right are warning icons and short explanations and a frustrated website user.

SIMPLE SEO

Due to the ability of search engines utilizing AI to understand searches in natural language, the SEO that has been the mainstay of marketing has changed. The process went mostly from keyword matching to a different strategy.

Reliable information that a search engine may use to provide answers to users is by far the most important ranking element after 'Traffic.' This material must be arranged so that a human or AI can quickly and clearly understand what the website is about.

When websites have identical content and structure, AI ranks them using data measures. Rather than just on-page quality, consider visitor behavior, brand familiarity, the length of time the website has been operational, and the availability of customer support.

Backlinks are still significant, but authoritative sources are less influential in AI SER. Cited backlinks in editorial material from relevant sites are an excellent way to create trust. Being recognized in trade journals demonstrates knowledge and improves a company's reputation.

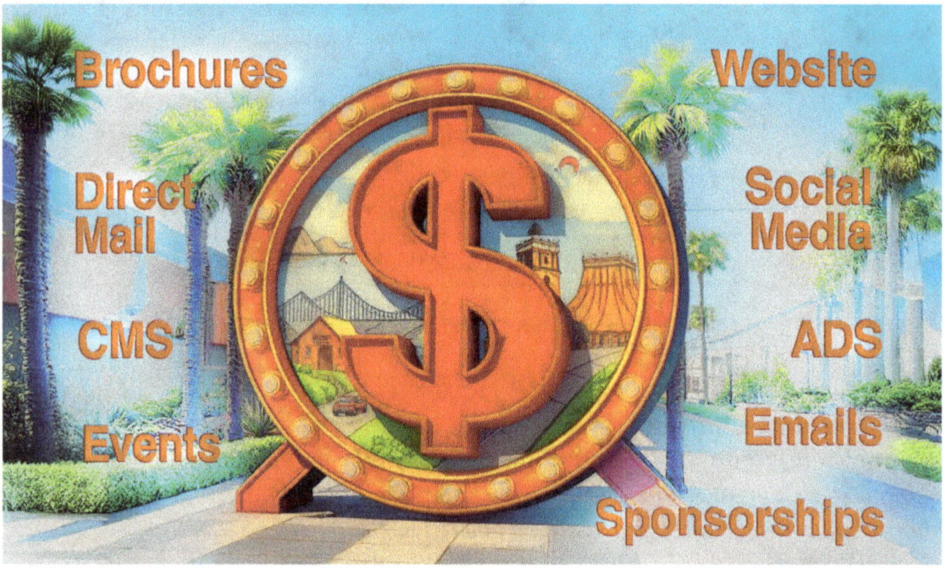

FIGURE 11.9

The mighty dollar

AI Practicum} Express Prompt: Large 3D decorative dollar sign with a website circling it like a planet.

HI Practicum: Blend images of an email, flyer, ad, postcard, radio, and social media created in Express and add special effects to be eye-catching.

Structure for Success

Designing for visitor interaction directly leads to higher rankings in search results. With AI-driven search results, designers must structure content for clarity, credibility, and intent to help websites rank and make information easy for humans and AI systems to understand and trust.

When building the website, include examples of 'trust' for AI searches. These signals can be supplied in multiple ways:

- The 'Home page' should not continue critical search content on another page; it should be found in the scroll. The copywriter will need to be concise with explaining an answer for a visitor.

- On the 'About page,' explain why the organization exists. Include an ownership or team biography with photos that are not in stock.

- Legal pages such as the privacy policy and terms of use need to be specific and not a template.

- Show photos of real work with before and after examples. These images require captions that are readable by potential customers and also included in the meta data for search bots. Images of locations help in searches for "near me" results.

Driving Traffic

Too often today, business owners still think all they need to do to build income is to have a professional website. Marketing strategies should include additional forms of brand promotion that are memorable. Email marketing and newsletters can lead visitors to a website, which is 'Traffic.'

The location and correct information in maps such as Google and Apple are important. Paid ads such as Google PPC, Facebook, and Instagram, if engaging, will drive traffic to the site.

Social and business public relations media integration that is meaningful and not a template has better results. A business not only needs a Google Business Profile, but it also needs star reviews with personalized replies from the administrator.

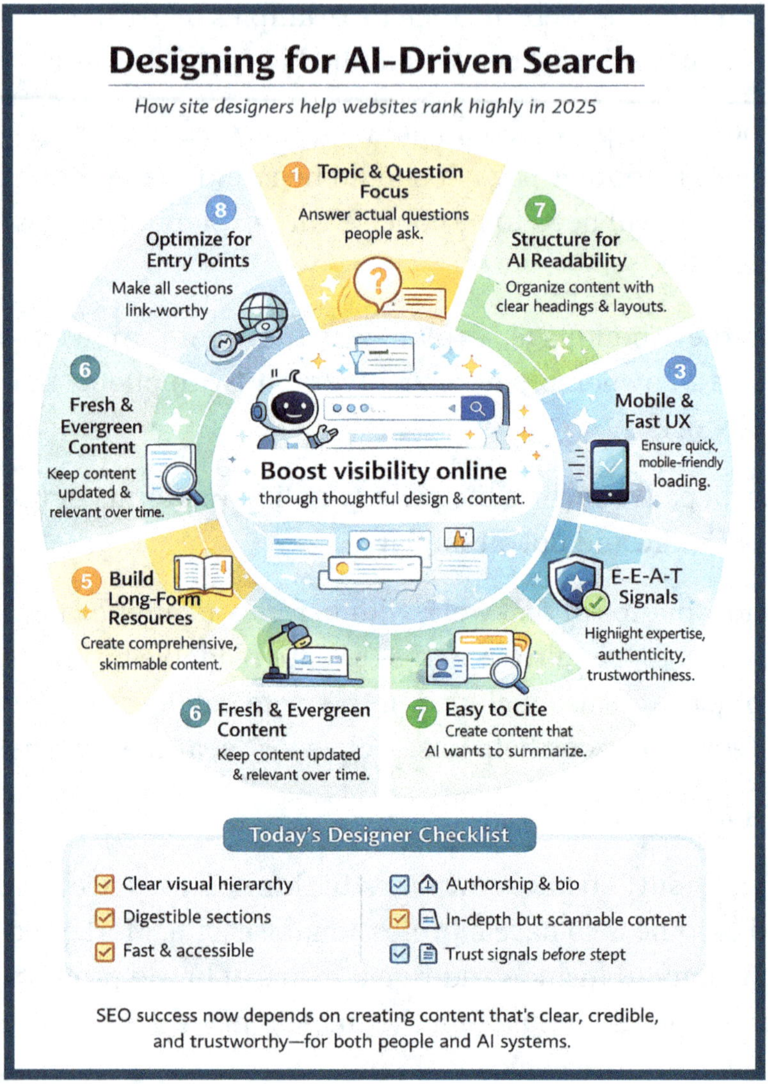

FIGURE 11.10

AI understands but make mistakes with spelling

AI Practicum} ChatGPT Prompt: Split screen, on left an infographic a designer's checklist, on pie shaped infographic with icons and short explanations of how to boost website visibility online.

Build Trust

Customer trust signals are supplied with testimonials, guarantees, and reviews. In a small survey of college students, websites with video testimonials ranked higher in trust than websites with written or no testimonials. The hypothesis was that website visitors would find video testimonials real, while written testimonials would not.

The small study of five graphic design classes at two different colleges with students ages 19 to 56 was too small a sampling to generalize across the entire internet. However, it provided some interesting generalities.

Each class was made up of 18-20 students who were given 15 minutes to look over three mocked-up service oriented websites and answer a 10-question survey about those websites. The questions were limited to color responses, content reactions, and testimonials as trust builders.

The customer video testimonials were perceived as real, while written testimonials were considered manipulated. A website without written testimonials ranked a little higher in trustworthiness than a website with written customer comments.

As stated, this survey was small and focused and not publishable due to its narrow field of respondents. However, for website designers who want to create successful websites, it was an intriguing and logical conclusion.

Hookwords, not keywords

Marketing strategy for websites has shifted. Search engines no longer rely on simple keyword matching to rank pages. Instead, they evaluate relevance first, then observe how people interact with a page to determine trust and value. Hookwords are the words or phrases that help earn that trust and encourage engagement. When a website is optimized for people, improved search ranking becomes a natural by-product. SEO no longer optimizes pages to be found—it optimizes pages to be trusted once found.

Hookwords, as defined by ChatGPT, are the "words or phrases intentionally chosen to signal clarity, credibility, relevance, or value to a visitor, encouraging engagement and trust. Their role is not to influence indexing, but to optimize human response—making ranking a secondary outcome rather than the primary goal."[1]

Verbal Queries

Be prepared for questions that are asked of a search engine with verbal cues. While only 27% of all users search with verbal instructions, as accuracies improve, so will the use of verbal questions or instructions on a website. It is estimated that approximately 77% of 18-34-year-old users are utilizing the voice options available in smartphones.

Users are in a "voice-first" shift approach. Typing has been the method for over a century. Writing was the non-voice communicative tool prior to the typewriter. Now users are able to say the AI agent's name and start a verbal communication.

Pretty or functional

If a website is made to look inviting and beautiful to a human visitor, it needs many images and very little content. Many websites are not looking to be found by searchers but to be used as an instrument of credibility and show a legitimate, successful business.

Most websites must appear in search results when potential customers are looking for specific information or answers to their questions. Rarely can the design be breathtaking and found in searches. The exception occurs when a website generates traffic through effective marketing, advertising, or newsworthiness. Even poorly structured sites that have a lot of visitors that spend thirty minutes on the site will show up on page one of searches.

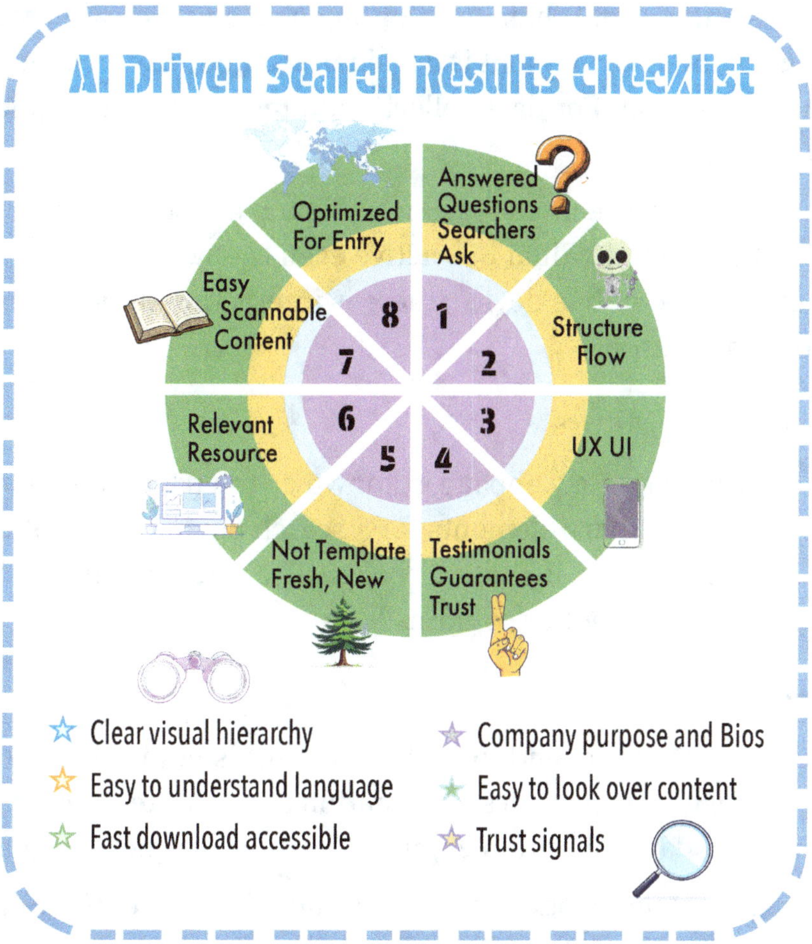

FIGURE 11.11

Target objectives search checklist

HI Practicum} Illustrator: ChatGPT diagram was too confusing and had typos.

Needed to be simplified to be understood and remembered.

Bounce Rate

The term 'bounce' refers to when a user visits a website did not interact such as clicking a link, video. When client see a high bounce rate, they assume the searcher left quickly and think that negatively reflects on the site.

It is misleading term because it is not necessarily a failure to engage a visitor. It refers to when visitors exit a website after seeing a single page. When a visitor lands on a website and reads the page before leaving, that is considered a bounce since there was no interaction. For data collection, it means the visitor did not select a CTA.

If a visitor calls the company from a desktop site, there is no activity, but the individual was active even though it could not be measured. On a mobile device, there is interaction if the visitor selects a call button.

Titles

The code that labels a webpage is known as the page title. They are one of the primary elements for a search engine. It should be kept to 60 characters, including spaces. The words should define what the page is about or contains.

Metadata

Inputted into the backend tools, this content is not immediately seen by a visitor. It provides information such as site descriptions or structural data for search engines to display in query results.

Page and meta descriptions provide a short informative summary of the webpage for potential visitors and search engines. These 160-character-long search snippets are shown in search results.

Site descriptions are the visible sentences structured with Hookwords and CTAs that provide detailed information and engage visitors. They are concise sentences made up of 160 characters. Media descriptions should be limited to 125 characters using descriptive and Hookwords for SEO.

A WP plugin that is used to copywriters and designers in optimizing the website content is AIOSEO, an AI-assisted SEO tool. It will offer suggestions and score how effective a snippet's content will be with searchers. By adding relevance and explaining the website's content, it formats the optimized content for Google to review.

RankMath is a slightly different WP plugin that assists in how a page is presented to Google for indexing. It uses best practices on clarity, intent, and will not keyword stuff. It will control the length of what is submitted to Google and improve the click-through-rate of a page. RankMath labels the website so search engines understand the intent of the website. This structure assist AI in understanding what a page is about for more accurate search results.

Local SEO: Google Business, reviews, and maps

Google offers a free business profile listing. It is an opportunity to explain and summarize its offering. Customers can review these offerings and grade them with stars. Apple Maps, Google Maps, and Bing Maps (or Azure Maps) allow a business to pinpoint its location for potential customers as well as include hours, menus, photos, and answers to questions. This is crucial for search results and to allow visitors to quickly learn about a company before going to its website.

> This is where the Title Tag will go that is clicked
> url.thewebsite address.website/page-link
> The summary text goes here with the purpose of reinforcing the website intent and answering the search query. Terms may be called out in bold.

FIGURE 11.12

Snippet is a visual block of information
HI Practicum} Created in Illustrator.

REFERENCES

1. Neal Hettinger, *Hookwords and Visitor-First SEO*, conceptual framework developed in collaboration with ChatGPT (OpenAI), 2025.

INSETS

FIGURE 11.3

Question Mark fantasy

AI Practicum} Express Prompt: 3D question mark made of melting on ice in a fantasy jungle with bright pastel colors.

FIGURE 11.4

Question Mark photo real

AI Practicum} Express Prompt: Close up of 3D question mark melting in ball of ice in the desert.

FIGURE 11.5

Question Mark opulent

AI Practicum} Express Prompt: Vintage ornate 3D question mark with gold and jewels on dark background.

FIGURE 11.6

Question Mark Pop Art

AI Practicum} Express Prompt: Pop art 3D question mark made of ice rising in front of the sun.

FIGURE 11.7

Question Mark of the future

AI Practicum} Express Prompt: Cartoon High tech 3D question mark made of melting ice in metal room.

The Artistry in Design

C12

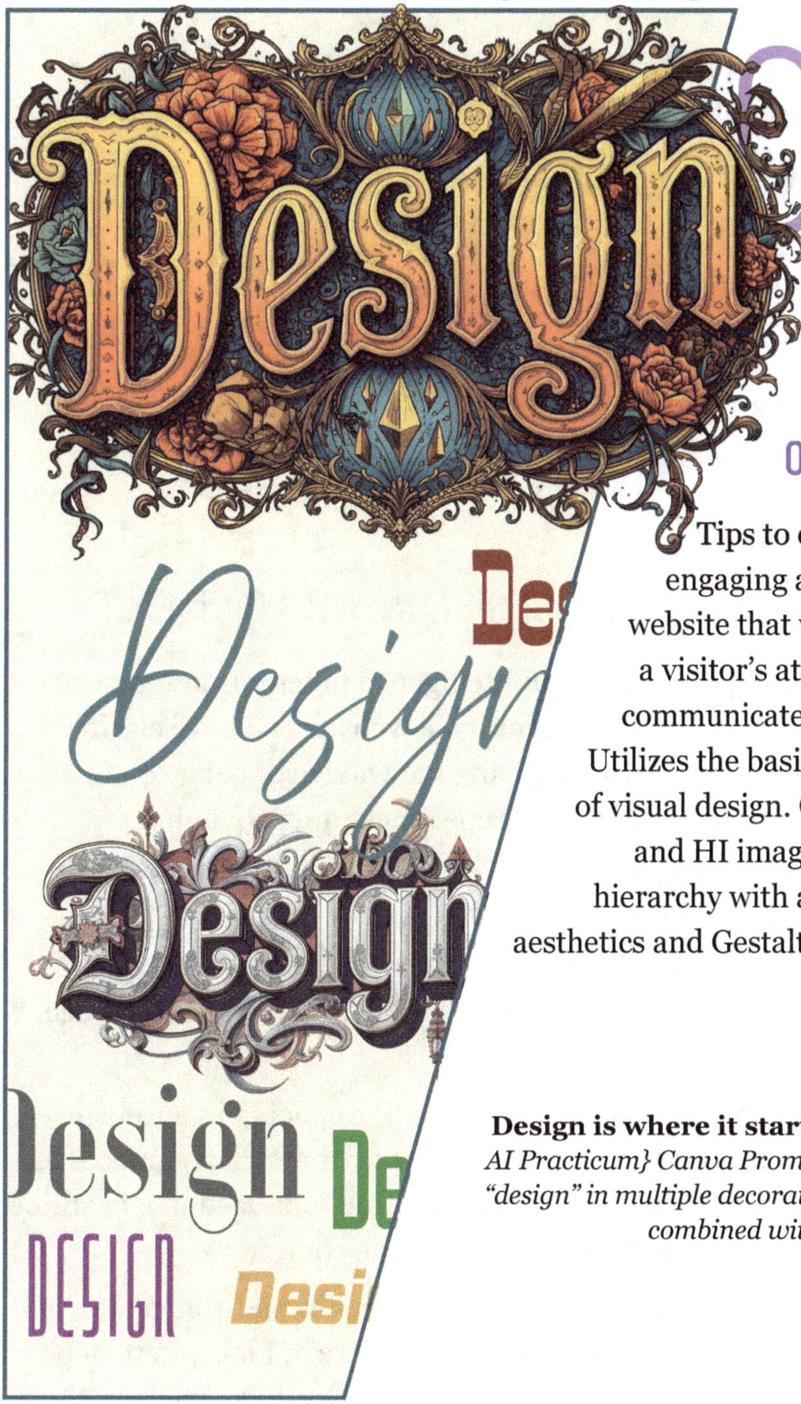

OVERVIEW

Tips to compose an engaging and striking website that will capture a visitor's attention and communicate effectively. Utilizes the basic principles of visual design. Curating AI and HI images creates a hierarchy with a balance of aesthetics and Gestalt principles.

Figure 12.1

Design is where it starts and ends

AI Practicum} Canva Prompt: The word "design" in multiple decorative fonts and combined with Photoshop.

PROFESSIONAL TERMINOLOGY

Gestalt: A school of psychology that viewers see designed as a whole element and not parts.

Harmony: Arrangement of elements into a unified visual message that feels complete to the viewer.

Pop-Up: A window that appears when an element on a website is selected.

Typography: The fonts used on a website to evoke a response.

Z-Pattern: One way visitors read a webpage.

EYE-CATCHING DESIGNS START WITH CONTRAST.

Designers using only artificial intelligence functions are focusing on emotion. With human ingenuity, a website can have clarity, emotion, and evoke trust. Applying knowledge of balance, contrast, hierarchy, alignment, repetition, and proximity.

Contrast is the number one method of drawing attention to a design. Nearly every element used in design, such as scale, color, space, or balance, can create contrast. Nothing in a design should be placed haphazardly. Everything relates to the rest of the page, including alignment.

Using three fonts or less and the same line spacing in a website design creates a consistency in typography that will feel readable and intentional to the visitor. A contrasting font used in a headline can visually pull a visitor to notice specific content.

A professional graphic designer or artist relies on three main tools: space, color, and fonts to create contrast. Flat color can be plain. Gradations of color can suggest mass and a contour of the areas that are in contact with each other. Space suggests effortless reading, and contrasting colors can be an attention magnet.

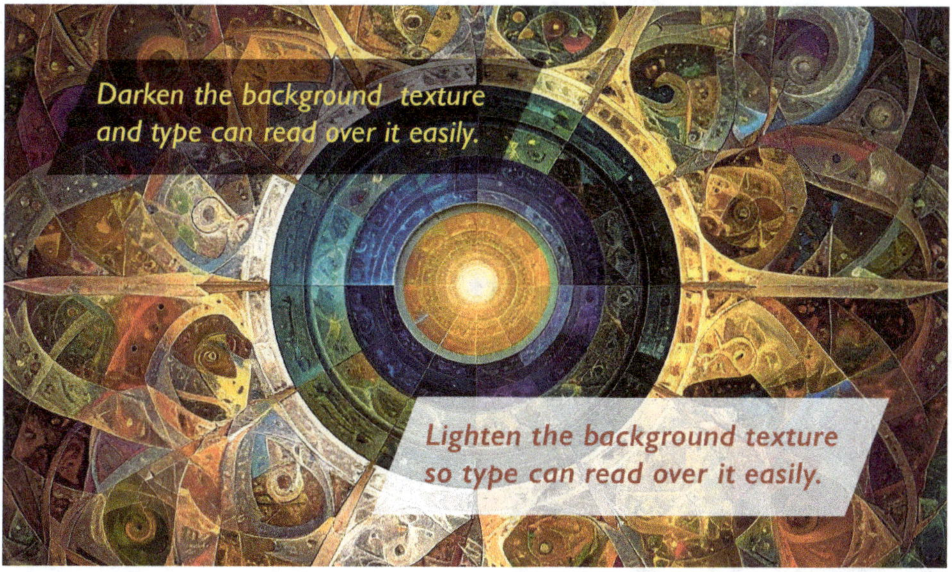

Figure 12.2

Color, space, and fonts attract

AI Practicum} Firefly Prompt: Artwork with cool tones demonstrating design symmetry

DESIGNERS USE THE GESTALT PRINCIPLES.

In the 1920s, a group of psychologists in Germany developed six theories of visual perception. The theories describe how we perceive visual objects, so their arrangements create a unified concept. These principles describe how the eye and mind use groups of images.

Today, these Gestalt principles are the basis of design layouts. When individuals look at the visual arrangement of elements in a design, they organize these elements to form a whole or complete design.

As a designer, these principles will help the layout look coherent, pleasing, balanced, and most importantly, professional. To transform a website layout from a generic template to a unique message, a designer should understand the six main principles of Gestalt theory. Gestalt theories.

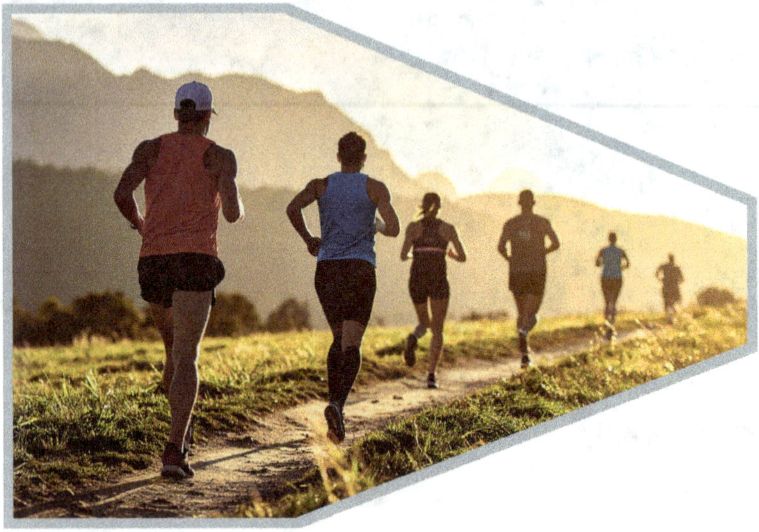

Figure 12.3

***Figure-ground* not only creates depth, but it can create an implied shape to use with cropping**

AI Practicum} Firefly Prompt: color image people running cross country into sunrise demonstrating the gestalt principle of Figure Ground.

Figure-Ground

The eye will see separate objects from their surrounding background, surrounding area, or a form, silhouette, or shape. Balancing figure and ground can make the perceived image clearer. Using unusual figure/ground relationships can add interest and subtlety to an image.

Correctly cropped, an image could lead the eye into the distant horizon. The figure and ground relationships change as the eye perceives the form of a shade of hands drawing with positive and negative space.

A third figure-ground concept is where an image is hidden within an image. The eye will see separate objects from the surrounding background using positive and negative space.

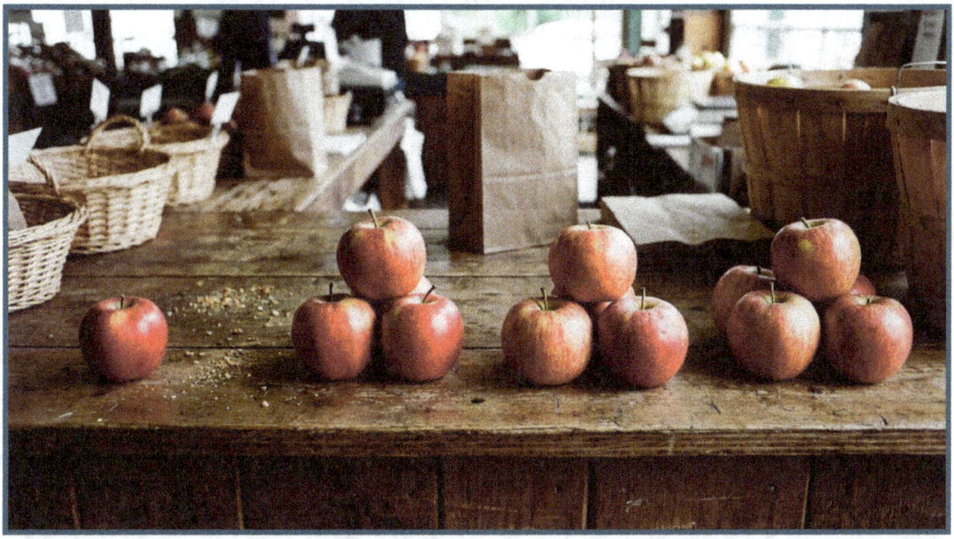

Figure 12.4

***Proximity* causes the viewer to focus on the single apple**
AI Practicum} Gemini Prompt: in a horizontal layout show on a grocery counter 3 groups of 3 red apples and off to the left is another red apple by itself in a photo real style.

Proximity

When related elements are grouped together, they are perceived as a group. When unrelated elements are spaced away from other elements, this positioning communicates which elements are not part of the other elements.

On a website, the header elements are the logo, tagline, navigation menu, and telephone number. This info is at the top to help visitors identify the site and use it. The content outside the header conveys messages specifically intended for the visitor.

If the menu is placed somewhere in the website body area, the visitor will be confused. If the header or sidebar had body content and the navigation was placed in the footer, the visitor would be frustrated and leave. They searched the internet and wanted to easily find the answer to their query.

The information in the body of the website needs to be grouped and placed in proximity to allow the visitor to quickly scan the content. While they continue to be separate shapes of information, such as an image, headline, and subhead, they are now perceived as one group.

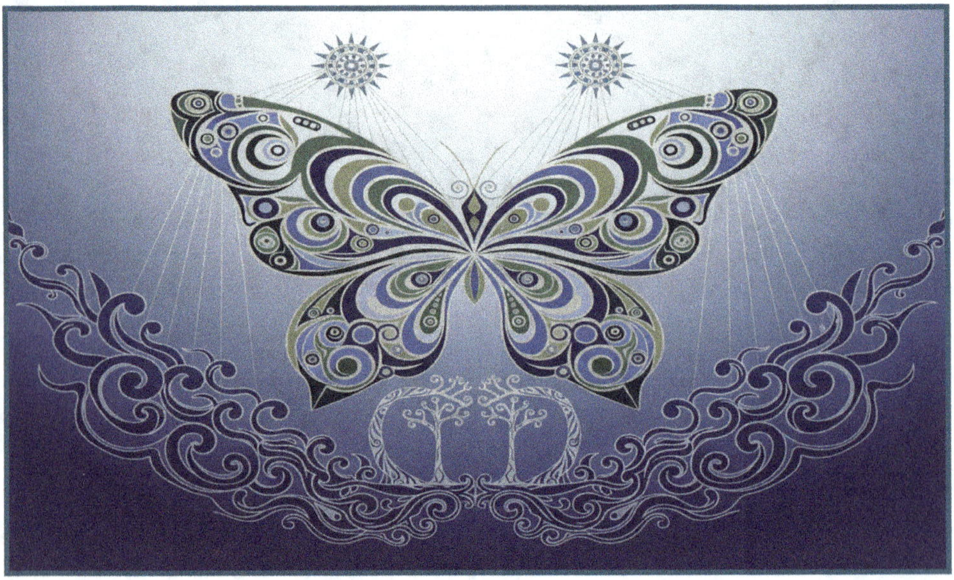

Figure 12.5

***Symmetry*—the complete butterfly is seen at first and then its parts**
AI Practicum} Firefly Prompt: Symmetrical layout of decorative butterfly and graphics in blue and green tones.

Symmetry

The principle of symmetry describes an instance where the whole of a figure is perceived rather than the individual parts that make it up. According to the principle of symmetry, designers can achieve a comfortable balance by mirroring the weight and shape of the design elements on equal sides of the layout.

Subconsciously a symmetrical website layout provides the visitor with a feeling of harmony.

More than five lines of type should not be centered due to the difficulty of reading the paragraph. Viewers prefer to read in an 'F pattern', where their eyes start at the top left of the content, go across the first line, and then scan down on the left edge until they come across something of interest or an answer to their query.

While a symmetrical layout is the easy design method, it is also overused. An asymmetrical layout creates energy and a visual hierarchy, but the design takes work and adjustment to flow correctly.

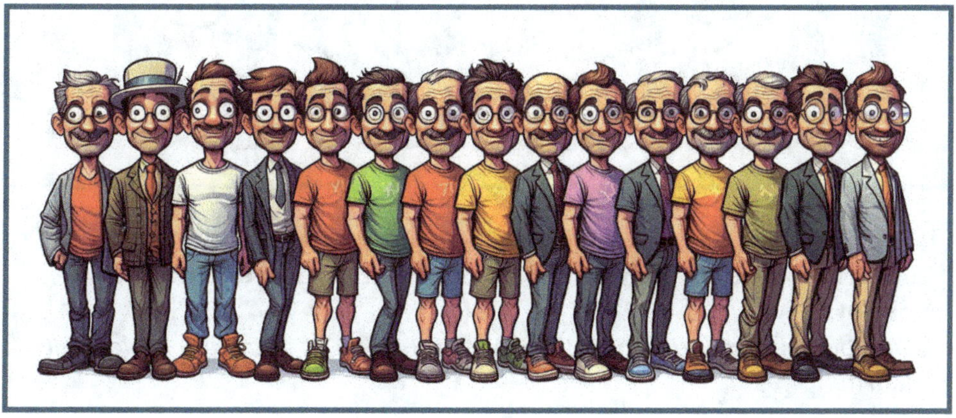

Figure 12.6
Similarity is a strong visual attraction
AI Practicum} Firefly Prompt: Similarity demonstrated with same cartoon character looking at viewer in different clothes.

Similarity

When objects look like one another, individuals may perceive them as a group or pattern. The similarity between different elements can be in shapes, colors, scale, texture, and value. The lightness and darkness of a color creates contrast and draws attention. Multiple distinct objects can be manipulated to form a single memorable image for a visitor. In a group, an object can be emphasized by being dissimilar to the others.

On a website, to increase retention and to be scanned quickly, the same fonts, colors, and spacing need to be used. To highlight specific information for the visitor, it should stand out. Headlines should be a different size and color than subheads and body content. The headline fonts should be similar so visitors can quickly identify what they want.

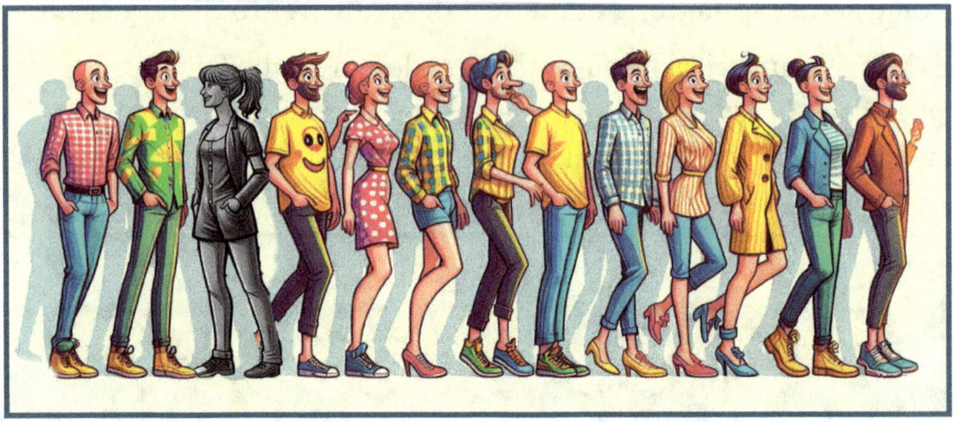

Figure 12.7

Similarity principle can be used to draw attention to a dissimilar element.

AI Practicum} Firefly Prompt: Cartoon illustration of a line of people showing similarity.

HI Practicum} Photoshop: Flip lady to face opposite of everyone and remove the color to stand out.

Closure

A strong design technique is to make a plain image memorable through closure. This graphic art technique is based on viewers perceiving an incomplete but recognizable object. They naturally fill in the missing parts. Graphic artists will intentionally design a logo as an incomplete image with missing lines or through positive and negative space.

This approach engages the viewer's imagination and builds more interest in the brand. Applying the closure principle in design prompts the viewer to pause and recognize the element. The art will cause curiosity and intrigue. This type of engagement can create a lasting impression.

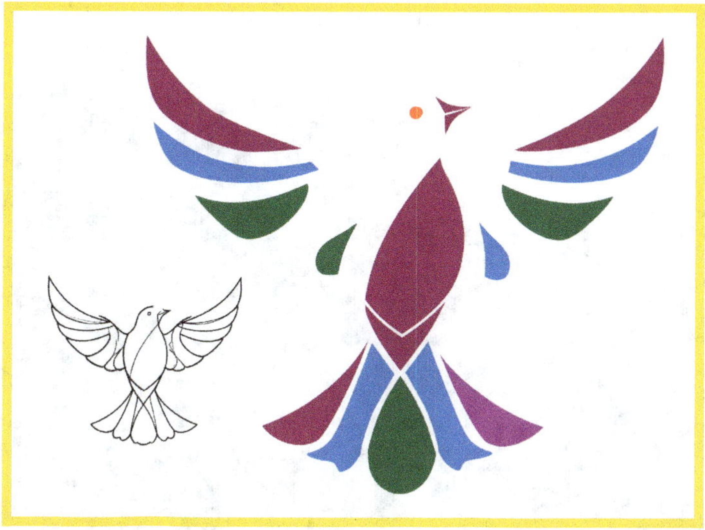

Figure 12.8

Closure lets the viewer solve the puzzle

HI Practicum} Used Illustrator Prompt: Draw black and white linework of bird with open wings demonstrating the principle of closure. Full bird drawn but edited with human ingenuity to demonstrate closure.

Continuation

This Gestalt principle of visual perception explains how people naturally follow lines, curves, and directional paths in a design. By strategically using lines and curves, designers can guide users seamlessly from one section to another, enhancing the overall user experience. Viewers

The eye will naturally follow a line or curve and prefers smooth, continuous paths over abrupt changes. The principle of continuation allows the designer to keep a visitor on a website through interest and a sense of movement. Using a diagonal image edge to point toward a headline or content creates an implied line to direct the visitor's attention.

They utilize continuation in a website design to engage the visitor and help convey information visually. Ultimately, the goal of a website design is to increase user satisfaction and encourage repeat visits. The website needs to appear professional to build trust.

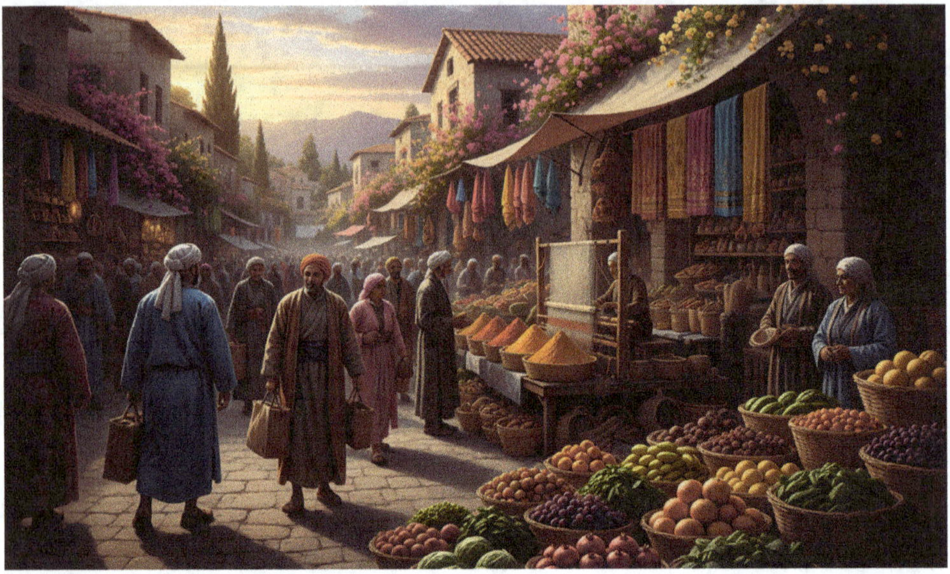

Figure 12.9

Continuation leads the eye into a story to engage a viewer
AI Practicum} Firefly Prompt: Middle ages Bazaar setting with dramatic light in an asymmetrical layout.

In a professional website design, continuation is used to guide the eye through content and create visual hierarchy. The best use of this gestalt theory is to lead users toward a call to action. The visitor will follow where the design leads them.

An example of continuation is when two lines intersect, the viewer sees two continuous lines crossing, not four separate line segments. A dashed line in a layout will be perceived as a single continuous line, not disconnected marks.

Eye flow can create higher visitor traffic. If a visitor can easily view a website because of a continuous design, they will feel the information is on the page.

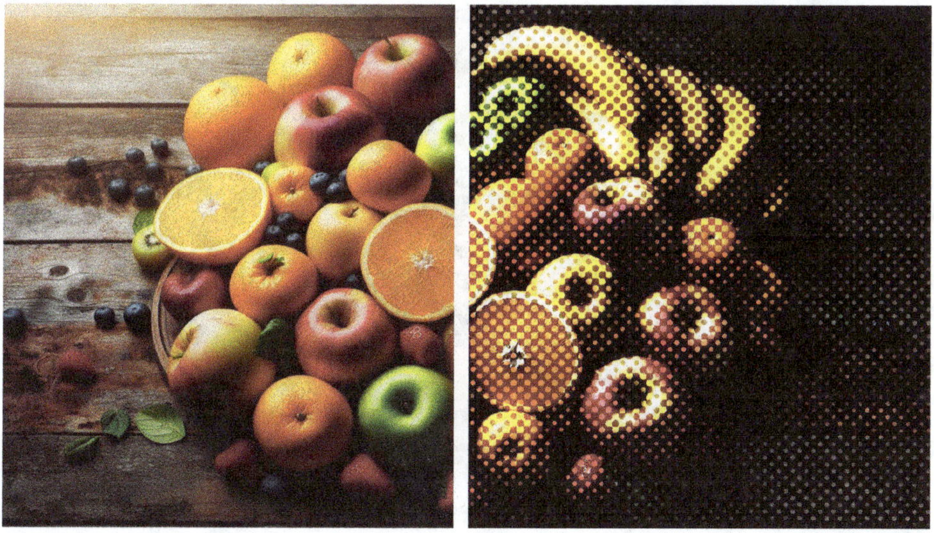

Figure 12.10

Color and design have always been a partnership

AI Practicum} Firefly Prompt: Photo of bowl of fruit showing appeal of color

COLOR IS A DESIGNER'S SECRET TOOL

Many beginners are afraid of color and will argue that they use black, grey, and white for logos and websites to be 'different.' This crutch is a weak attempt to avoid using one of the greatest contrast tools. A complementary color palette can be used to stop a visitor from selecting the back button. It is a powerful design tool to sell a brand. To use black and white powerfully requires experience and finesse.

An easy way to choose a color for a font or line is from a color in an image. Find a neutral tone and adjust it to develop tints and shades.

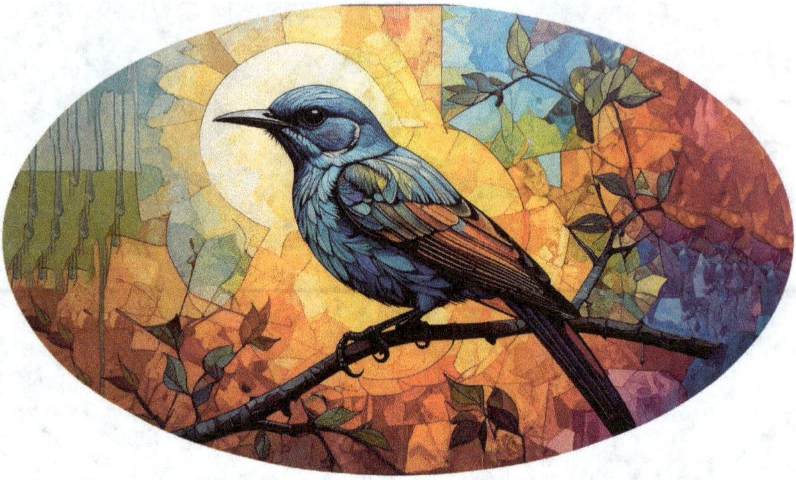

Figure 12.11

Texture and color can emotionally affect the visitor

AI Practicum} Firefly Prompt: In artwork with brush strokes show a songbird sitting on a limb with the sun in a colorful background.

FIVE WEBSITE FORMATS

#1 Hero Layout

When the visitor enters this popular style of page layout, they see a large image and limited content. They have an immediate understanding that this website will not take long to scan to know what is being offered. The potential customer will have a strong impression and will recognize the site when they return. This simple, clear visual flow takes them to the CTA.

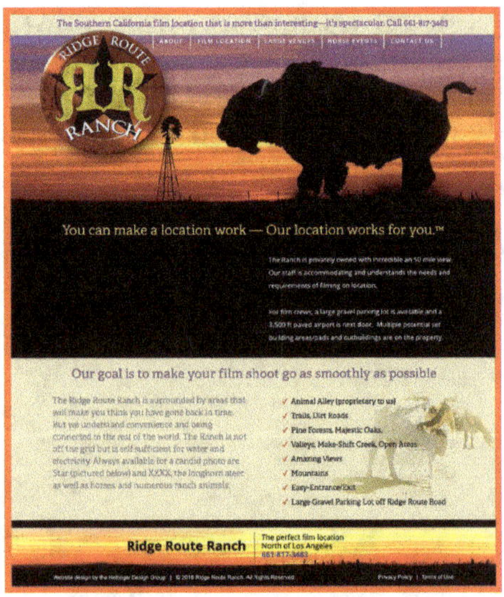

IMAGE 12.12

USES	FEATURES	EMPHASIS	POSITIVES	NEGATIVES
✦Restaurants ✦Personal services ✦Contractors ✦Retailers	✦Large hero image at top ✦Headline 7-9 words ✦Subhead 9-13 words ✦Limited content ✦CTA button ✦Sections stacked vertically	Brand offering follows go yo market strategy	Immediately communicates the purpose and prompts user action	Layout is not special, with minor focus on the brand

Table 12.1 | Hero Layout attributes breakdown

#2 Content-Driven Layout

This editorial-style website targets detail-seekers. The verbal flow with negative space minimizes UX interruptions resulting in long visitation times. Cognitive loading and reading ergonomics suitable for UI information design.

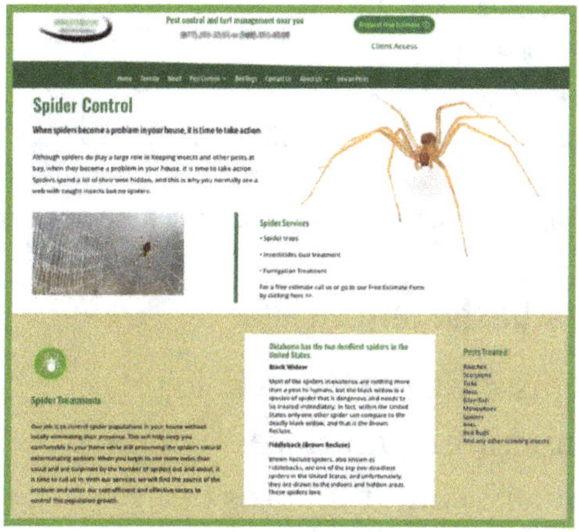

IMAGE 12.13

USES	FEATURES	EMPHASIS	POSITIVES	NEGATIVES
✦Information ✦News ✦Articles ✦Online books	✦Narrow text columns ✦Strong typography ✦Minimal distractions ✦Medium-sized images ✦Smaller content and section images	✦Typography ✦Scannable content flow ✦Easy to read	Typographic hierarchy arranged to allow ample space to encourage reading	Limited visuals are inconsistent with modern tech generations

Table 12.2: Content-Driven Layout attributes breakdown

#3 Modular Grid Layout

A grid-based modular layout that allows scanning, comparing, and visual balance. Since website software is made up of squares and rectangles, this layout promotes these traits.

USES	FEATURES	EMPHASIS	POSITIVES	NEGATIVES
✦Creatives ✦Financial firms ✦Institutions ✦Legal firms ✦Online stores ✦Galleries ✦Portfolios	✦Card-based modules ✦Hover to expand. ✦Image thumbnails ✦Iconic info buttons	Swiss and Bauhaus style that is repeatable on each page	Visual consistency with symmetrical balance builds a feeling of trust	May overwhelm some visitors and is not a memorable design with impactful images

Table 12.3 | Modular Grid Layout attributes breakdown

#4 Dashboard Layout

This style of design is for functional interfaces, which means that it focuses on providing mass amounts of information by using lengthy navigation and task-oriented components. Areas with dense information may overwhelm viewers.

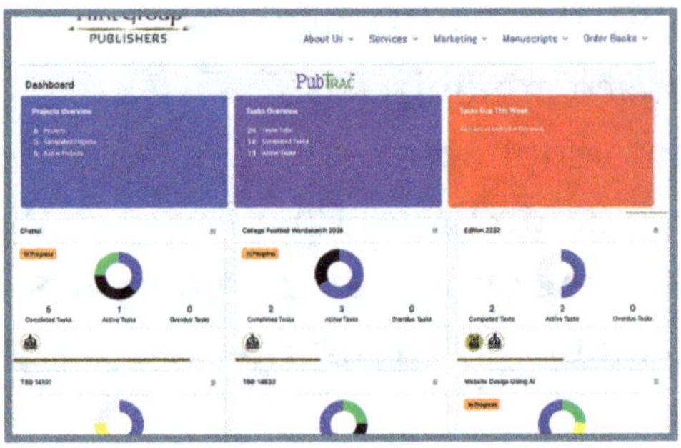

IMAGE 12.14

USES	FEATURES	EMPHASIS	POSITIVES	NEGATIVES
✦Web apps ✦Internal tools ✦Analytics platforms	✦Data visualization tools ✦Side navigation ✦Header navigation bar ✦Tables, charts, controls	Efficient navigation that visually presents mass amounts of data	Prioritizes function over emotion	The utility look with deep navigation makes it difficult to find items

Table 12.4 | Dashboard Layout attributes breakdown

#5 Narrative Layout

This layout arranges content chronologically, guiding readers via a structured visual and informational narrative.

USES	FEATURES	EMPHASIS	POSITIVES	NEGATIVES
✦Brand stories ✦Campaigns ✦Long-form features	✦Full-width imagery and sections ✦Visual storytelling ✦Movement triggered as user scrolls ✦Minimal navigation	✦Story-telling images ✦Ample negative space ✦Short sentence structure	Aimed at visitor emotional engagement by creating a memorable experience that builds a strong brand message	Visitors may be impatient to find the information that brought them to the site

Table 12.5 | Narrative Layout attributes breakdown

PHOTOGRAPHY LAYOUTS

Lifestyle shot

Shows the product in a natural, real-world setting, often with people, helping customers imagine it in daily use. Lifestyle shots can portray the product or company as the hero and convey a specific message.

Pack shot

A clean, consistent image on a plain background that focuses solely on the product.

Hero shot

A professionally styled photo that emphasizes branding, emotion, and desirability—often the centerpiece of a campaign.

Detail shot

A close-up highlighting specific features such as texture, finish, or design elements.

Flat lay

An overhead photo of products and props arranged neatly on a flat surface.

Group shot

Displays multiple related products together to showcase a set or collection.

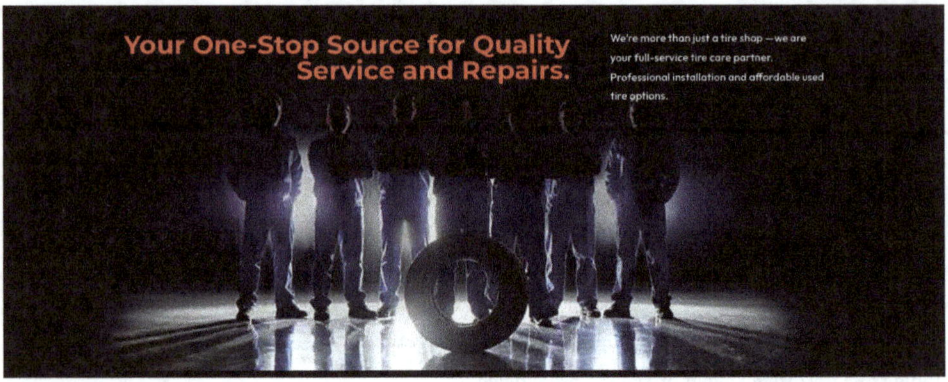

Figure 12.15
Depth Stack hero image

THE ART OF A HERO IMAGE

When a visitor reaches a website, they see a large image at the top of the page that stretches across the page. That is the hero image. This high-impact work acts as a hook to encourage the individual to stay on the website. By immediately grabbing the guest's attention, the website clearly conveys its primary goal. Visitors do not need to read or scroll; they can immediately understand what the website is selling or explaining.

Visually telling the visitor what the website is about is more effective and allows for more white space. Individuals understand images 60 times faster than they do text; it triggers a motion response that could build trust or explain a service. If the main headline is above, below, or inside the image, the subject must complement the wording.

Search robots catalog content but not images with type embedded into the artwork. The type is art and not readable information for AI bots.

Hero formats

Due to their strong image and large size, heroes are the standard in today's website design. Scale is established to start the visual flow. Loading time and information for search bots is weighed against visitor engagement.

Headline and subhead type can be placed over the hero image. If it has a lot of contrast with light and dark tones and colors, the type will be difficult to read. The robot will have the same difficulty as a human. Use easy-to-read type, which means it cannot be very small.

Cover
Has the most impact on the home or landing page since the image fills the entire page from header to footer. The image fills the page across the entire monitor or across the page and down to the fold.

Window
Adjacent to content, which leads the visitor to more information. The image may show white margins if the monitor is larger than the page.

Splash
Intended to immerse visitors immediately in the story.

Landscape
The standard marketing image which attracts visitors without as much impact as larger heroes but allows for more content and less scrolling to find the searched information.

Banner
The best hero for search engines since it allows the image and content to be above the fold. However, among the available options, the Banner has less impact. Search engines focus on content. But visitors can be drawn to the image and then read the content below, which the bots will also read.

Figure 12.16

A strong prompt can create a strong image.

AI Practicum} Firefly Prompt: Artwork of author standing on a stack of books with one knee on a book cover and one arm raised like a superhero, backlit by the sun.

Hero Types

To access the internet, different devices are available and need different hero formats. For instance, a desktop needs a horizontal image, while a mobile website needs a vertical image. For e-commerce sites a product-focused image tells visitors what is being sold. Videos will keep individuals interested longer than one photo or a slideshow as long as they load quickly. Above all, make sure the image is legible and there is adequate padding for margins.

Eight basic layouts are used to assemble hero images on websites. The size allocated for a hero image will influence the visual approach, and typically, the designer determines which approach will establish a connection with the visitor.

1. **Dominant Figure**
   One primary product, spokesperson, or owner person fills most of the frame. Supporting elements are minimized or pushed to the background.

2. **Depth Stack**
   Multiple products or team members are layered horizontally. Usually the most well-known product is in front, with other products placed behind.

3. **Ensemble**
   Several products are presented at similar visual weights, often arranged symmetrically or in a grid.

4. **Montage**
   Multiple scenes are displayed in a slideshow format that will showcases the product or service, often with autoplay enabled.

5. **Scene-Based**
   A lifestyle shot where people using a product or service are integrated into a specific scene or setting and implies a story.

6. **Split**
   The hero space is divided into sections showing products or scenes that contrast each other.

7

Typographical
The brand or product dominates the composition, with very little supporting imagery.

8

Symbolic
Minimal or iconic imagery depicted within a background setting.

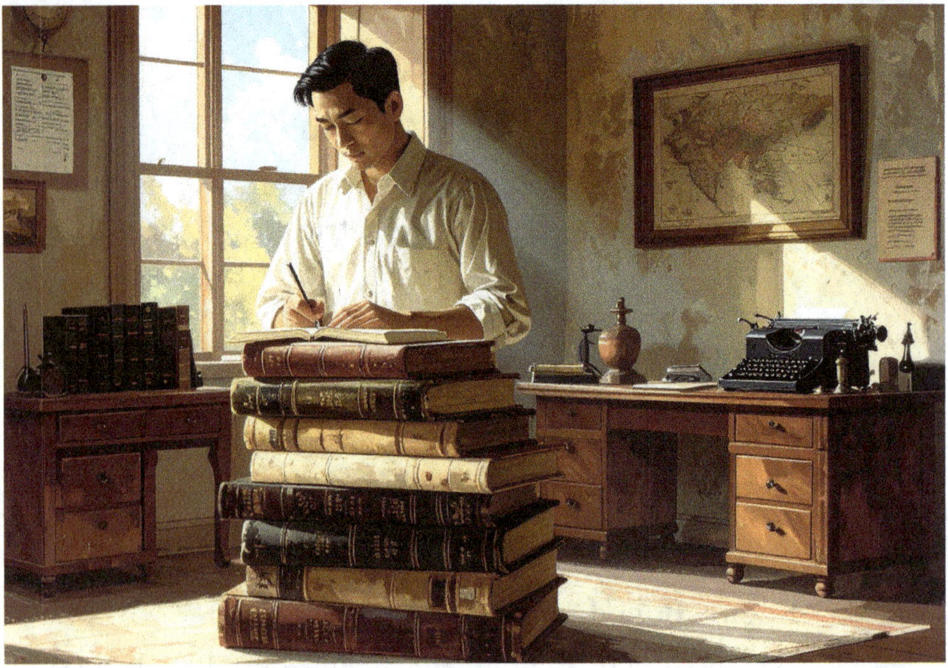

Figure 12.25

The power of words
AI Practicum} Firefly Prompt: Photo-real art of a person signing a stack of books with sunlight shining into a retro office.

CONCLUSION

A website designer who understands the influence exerted on visitors by visual tools like contrast, scale, space, and alignment directs the viewer's attention. They make it easy to discover a website's message.

By directing the visual flow, the searcher will not feel frustration or confusion. Storytelling images and Hookwords in content are not only instruments of visitor engagement but also builders of trust.

Color palettes that utilize complementary image colors and adjacent branding tones with distinctive fonts build on trust. The harmonious use of complementary and adjacent colors subconsciously establishes a reaction to the company, product, or service.

Understanding the art in design enables a website creator to generate innovative ideas that resonate with viewers and effectively communicate the message. The website that is created will address the issue.

INSETS

Figure 12.17

Dominant Figure

AI Practicum} Express Prompt: 3D diamond prism artwork of the number 1 on a white background.

Figure 12.18

Depth Stack

AI Practicum} Express Prompt: 3D artwork of a vintage number 2 on a white background

Figure 12.19

Ensemble

AI Practicum} Express Prompt: 3D artwork of a retro number 3 on a white background.

Figure 12.20

Montage

AI Practicum} Express Prompt: 3D sand sculpture artwork of the number 4 on a white background.

Figure 12.21

Scene-Based

AI Practicum} Express Prompt: 3D glass artwork of the number 5 on a white background.

Figure 12.22

Split

AI Practicum} Express Prompt: 3D floral artwork of the number 6 on a white background

F Figure 12.23

Typographical

AI Practicum} Express Prompt: 3D leather artwork of the number 7 on a white background

Figure 12.24

Symbolic

AI Practicum} Express Prompt: 3D ruby red artwork of the number 8 on a white background

Launch Sequence-Go

C13

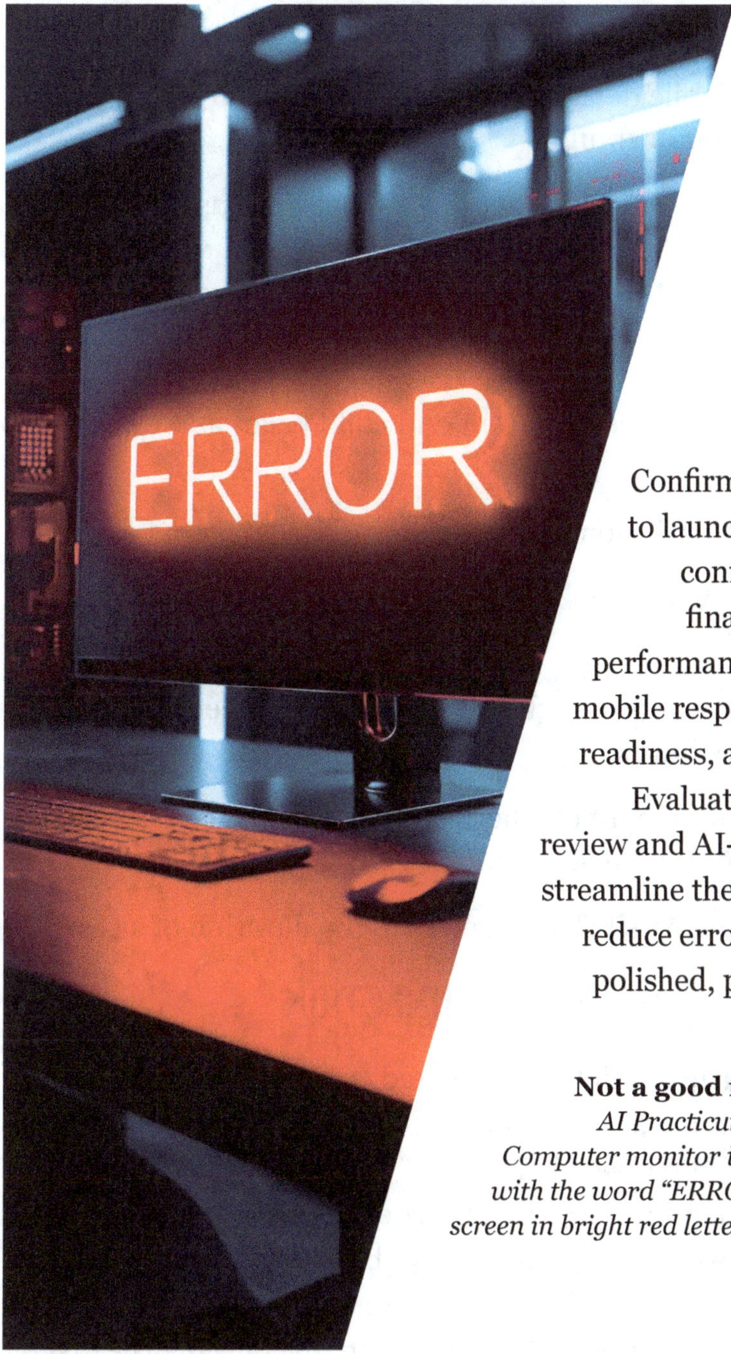

OVERVIEW

Confirms steps required to launch a website with confidence. Reviews final quality checks, performance optimization, mobile responsiveness, SEO readiness, and accessibility. Evaluates using manual review and AI-assisted tools to streamline the launch process, reduce errors, and deliver a polished, professional site.

FIGURE 13.1

Not a good first impression
AI Practicum} Canva Prompt: Computer monitor in a futuristic office with the word "ERROR" glowing on the screen in bright red letters, Photoreal style.

PROFESSIONAL TERMINOLOGY

Actor: Website development group member.

Fat Finger: Mobile device users press multiple targets at once with their finger or thumb.

Hamburger: Navigation term for the three lines used in mobile devices.

Indexing: The process of Google discovering and listing a website.

Mega Menu: Includes all parent and child pages as well as design elements.

Player: Client or liaison who provides needed information.

Screen Grab: A capture of a selected portion of the monitor screen.

Screenshot: A capture of the entire monitor screen or of an application's window.

Session: Measurement of when a visitor is active on a website until 30 minutes of inactivity.

TOS: The "time on site" term refers to the duration of a session.

MAKING A CONNECTION

The internet started with the two linked computers that, on the first try to communicate, attempted to type in "Login." The system crashed after the first two characters, "Lo," were input. From that inauspicious beginning, the internet has grown to over 100 million servers worldwide with over 30 billion connected devices. When a website goes live, it takes time to be active in all of the areas that access the internet. After launch, the designer needs to be patient and realize that when errors crop up, the adjustments may not be corrected immediately.

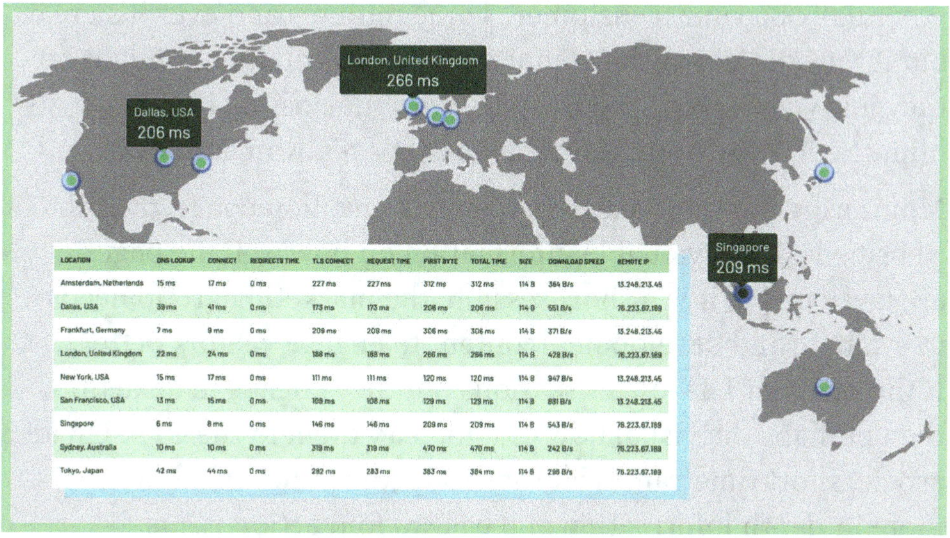

LOCATION	DNS LOOKUP	CONNECT	REDIRECTS TIME	TLS CONNECT	REQUEST TIME	FIRST BYTE	TOTAL TIME	SIZE	DOWNLOAD SPEED	REMOTE IP
Amsterdam, Netherlands	15 ms	17 ms	0 ms	227 ms	227 ms	312 ms	312 ms	114 B	364 B/s	13.248.213.45
Dallas, USA	39 ms	41 ms	0 ms	173 ms	173 ms	206 ms	206 ms	114 B	551 B/s	76.223.67.189
Frankfurt, Germany	7 ms	9 ms	0 ms	209 ms	209 ms	306 ms	306 ms	114 B	371 B/s	13.248.213.45
London, United Kingdom	22 ms	24 ms	0 ms	188 ms	188 ms	266 ms	266 ms	114 B	428 B/s	76.223.67.189
New York, USA	15 ms	17 ms	0 ms	111 ms	111 ms	120 ms	120 ms	114 B	947 B/s	13.248.213.45
San Francisco, USA	13 ms	15 ms	0 ms	108 ms	108 ms	129 ms	129 ms	114 B	881 B/s	13.248.213.45
Singapore	6 ms	8 ms	0 ms	146 ms	146 ms	209 ms	209 ms	114 B	543 B/s	76.223.67.189
Sydney, Australia	10 ms	10 ms	0 ms	319 ms	319 ms	470 ms	470 ms	114 B	242 B/s	76.223.67.189
Tokyo, Japan	42 ms	44 ms	0 ms	282 ms	283 ms	383 ms	384 ms	114 B	298 B/s	76.223.67.189

FIGURE 13.2
Watch the site go live across the world internet
HI Practicum} Screen grab of test results.

A fun and informative check of the website as it goes live can be seen at Global Uptime Test. Results for domain health DNS performance and website page speed. Located at uptime.com/freetools, this is free service is availaoble for a limited number of uses.

The average visitor skims a home page or landing page for 30 to 60 seconds. Blog articles have up to two minutes interaction while om an e-commerce page. The potential customer spends 20 seconds looking for an item and up to 60 seconds reading more of the information.

Website designers know if the searcher is gone in under 10 seconds, visitor did not find a headliner or visual that rather attention. If they spend anywhere from 30 to 60 seconds, that's good because they realize the visitor did skim the page and evaluate whether needed more attention or if they should move on. Under two minutes means they were interested and could potentially become a customer. Three minutes and over it's great but if they did not click for more interest or call then it might be they just went away from the page without closing. If they see 30 minutes of a visitor on the page, then it's really in activity.

Monitoring the time a searcher spends on a homepage gives the website designer valuable information on how well the pages are layed out. If it is a short session, the marketing group needs to evaluate and develop new content to engage visitors better. If the searcher has longer sessions but they engage in an action, then perhaps the visual flow did not lead them to the CTA. On an article, short timeframes let the group know they need to have more in-depth information and easy to find action items.

PRE-LAUNCH CHECKLIST

When preparing a checklist prior to launching the website, outline the key topics to be addressed. If they are required, store the details in a separate file. In Chapter Nine, the setup of the CMS website was detailed and must be completed prior to the prototype phase. Avoid combining items across checkoffs, as this will render the list excessively burdensome. By implementing distinct stage lists, a sense of achievement will motivate the actors for the subsequent stage and foster a sense of inclusion among the players, affirming that the site is advancing. Names may be utilized; however, at times greater progress is achieved by refraining from explicitly assigning responsibility for omitted elements to an individual.

Note the efficiency of short lists set up in columns and rows. Allowing a space for notes and the individual assigned to that action allows for communication. If possible, share on a network that the entire team can access. Workflows that are set up with an automatic action that informs the responsible party that their assignment is up next keeps the project in motion.

Website Name and URL here						
Prelaunch Checklist						
	Main Lisitng	**Subsets**	**Delivered**	**Approved**	**Champion**	**Notes**
✓	branding guidelines		✓	✓	Actor 1	
		Color call outs	✓	✓	Actor 1	
		H1 Fonts light, dark sizing	✓	✓	Actor 1	
		Subhead fonts	✓	✓	Actor 1	
		Tests, captions, emphasis	✓	☐	Player 3	On Holiday
☐	Target market guides	Breakdowns	✓	☐	Player 2	
		Stories	✓	☐	Player 3	
✓	Wireframe	Mock up	✓	✓	Actor 4	
☐	Visual hierarchy		✓	✓	Player 1	
☐	Header info		✓	☐	Actor 2	
☐	Footer Info		✓	☐	Actor 2	
✓	Page descriptions		✓	✓	Player 2	
☐	Page Meta content		✓	☐	Player 2	
☐	Social Media links		☐	☐	Player 5	

FIGURE 13.3
Goblin Pre-launch Check list
AI Practicum} Goblin Prompt: Create a new website pre-launch Checklist.

The pre-launch phase of any website encompasses three primary steps: selecting the hosting provider, gathering optimized components, and designing the website. Maintain two lists to ensure each task remains focused and manageable. After the host has been established, configure the backup and a testing environment that does not utilize the domain. Once the website has been thoroughly approved, tested, and finalized, it may then be deployed to the live site associated with the domain.

Website Name and URL here

Contents Checklist

Ready	Champion	Elements /Parent	Subset/Page	Collected	Opt	Meta	Notes	H1	H2	H2	H3	H3	Txt	Comments
✓	Actor 1	Branding	X	✓	✓	✓	✓							
✓	Actor 1	Guide	X	✓			✓							
☐	Actor 1	Home Pg		✓	✓	☐	✓	✓	✓	✓	✓	✓	✓	Waiting on approval
☐	Actor 1	About Us		✓	☐	✓	✓	✓	✓	✓	✓	✓	✓	In Progress
☐	Player 3		Newsletter	✓	☐	☐	✓	☐	☐	☐				Player 3 on holiday
✓	Player 2		Locations	✓	✓	✓	✓	✓	✓		✓		✓	
✓	Player 3	Team Page		5	✓	✓	✓	✓	✓	✓	✓	✓	✓	
✓	Actor 4		Career Opps	7	✓	✓	✓	✓	✓	✓	✓	✓	✓	
✓	Player 1	Services		✓	✓	✓	✓	✓	✓	✓	✓	✓	✓	
✓	Actor 1		Installation	✓	✓	✓	✓	✓	✓	✓	✓	✓	✓	
✓	Actor 1		Repair	✓	✓	✓	✓	✓	✓	✓	✓	✓	✓	
✓	Actor 1		Maintenance	✓	✓	✓	✓	✓	✓	✓	✓	✓	✓	
✓	Actor 1		Referral Prog	✓	✓	✓	✓	✓	✓	✓	✓	✓	✓	
✓	Player 2		Online Sched	✓	✓	✓	✓	✓	✓	✓	✓	✓	✓	
☐	Player 3	Product		☐	☐	☐	☐	✓	☐	☐	☐	☐	✓	Compiling
✓	Actor 2		Main	✓	✓	✓	✓	✓	✓	✓	✓	✓	✓	
☐	Actor 2		Ancellary	✓	☐	☐	☐	☐	☐	☐	☐	☐	☐	Waiting on approval
☐	Player 1		TBD	☐	☐	☐	☐	☐	☐	☐	☐	☐	☐	After launch
✓	Actor 2	Warranties	Icons, Terms		✓	✓	✓	✓	✓	✓	✓	✓	✓	
☐	Player 2	Certifications	Logos, Links, #S		☐	☐	✓	✓	✓	✓	✓	✓	✓	Player on holiday
☐	Actor 4	Contract Us	Info Required			☐	✓	✓	✓		✓		✓	In Progress
☐	Actor 4		Info Optional			☐	✓	✓	✓		✓		✓	In Progress
✓	Actor 1		Recepients			✓	✓	✓	✓		✓		✓	

FIGURE 13.4

Goblin Content Check list

AI Practicum} Goblin Prompt: Create a website content Checklist.

The required elements list should encompass all forms of content necessary for the website, including text, images, videos, and downloadable assets. It is an inventory designed to systematically document and monitor all content elements. This list should include all required approvals from relevant stakeholders for all textual content, as well as note the sources or the necessity of creating images such as product photographs, banners, iconography, and illustrations. This Elements List guarantees that all images are of high quality, optimized for web usage, appropriately sized, and accurately named.

By setting up a Pre-launch List before beginning the website design, all of necessary website features and functionalities will be spelled out. If the design is done on the fly, there is a lot of back tracking and redoing which will lead to mistakes and a bloated media storage gallery. Develop and finalize website wireframes before the design. Consider it building the skeleton with muscles before adding skin.

As soon as the website preliminary layout begins, make sure a timely backup test is conducted. It is advisable to conduct an hourly backup to ensure the absence of errors for sites in progress, as this is typically when the majority of issues arise. Errors may result in a malfunction, potentially leading to the loss of one or more pages. This issue will result in the loss of all data unless a backup has been created within the past hour.

WEBSITE FUNCTIONALITY TESTING

The pre-production website is developed on a staging site. To make this environment difficult to be found before it is a live functioning site, usually the domain name is whatever this staging site uses as an URL. The designer and marketers should test for the visual differences between browsers and functionality of the buttons, links, and animations.

Once the website has been completely uploaded and approved by the marketing team, arrange and execute a hidden launch, also known as 'beta testing,' with a selected group of users. Reviewing the website will require over one hour. Plan enough time within the schedule for testing, website revisions, and additional testing.

A protocol should be established for these participants to utilize while reviewing the website. Do not anticipate that they will generate a large number of scenarios. Designate sections on the checklist pages for remarks and incorporate several open-ended questions to elicit candid responses. These evaluators should be positioned in a quiet environment with a designated time allocated for reviewing the website without interruptions.

This stage of development is crucial. It is easier to make changes, revisions, and corrections at this pre-production stage than when the website is live. Once the site is in production anyone who accesses the site that is under construction, they will become frustrated and may not return. Non-participants in the client's company will focus on the errors and instead of the site's first impression.

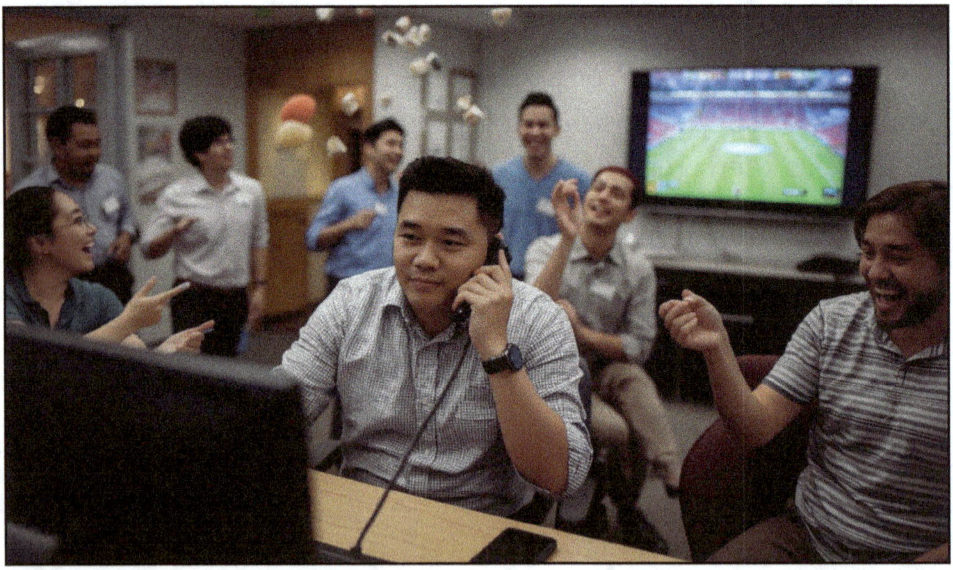

FIGURE 13.5

Not a good testing environment.

AI Practicum} Canva Prompt: Person with a phone trying to use a computer in an office break room that has people laughing, eating, throwing things at each other, and a TV with a sports game on.

Testing protocols

To establish a checklist, clearly identify the objectives, such as testing usability or detecting performance issues. Avoid setting an excessive number of objectives. Maintain a focused testing approach without adding confusion.

Identify the intended consumers in accordance with the target market. Provide explicit written instructions and facilitate monitoring without interrupting the participant. This approach enables the testers to inquire or seek clarification regarding something in particular.

The goal is to gather real-world user experience. If the designers and marketers are the only source of testing, it will be biased since they know what is supposed to happen. When a beta tester sees the website for the first time, the reactions and overall satisfactions will be similar to how a visitor should respond.

For small businesses that are unable to budget for a beta testing firm, consider requesting previous customers to review the new website over a designated period in exchange for a complimentary meal. Invite the selected group to the office for a catered luncheon and utilize this opportunity to foster a deeper understanding of them. Upon completion of the testing, express your gratitude and present them with a branded gift or gift certificate as a token of appreciation for their time. Follow up with them via a phone call or letter to continue the customer relationship. Do not send a canned email.

Give the participants different tasks, scenarios, and they should not be together in the same room. The environment needs to be quiet, comfortable, and free of distractions. It is not a race.

Choose participants that have diverse experiences, different levels of technology proficiency, with basic devices. Based on the pool of testers, have them try out the website on different browsers.

After wrapping up the beta testing, elements may be changed or deleted. Further testing should be included with previous visitors for insight into returning visits and how they navigate the website.

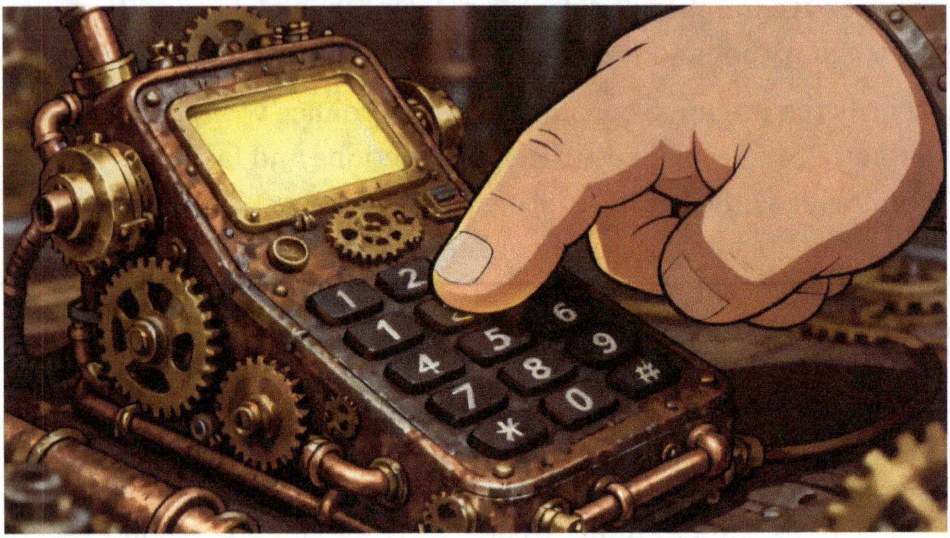

FIGURE 13.6

Not a new skill: fat finger typing

AI Practicum} Picsart Prompt: Cartoon of fat finger typing on vintage technology phone.

Device format problems

When a desktop site is adapted for mobile and tablet devices, the biggest risks arise from the assumption that the same design, content density, and interactions will be effective across all platforms. Google will evaluate the mobile site for speed and performance before indexing the desktop site.

Download speeds for a Wi-Fi enabled desktop computer will be slow and too heavy for a mobile device that relies on cellular data. Images need to be optimized for all three types of devices and cropped differently. Videos that load and play quickly on the desktop can cause an error on a tablet.

Desktop pages frequently include too much content for a mobile layout. Not only does a visitor not want to read all of that material, but CTAs might become buried or difficult to spot among all of the other pieces. A mobile site's objective is to direct visitors to take one major action. In a tablet design, the goal can have two CTAs, whereas a desktop can have numerous CTAs depending on how the page scrolls.

The font sizes need to be adjusted and the line spacing. Light fonts become less legible, and the line breaks will be awkward. To engage the visitor on a mobile layout, keep content to short sentences or bullets.

Designers should not assume the answer it to simplify the mobile design by hiding or removing elements. Tablets can be slightly modified from the desktop but mobile still needs to be effective. Best practice is to think of the smaller vertical format designed with the intent of speed.

Desktop grids that do not collapse smoothly are areas for refinement. When reduced to a vertical form, columns may become overly thin or stack incorrectly.

Navigation is represented by three lines commonly referred to as the 'Hamburger' icon. These lines conceal a drop-down menu for a vertically arranged menu listing. The page links should be concise for mobile screens and a little longer for tablet screens. The navigation opens up in a vertical format for the visitor to select a linked page. Due to the smaller screen size and the use of a thumb by the visitor, the menu words need to be concise, and the number of options should not cause the visitor to scroll. The menu and interactive components should be positioned within the natural reach of the user's forefinger.

Scale and space are usually the problems when the visitor tries to read the pages or tap just one of the links. Hover states do not exist on touch devices and buttons, and form fields need to be thumb-friendly. Watch for abandoned "contact us" pages due to the forms or contact buttons not being sized for the phone.

Visual builder concerns

Many of the visual builders, such as Divi and Elementor, allow the core design for desktop first, then use the visual builder's tablet and phone views to make specific adjustments for those devices. They have seamless views, and the specs can be changed based on the type of mobile phone, allowing for a responsive design.

For text, image, and button modules, responsive icons symbolizing desktop, tablet, and phone formats are in the design settings. They allow the designer to change settings like spacing with different padding and margin based on the device. Font sizes and alignments can be set for each device, and text blocks and image windows can be hidden just for the selected device without affecting other formats.

The inherent problem of allowing the visual builder to adjust the desktop site to a mobile device is publishing an awkward design. Spacing, sizing, and the positioning of images will not visually be as effective when the format changes.

Watch for awkward spacing, misaligned sections, and excessive scrolling. Use familiar icons such as a magnifying glass for searching or the map point to illustrate a location. Use common symbols for the call button or email link. Colors should contrast and not blend for CTAs.

One area to always consider is that the mobile or tablet can be turned vertical or horizontal and change what can be seen. People usually take photos with their phones vertically, even though the formats are horizontal. Website images will need to be retouched to allow more impact or at the background color on each side, so the image appears vertically.

Tablet layouts often get ignored, but they are used for different reasons. Unlike a desktop, they are mobile, and unlike a phone, they have a large screen. The navigation menus will not be hidden in a hamburger but will show words.

Unless the user has set all webpages to display the phone website, they will show the desktop site. If they have changed the default on the phone, they would get a zoomed-in, large, and somewhat distorted version. Some browsers, such as Chrome, will scale the mobile version down, and other browsers offer the desktop site as an option. The design should automatically adapt the layout to the screen size of the tablet.

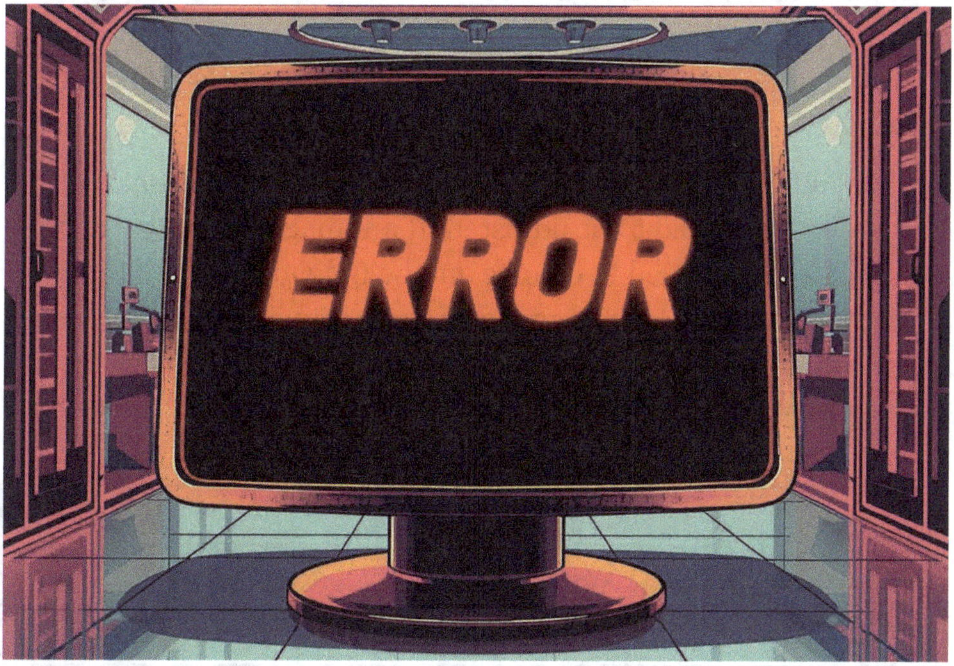

FIGURE 13.7

Not what anyone wants to see on a published site.
AI Practicum} Canva Prompt: Computer monitor in a futuristic office with the word ERROR glowing on the screen in bright red letters. Pop art style.

Final pre-launch website areas to check

Responsive design refers to a large screen, mouse/keyboard focused layout to a small screens, touch-only on-the-go format.

The layout will need to change from desktop dense layouts of multi-column grids to mobile screens with stacked content in a single-column. The difficulty for the designer is appraising the effect of this responsive layout. On a mobile site, the navigation should be adjusted for the change and there should be a single CTA that needs to stand out.

Links on a desktop can be smaller for a cursor unlike a mobile which should be set up for 'fat finger' use. The mobile design should be adapted with larger target areas.

A desktop user has more patience for a two second download than an on the go user where performance is mandatory. The mobile user wants the information quickly while the desktop and tablet users have longer attention spans.

Broken links need to be relinked and checked for meta data. Image size may need to be adjusted. If an image needs revisions, the file name still need to change and be uploaded even if the changes are minor. If the name is the same it will cause confusion on the link. Copy the meta data to the revised image and then delete the old image from the media gallery.

Trust Your Financial Future To The Proven Advisor.
www.isitwp.com/headline-analyzer
Here is how your headline will look like in google search results page.

FIGURE 13.8
Screen grab of snippet example by IsItWp

View each page for consistent fonts, color palettes, and visible branding elements. Check to make sure the line breaks do not loose content when changing format. Look for placeholder text and images.

Forms should be filled out and partially filled out to test for errors and the proper recipient received the message. Since the communication will be coming from the pseudo-name domain, it may go to spam.

POST LAUNCH FOLLOW UP

All elements need to be checked to make sure nothing dropped off or has a broken link. Forms need to be tested, submitted, and spell check the automatic received message. The recipient may need to add the form address to their contacts. The designer may want to be copied on all forms in case there is a problem. The designer can forward the form information to the necessary parties to discover if all the messages are not going through.

Even though the website has been tested multiple times by multiple individuals, it needs to be tested again. All content should be proofread and make sure the sizing has not changed.

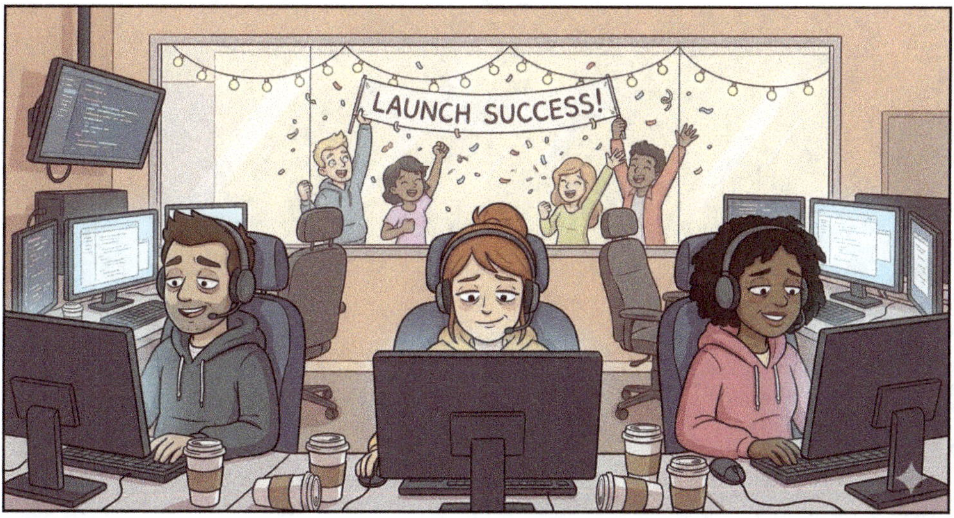

FIGURE 13.9

A job well done

AI Practicum} Gemini Prompt: Cartoon of people looking at computer monitors in tech room smiling but tired. People in background celebrating.

Run a complete backup and download the zipped file. Expand and visually look at the files. Check with the traffic plugin such as Statcounter for errors. Once the data is being collected, turn off counting the designer's IP address in the statistic gathering. Ensure CRM or integrations are syncing properly.

Once Google and other search engines have indexed the site, check the snippets. They should look like the examples created in the SEO plugin.

Plugin and theme should be checked for conflicts. Set up a monitoring plugin or hosting notice for any problems. In two weeks check for updates and learn how the new plugins may change the layouts or create problems. Before activating, run another backup.

Hiring a Web Designer

C14

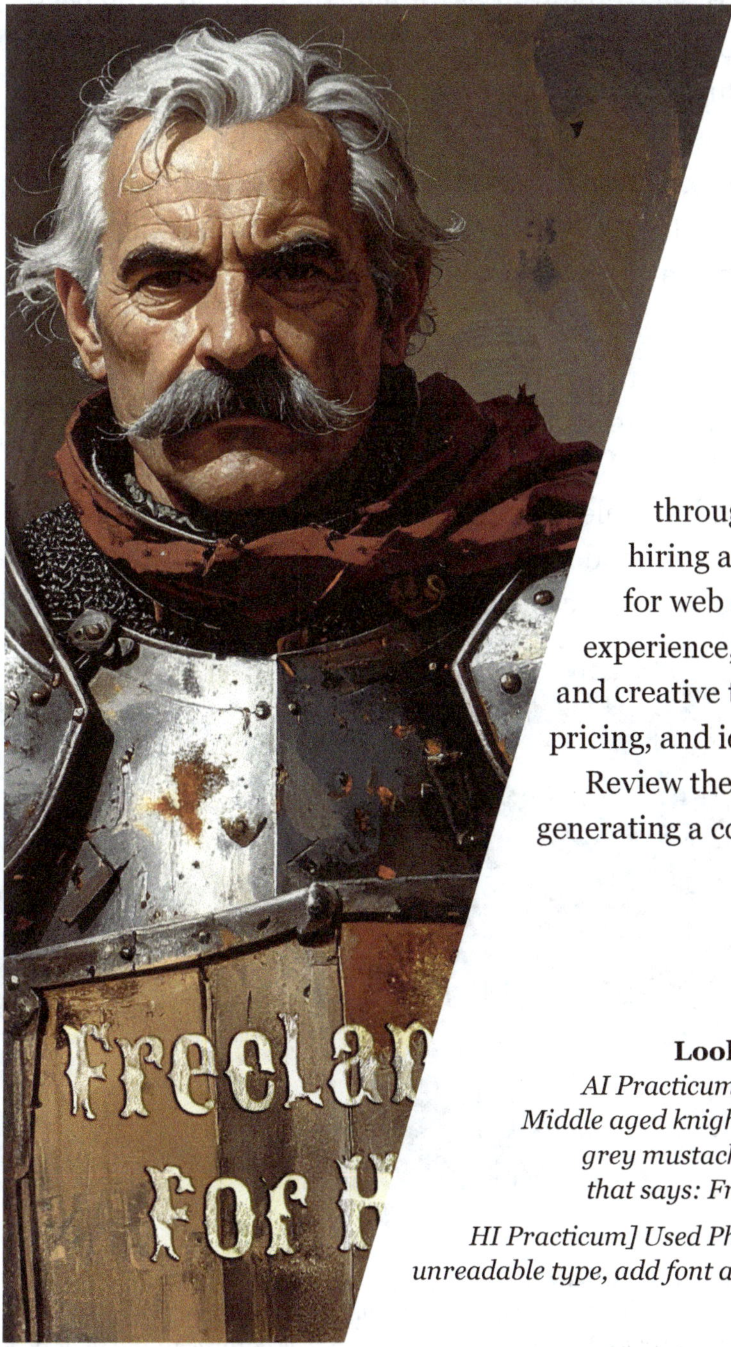

OVERVIEW

Chapter guides through assessing and hiring an outside source for web design. Evaluate experience, gauge technical and creative talents, compare pricing, and identify red flags. Review the four options for generating a company website.

FIGURE 14.1

Look for experience

AI Practicum} Express Prompt: Middle aged knight in dented armor, grey mustache, holding a shield that says: Freelancer For Hire"

HI Practicum] Used Photoshop to replace unreadable type, add font and distressed type.

HIRE BASED ON KNOWLEDGE—NOT HOPE

For the most part, self-taught practitioners do not know the best methods to index a website for search engines that lead to being found in the results. A common complaint by small business owners is that the designer said they would build an SEO website, but the site is on page five in search results. After reading the previous chapters, the owner should know when an outside source refers to SEO, they are speaking about an indexable website for Google and not search results.

When hiring a design firm or freelancer, the owner has two choices about what plan to select. For a credible brand marketing item, there should be a lower-priced option to have the site built, indexed, and used for sales and marketing. The owner would host the site, domain, etc., and fully control its look, updating, and checking backups upon occasion.

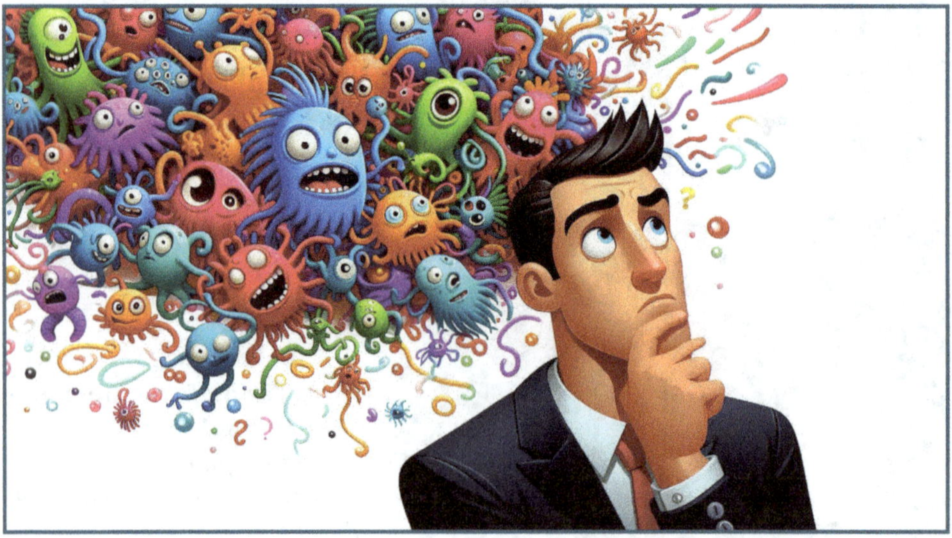

FIGURE 14.2

With knowledge comes options

AI Practicum} Creator Prompt: Cartoon of a businessman thinking by tapping a finger against his chin and looking at the small, strange creatures flying around his head.

This cost of building the website can be paid upfront or broken into payments set by approved milestones. The payment process usually has a start-up fee,followed by one or two payments, and then a final payment due once the site is live and functioning.

Make sure there is a window of corrections at no additional costs in the agreement. Payments should be tied to hard milestones dates such as the project would start as soon as the Deposit is received. Address the concept stage, specifically revisions, and how many stages are included. Set a fee for additional stages and what if any additional costs will be due on Final Delivery of the live website.

The company or independent contractor may also create and manage the website, which includes updating the site for search engines in addition to keeping components and plug-ins current. This all-in-one choice of web design encompasses both front-end and back-end development.

The packages price typically require a monthly contract. The contract should include the website's construction costs that should be paid over six to eighteen months. The part of the monthly fee that includes the building costs should expire after that fee has been paid. Only the service and maintenance payments are due from that point on.

As time goes on and the cost will increase for the plugins that help with SER. Maintaining the website will always be necessary and it will always become more expensive. Installing tracking software, like Statcounter, will allow the owner to receive monthly reports via email but it is not a free service.

The frequency of website changes made by competitors affects search results. It is a continuous procedure. Users change their search keywords, Google adjusts its algorithms, and AI bots assess fresh and pertinent material in different ways.

BRIEF HISTORY OF SEARCH RESULTS

From 2005 to 2012, blogs with keywords were an effective method to be found by Google. Since "blogs" were popular and a known item to non-professionals, SER seminars developed showing how to write blogs to use them for rankings. Of course, Google realized blogs were being used to manipulate search results knew long before the seminars began. It is easy to see that if a blog has no comment and not followers that it has only one purpose and it is not the dissemination of relevant content.

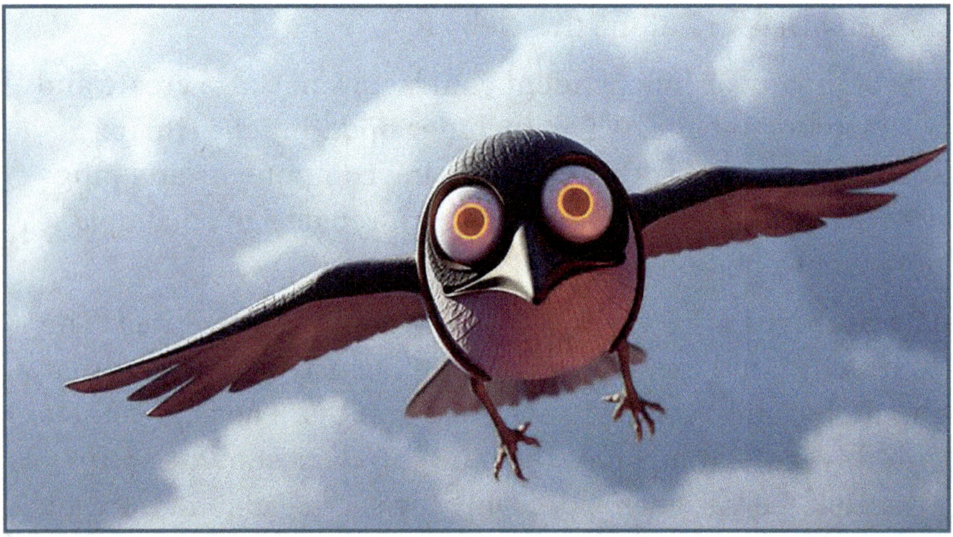

FIGURE 14.3

Ready or not it's time to fly

AI Practicum} DeepAI Prompt: Bird in the sky with very large eyes with a scared expression wearing a parachute.

Google then moved toward keyword matching for search results. Keyword stuffing such as having the terms in white on a white background interspersed with the other content became popular. Very quickly Google saw the white type of method and blacklisted those sites. Then SEO experts heard that if they put their industry in a search term followed by "near me" the website would rank better and used location services so the "near me" term did not work outside of the business's office location.

Next marketers went to buying pay per click ads when they found out the organic website would rank higher. The problem with this attempt was when PPC ads were stopped, the website dropped. With the depth of the trademarked search generative experience, website did not move up if the coincidentally had paid ads.

SGE evolved into the AI overview in Google searches. It is an AI-powered evolution of Google Search that provides common answers at the top of search results, While it is related to Google Gemini, it is only a small portion of the model create direct summaries and insights for queries, appearing above standard organic results.

Today, Google is still searching for information on websites for users. Consider having an info or news page on the website. It should be relevant to searchers and give visitor information which includes Hookwords.

Seminars that were developed for non-professionals to tell them the "secrets" of being on the first page of results will have old information. By the time a practicing SER expert discovers how to show up in result and then a teacher puts those practices into a seminar, Google has already discovered these maneuvers and moved on.

That is what is so difficult, the details are always being remade. Suddenly, the traffic will drop off, and the website champion has to scramble to catch up. It is not quickly which makes changes even more difficult to see what results work.

DECISIONS...DECISIONS...DECISION.

A business proprietor recognizes the significance of a website. They recognize that it functions as a marketing instrument capable of establishing credibility and generating a new revenue stream. To access the income stream, being discoverable through search engines is the most essential prerequisite. The subsequent requirement is to persuade visitors to convert into customers. The proprietor must understand what achieving these objectives entails in order to decide whether to develop a site independently or to hire a professional.

Option 1

This publication has examined two alternatives. The initial approach to creating a website involves utilizing an existing template.

The template will streamline the process but does not generate a distinctive website tailored for the targeted visitors or optimized for Google. It will appear professional; however, the images need to be substituted, and the content requires modification. That requires a certain amount of time.

Option 2

The second solution involves the proprietor developing a website that is memorable, distinctive, and optimized for search engines. This book covers many of the details; however, the web designer will still need to understand the extensive applications of the website design software.

Generally, proprietors lack the time to develop a website that is discoverable or to acquire the knowledge of all the necessary components that must be properly configured. The villain resides in the numerous intricate details involved in designing an effective website.

If an owner or marketer has time, they should build the site to save money. Without affecting the marketing budget, they can maintain control of the site and make necessary updates and additions. Time is valuable, which brings us to the third choice.

Option 3

Hiring a professional is the third and most popular process for building a website. Experts will build the website correctly and save the owner time, but not money. When employing an outside source, the initial worry is that even if the freelancer or company creates a visually appealing and representative website, it won't be discovered. Web designers are more self-taught than established experts.

HIRING TIPS

When business owners start the hiring process, they have a realistic expectation—who they hire will know how to create a website that will be found and highly ranked. A plumber is expected to put in and develop a system that operates as it was intended and not leak. That same reasoning does not apply to graphic designers who have learned how to make an attractive website.

Some freelancers and firms are strictly frontend web designers. That means they are concerned with the visuals and user experience. They do not program or write code to create the site but use drag-and-drop tools through content management systems.

The full stack designer not only handles what the user sees and the UX flow, but also the hidden meta areas and backend server-side functionality.

The problem is that many web designers will not inform the owner that they only handle frontend. They will use the term SEO correctly, but the owner will usually confuse that term with SER. Some frontend web designers think all that is needed is to put the correct paid plugins into action.

The owner should be aware that Google may require approximately six to eight weeks to index the website, ensuring that it appears in search results when someone searches for the company's precise name. For term and phrase inquiries yielding results within the first three pages, the process generally takes between six and eight months.

One method to initiate the process of being discovered promptly is to display an 'Under Construction' image on all pages. Refrain from placing the words on the pages, as Google will interpret that and fail to index the site. Many specialists contend that this measure is ineffective, and Google will explicitly assert that it is not beneficial. This sizable image should lack meta elements and be exclusively displayed on the site for visitors to view.

The image should not say "Check back soon" since no one will keep returning to see if the site is available. Schedule a date marked with an asterisk indicating potential change, but endeavor to confirm it. Draft content must be positioned on each page; however, it may be modified at a later stage.

SECTION	ELEMENT	DESCRIPTION
Business Overview	Business Name and info	Industry or type of business, main products or services
Contacts	Telephone and email Info	Who provides elements
Target Customers	Primary audience, secondary audience	Describe your ideal customers
Primary Function	Website goals	I.e. Increase leads, sell online, improve branding, credibility
Branding	Preferences and requirements	Logo style guide, color palette, fonts
Research References	List websites, Design styles	Modern, classic, minimalist, bold
Content	Pages needed, hierarchy	List including cookies, terms, privacy
Domain, Hosting	Credentials	Set up separate user access
Platform preference	WordPress, Wix, Divi, Elementor	System to use if CMS
Timeline	Target launch date	Date ranges, include time for corrections after Live date

Table 14.1 | Breakdown of items needed for the web designer brief.

PROJECT BRIEF FOR PROPOSALS

Small business owners need to know what to prepare before hiring a web designer. Otherwise, a lot of time will be wasted. The purpose of the brief is to streamline communications with a freelance web designer or developer. Prepare it before the first meeting to save a lot of time and ensure both parties clearly understand the project.

THE WEB DESIGN CONTRACT

In a search of the internet, multiple options of examples of contract are available. There are web legal services and attorneys who can draw up the contract. Since their fee is based on the time needed to create the agreement, it is recommended a web designer prepare a list before contacting them. A sample contract created by ChatGPT will NOT be a legal document. .

1. **Open ChatGPT and prompt**: I need to create a contract for Small Business Website Project. What information should be included?

2. **ChatGPT will reply:** A contract needs a number of items, See Table 14.2 as a reference only. The practitioner will need to use their own prompted list.

3. **Collect the information** in the same order ChatGPT presented it. It should be practical, easy to customize, and checked for spelling errors.

4 **Save the original file**. Then save as an optimized pdf suitable for uploading. Have ChatGPT pause while the PDF is uploaded

5 **Prompt ChatGPT**: In plain language for my business hiring a firm to design a website, list how the contract should be organized to be adapted for Word. Download the document

The items that need to be covered in a contract are provided in the list below solely for educational purposes and do not constitute legal counsel. Readers are advised to seek guidance from a qualified attorney prior to utilizing or modifying this agreement

Items to include in a contract.

If using ChatGPT for a draft it will need to contain the specifics of the company and what is needed to produce a custom list. ChatGPT can supply the wording needed in a contract for reference. This list may seem overly concerned about small items but they happen and can cause a lot of frustration.

Many of these elements were covered in the brief but when drafting the contract, nothing should be assumed. State everything that could be a question or problem once the project has begun. No surprises for a project is very satisfying.

In case an AI tool is used to generate a contract, the practitioner should understand that it is a facsimile and not intended for use as a legal document. An AI tool is not a legal identity which leaves the contract up for interpretation. For a legal document consult with an attorney or legal AI service.

Optional add-ons

The contract may need an addendum for a maintenance plan. That template would address monthly updates, backups, and monitoring.

To make sure everything is covered, use AI such as Goblin.tools to create a Website Launch Checklist. It should identify the owner of the domain, the creation of an SSL certificate, mobile testing by Google, and an analytics setup. The business owner should own and control the renewals of the domain.

ITEM	SPECIFICS
Effective date	This is date the agreement is drawn up. It may not be the date everyone signed the agreement.
Parties involved	Telephone and email Info of contact, wording on website for webmaster and where it links. State how elements are to be sent to the designer such as email or portal.
Scope of Work	Website description in bullets. Include a limit on pages, layout, additional info, SEO and SER, plugins used may not be free, indicate who is responsible for renewals.
Timeline	Set realistic dates and have options when the dates are missed. That will preclude drawing up a revised contract.
Payment	Terms, milestones and goals., Optional bonus if Live early, discounts if late.
Responsibilities	In clear language and bullet points explain the Client and Designer duties, approval timeframe and if communication is by email or text, and expected response times.
AI generated elements	Specific instructions on whether AI can or cannot be used and on what elements, stock photography ownership.
Maintenance	What happens if server crashes, or updates are needed, have a timeline, bullet where is covered and what is not included.
Domain, Hosting	Many large firms will offer to buy and renew the domain which will put a company in the position of not being able to change to a different source later.
Ownership	Do not assume all images and content belong to the company.
Approvals	Authority to approve website concepts, stages, approve costs incurred for revisions, cap on unexpected problems or expenses.

Table 14.2 | The major items to include in a contract.

OPTION 4: BELIEVE IT OR NOT!

There is one remaining alternative for creating a distinctive and tailored website for the business. After reviewing the manuscript, several small business owners inquired why this option was not presented in the first chapter.

The straightforward answer is that if a designer employs this option, they will lack the knowledge to verify, test, modify, or enhance the website. AI generators, such as the Hostinger proprietary website builder, have the capability to construct the entire website when provided with an appropriate prompt. It will produce a comprehensive website with pertinent content and design for a small business. The secondary reason for including it in this chapter is the author at the time of writing the manuscript has not used or tested the website builder.

Research from the information on the Hostinger website and online searches of ChatGPT, Gemini, Reddit and Wikipedia, has discovered some basic information. Without going into too much detail, here is what was discovered.

An editing function enables the digital practitioner to insert, reposition, and format elements such as text, images, icons, and sections. It allows for the inclusion of custom sections, videos through YouTube links, and precise adjustment of elements.

Two types of websites can be produced when utilizing Hostinger's website builder platform: Option 1 is a non-WordPress format and Option 2 is a WordPress site. The generation takes about the same amount of time. The first option is a closed website that will always need to be used on the Hostinger platform, and the second option will need adjustments, but it allows for long-term control and can be migrated to another hosting server.

Option 1, the non-WordPress generates a website will allow adjustments using its drag and drop editing feature. It is recommended for small business sites that want the brochure approach. The generated elements are not designed to be exported into WordPress or themes such as Divi and Elementor that use WP.

Option 2 generates a WordPress website that is theme based and uses the block editor. Using this option allows for changes and control of the SEO. The practitioner can install Divi and rebuild the pages.

The Hostinger Builder provides a wide selection of mobile-responsive templates suitable for various specializations, including contractors, small businesses, and marketing firms with portfolio galleries. The site cannot be too deep and should consist of the core pages of an average website.

The AI incorporates features for creating online stores with product pages and sales functionalities. The blogging feature can serve as a platform for news and articles. SEO tools designed to enhance user experience and visibility can be implemented.

A negative to generating a website with AI is that the website cannot be copyrightable. This means that your company's website can be copied by other companies.

It will require time, to create the prompt. It must be meticulously and comprehensively crafted. The practitioner must try a number of options and formats to produce the correct prompt.

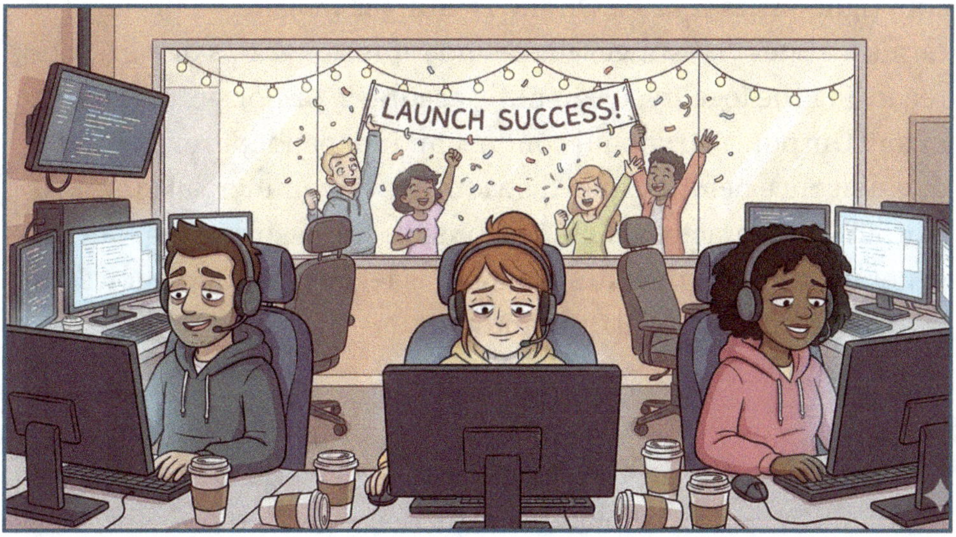

FIGURE 14.9

A job well done

AI Practicum} Gemini Prompt: Cartoon of people looking at computer monitors in tech room smiling but tired. People in background celebrating.

A suitable approach is to provide ChatGPT with the necessary information required to generate the prompt. It has the capability to generate a lengthy AI website prompt applicable to virtually any industry.

Create a checklist of all the necessary details to include before crafting the prompt to guarantee the accurate generation of the site. Explain the purpose of the prompt and inquire about the information required for it to be as effective as possible. The list should encompass ten primary items, including a branding guide, business information, target audience, services or products, and the stylistic approach of the website. Please consult this book for specifications regarding layout, color schemes, typography, and stylistic elements.

The images supplied by the AI Builder need to be checked or replaced due to issues with using them. The images may be AI generated, from the Hostinger royalty-free library, or may have copyright issues if used. On the Hostinger website, in the legal terms it states "Hostinger makes no representations or warranties regarding the legality, originality, accuracy, or non-infringement of any Output. You should conduct an independent review and due diligence before using, distributing, or commercializing any Output." The practitioner is responsible for ensuring that any AI-generated output, including images, is legally safe and allowed to be used for commercial or brand use.

CONCLUSION

Ultimately, mastering the design principles leads to innovative solutions. A website should resonate deeply with the visitor, enhancing both aesthetic appeal and communicate a trust for the offering.

By skillfully balancing the design of the website parts with content, website designers can create a memorable message of trust that is memorable. This understanding allows for the creation of websites that not only capture attention but create the desire to discover the story.

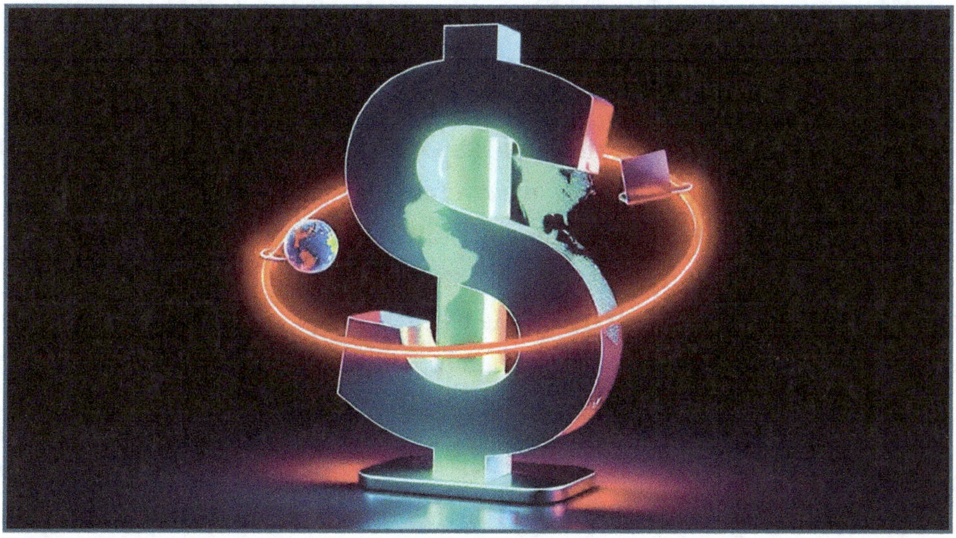

FIGURE 14.10

Congratulations—you have earned your pay.

AI Practicum} Express Prompt: Large 3D decorative dollar sigh with a website circling it like a planet.

INSETS

FIGURE 14.4 - 14.8

Plain B&W numbering

AI Practicum} Firefly Prompt: Create black and white 3D numbers 1,2,3,4,5 on a white background.

HI Practicum] In Photoshop clean up numbers, add shadows and optimize for printing.

ABOUT THE AUTHOR

A

Professor, designer, and author Neal Hettinger combines graphic design, website development, and AI. After years of teaching, Neal realized that most web and design courses focus on software tools or technical standards rather than how design, search visibility, and human trust interact in real-world digital contexts.

Website Design Using AI educates students, designers, and company owners on how to create visually appealing, discoverable, reputable, and effective websites. After decades in graphic design, branding, advertising, and web development, Neal has created a teaching method that combines basic design concepts with AI-powered workflows. He teaches design, user purpose, and search behavior in an AI-driven environment, not just tool use.

The accessibility of AI allows non website designers access to the tools and the ability to make images .

Neal has an MA in Mass Communications, a BA in Graphic Arts, and a second BA in Advertising. He learned branding, marketing, and digital production first hand at design and advertising agencies in Los Angeles, Nashville, Oklahoma City, and Birmingham. Neal was the Creative Director on projects for Nissan Motors, Universal Studios, Paramount Pictures, Adidas, Pioneer Electronics, and the UFC. He was the managing partner at The Lead Pencil Advertising and Design Firm in Los Angeles.

He later began teaching as an adjunct professor at Oklahoma City Community College, where he received the Outstanding Adjunct Professor award, and has also taught at the Oklahoma State University Institute of Technology. Neal is known for integrating emerging technologies into creative education, helping students understand how AI, design, and marketing intersect in today's web-driven economy.

Neal teaches how AI is changing website design, SEO, and digital marketing. He lectures at colleges and civic groups on AI and teaches courses on personal and business AI applications to enable the next generation of designers and entrepreneurs to create better, more trustworthy digital experiences.

GLOSSARY

TERM	PAGE
Accessible	46
Actor	234
AI Learning	2
Alternate Text	196
Analytics	162
B2B	140
Backend	64
Bounce	196
Brand	46
Browser	2
Cache	162
Caret	140
Chatbot	2
Chevron	140
Child page	140
CMS	24
Color space	122
Conversion	82
CSS	24
CTA	82
Domain Name	24
Dropdown	140
Dynamic Content	82
E-Commerce	2
Embedded	104
Fat Finger	234
Favicon	122
Footer	140
Frontend	64
Gestalt	211
Grid System	82
Hamburger	64
Hamburger	234
Harmony	211
Header	104
Hero	122
HI	2
Homepage	82
Hookwords	196
Human Ingenuity	180
Indexing	234
Keyword	180
KPIs	162
Landing Page	104
Layout	82
Links	104
Mega Menu:	234
Meta	196
Natural Language	2
Navigation	140
Open Source	122
Open-source	24
Optimize	122
Parent Page	140
Pixelated	122
Player	234
Plugin	24
Pop-Up	211
Prompt	104
Redirect	24
Responsive	64
Royalty Free	162
Screen grab	234
Screenshot	234
Search Bar	180
SEO	24
SER	24
Session	234
Sidebar	180
Site Map	46
Snippet	180
Stock Photos	162

LIST OF TABLES

Other Works with AI by Neal Hettinger

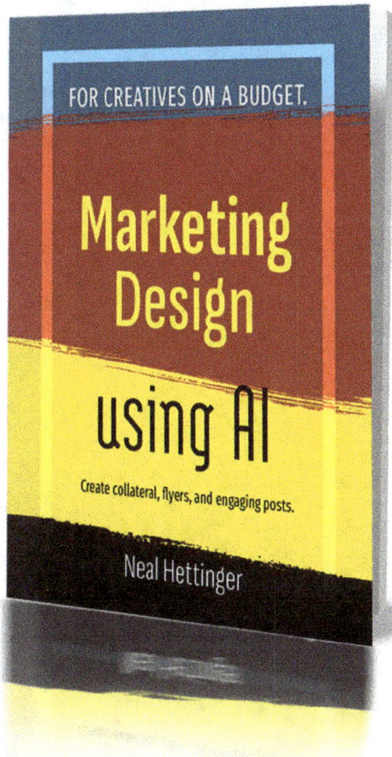

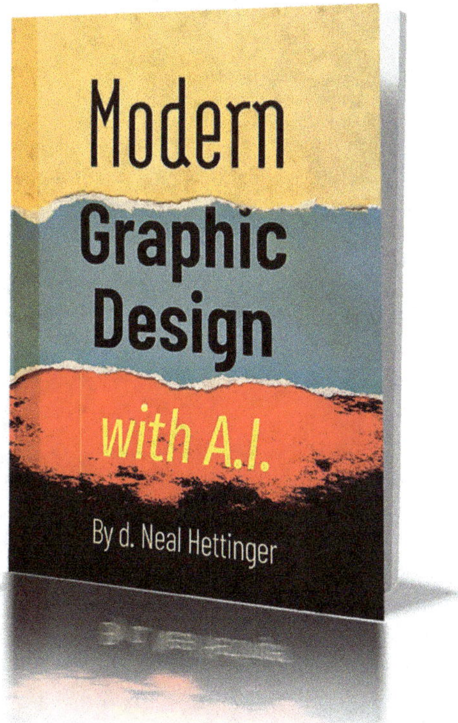

Marketing Design Using AI

(March 2026)

Whether you are a graphic designer, marketer, educator, or student, you will benefit from the explanations of graphic art styles and how to apply them to strengthen your own concepts. Modern Graphic Design with AI teaches how to create compelling solutions utilizing graphic design principles, integrated with software and artificial intelligence.

Modern Graphic Design with AI

(December 2024)

This book introduces the role of artificial intelligence within contemporary graphic design, emphasizing visual communication, creative workflows, and design decision-making. It provides a conceptual and practical foundation for students and educators while remaining accessible to working professionals seeking to understand AI's impact on modern design practice.

www.ingramcontent.com/pod-product-compliance
Lightning Source LLC
LaVergne TN
LVHW052259200926
848481LV00002B/411